# THE NEW SOCIAL WORKER®
# Volume 19, Winter-Fall 2012

The New Social Worker®
the social work careers magazine

## Linda May Grobman, Editor

White Hat **Communications**
Harrisburg, PA

# CONTENTS

THE nEW SOCIAL WORKER®
Winter 2012
Volume 19, number 1

## FEATURES

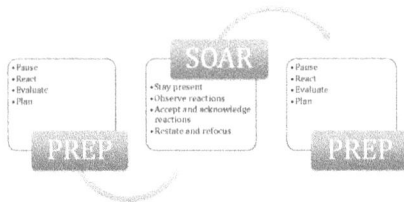

## DEPARTMENTS

# Publisher's Thoughts

Dear Reader,

Happy New Year! This issue marks the beginning of *THE NEW SOCIAL WORKER's* 19th year of publication! I cannot believe how my "baby" has grown and developed over the years!

Do you make New Year's Resolutions? Kryss shares hers with us on page 26. Whether you call them resolutions, goals, or a bucket list, knowing what direction you are headed–both personally and professionally–can help you get there!

Social workers encounter many difficult issues with their clients and in their everyday practice. Some of

*The publisher/editor*

these issues, such as child sexual abuse, have been prominent in the national and local news lately. (See Jenna Mehnert's letter to the editor on page 7.) The general public is, as a result, becoming more aware of some of the issues we all know all too well as social workers. It is unfortunate that it took some high-profile cases to get the attention of the press and legislators. Hopefully, this attention will result in improvements in reporting and legislation regarding child sexual abuse and other important social issues.

In this issue of *THE NEW SOCIAL WORKER,* we address some of the difficult issues.  For example, how do you approach telling a client something that you know he or she will not want to hear? How and when do you warn someone of potential harm? Can veterans learn a new way to think about surrender when in substance abuse treatment? And what can be done about sexualization of young girls in today's entertainment media?

In this issue, we are introducing a new feature called, "What Every New Social Worker Needs to Know About...." I am happy that Nicole Clark, an expert in and advocate for women's reproductive and sexual health, agreed to write our first installment in this series.

Two social workers write about passion in social work careers in this issue. Katie Ullman recalls how her field placement helped her find that passion. Then on page 18, Sonya Hunte provides tips for turning your own passion into a successful social work career.

Do you have ideas or experiences you would like to share with our readers? Perhaps you would like to write an article or serve as an expert interviewee for a future issue! Let me know.

Until next time–happy reading!

*Linda M. Grobman*

## Write for The New Social Worker

We are looking for articles from social work practitioners, students, and educators.

Some areas of particular interest are: social work ethics; student field placement; practice specialties; technology; "what every new social worker needs to know," and news of unusual, creative, or nontraditional social work.

Feature articles run 1,500-2,000 words in length. News articles are typically 100-150 words. Our style is conversational, practical, and educational. Write as if you are having a conversation with a student or colleague. What do you want him or her to know about the topic? What would you want to know? Use examples.

The best articles have a specific focus. If you are writing an ethics article, focus on a particular aspect of ethics. For example, analyze a specific portion of the NASW *Code of Ethics* (including examples), or talk about ethical issues unique to a particular practice setting. When possible, include one or two resources at the end of your article–books, additional reading materials, and/or Web sites.

We also want photos of social workers and social work students "in action" for our cover, and photos to accompany your news articles!

Send submissions to lindagrobman@socialworker.com.

**The New Social Worker®**
*the social work careers magazine*

## Winter 2012
## Vol. 19, Number 1

*Publisher/Editor*
Linda May Grobman, MSW, ACSW, LSW

*Contributing Writers*
Barbara Trainin Blank
Kristen Marie (Kryss) Shane, MSW, LMSW

THE NEW SOCIAL WORKER® (ISSN 1073-7871) is published four times a year by White Hat Communications, P.O. Box 5390, Harrisburg, PA  17110-0390. Phone: (717) 238-3787. Fax: (717) 238-2090. Send address corrections to: lindagrobman@socialworker.com

Advertising rates available on request.

Photo/art credits: Image from BigStockPhoto.com © Kirill Zdorov (page 16), Rachel Sellers (page 28), David Castillo Dominici (page 30).

*The New Social Worker* is indexed/abstracted in *Social Work Abstracts.*

Send all editorial, advertising, subscription, and other correspondence to:

**THE NEW SOCIAL WORKER**

**White Hat Communications**
**P.O. Box 5390**
**Harrisburg, PA 17110-0390**
**(717) 238-3787 Phone**
**(717) 238-2090 Fax**

lindagrobman@socialworker.com

http://www.socialworker.com
http://www.facebook.com/newsocialworker
http://www.twitter.com/newsocialworker

**Print Edition:**
http://newsocialworker.magcloud.com

# Carmelina Gilberto

## by Barbara Trainin Blank

One of Carmelina Gilberto's simple joys is going home for the weekend. She lives in a house in DC that she shares with her best friends near the campus of Catholic University of America, where she is pursuing her BSW degree. "Home" is Annapolis, Maryland, where she goes for birthdays, holidays, school breaks, and to get a home-cooked Italian meal from her mother or Nonna (grandmother). With her busy work and school schedule, it is something she doesn't do often.

"I love my family, coming home and talking to them," she says. "A lot of my family is in Italy, but there's a pretty large family here, too—one of my grandmothers has a lot of brothers and sisters."

Both sets of grandparents come from Italy. After Gilberto's parents' divorce when she was in sixth grade, her father moved back there. Gilberto, 21, has one sister three years younger.

Aside from academics, Gilberto is doing an internship at National Rehabilitation Hospital. She does intake evaluations and assists in family conferences with insurance companies. The hospital serves pediatric patients and adults who have suffered stroke, spinal injury, and other trauma.

"I learn something new every day," she says.

She is likely to be even busier and learn even more, now that she is serving as the national BSW Student Representative for the National Association of Social Workers (NASW).

She was first exposed to the helping professions when she underwent therapy to deal with her parents' split. But Gilberto's interest in social work blossomed during her sophomore year of high school, when she took a service trip for a week to Baltimore to work with kids from low-income families.

"I played with the children and had an interaction they didn't get with their parents," she says. "That sparked what I wanted to do."

Gilberto was a volunteer coordinator for the Jumpstart program of AmeriCorps at the Catholic University from December 2010 to May 2011. In that position, she was responsible for planning and involving students in volunteer events and recruiting, training, and managing volunteers for one-day, short-term, and long-term service projects.

The experience was so seminal that it formulated her goals. She knows she wants to work with children, and she wants to help low-income populations. After completing her BSW, in fact, Gilberto would like to work for Teach of America—another AmeriCorps program—probably before going on for a master's.

She has worked with children in other capacities, as well. In March 2010 as a team member, and again in March 2011 as a team leader, she participated in Mission Jamaica trips through her college. There, Gilberto taught first graders, helped in the assisted living home for the abandoned elderly, and helped refurbish homes and schools.

"Carmelina is a student with a bright smile who is always willing to help," says Emmjolee Mendoza, associate director of the Campus Ministry and Community Service at Catholic University, who led the second mission. "She has leadership qualities—having a positive attitude,

Carmelina Gilberto

engaging other people, and a willingness to help."

Gilberto was a team leader for DC Reads, a program in which she tutored low-income third and sixth graders in literature, among other responsibilities. On campus, she is vice president of BASSO, the student social work group.

Her selection as NASW representative was assisted by the nomination of Anthony J. Hill, who taught her in two policy courses.

"I nominated Carmelina because of her proven leadership in the classroom," says Hill, assistant clinical professor at Catholic University, National Catholic School of Social Service.

That leadership, he says, was demonstrated particularly in group projects.

"Carmelina is able to build group consensus to move the group forward," Hill adds. "She has also demonstrated leadership potential through her volunteer activities on campus and abroad. I knew about her work in Jamaica and saw her ability to build a consensus on group assignments."

Gilberto is "very articulate, not afraid to speak up," he adds.

Being elected was "huge" for the BSW student.

Influencing others definitely requires a certain outgoing nature and belief in oneself, and Gilberto admits she has

*Gilberto—continued on page 21*

# Duty To Warn, Duty To Protect
## *by Steven Granich, LCSW, MPA, DSW*

Since the Tarasoff case in 1974, duty to warn and duty to protect have become important as concepts in the field of social work and other helping disciplines. Being able to protect potential victims from harm and protecting clients from self-harm have become ethical obligations in social work practice. This area needs to be explored and understood by social work practitioners, educators, and social work students. Duty to warn and duty to protect have ethical implications for all social workers.

Walcott, Cerundolo, and Beck (2001) describe the facts of the Tarasoff case. Prosenjit Poddar and Tatiana Tarasoff were students at UCLA. Poddar stated to the university health science psychologist that he intended to kill an unnamed woman, who was identified as Tatiana Tarasoff. Although the psychotherapist did not directly warn Tarasoff or the family, the psychologist notified the police, who interviewed Poddar for commitment. The police only warned Tarasoff to stay away. After Poddar returned for the summer from Brazil, he murdered Tatiana with a knife. Tarasoff's family sued the campus police and the university health service for negligence. Walcott, Cerundolo, and Beck (2001) cite the second Tarasoff case, establishing a duty to protect.

*When a therapist determines, or pursuant to the standards of his profession should determine, that his patient presents a serious danger of violence to another, he incurs an obligation to use reasonable care to protect the intended victim against such danger. The discharge of the duty may require the therapist to take one or more various steps, depending on the nature of the case. Thus, it may call for him to warn the intended victim or others likely to appraise the victims of that danger, to notify the police or take whatever steps are reasonably necessary under the circumstances (p. 340).*

The Tarasoff case imposed a liability on all mental health professionals to protect a victim from violent acts. The first Tarasoff case imposed a duty to warn the victim, whereas the second Tarasoff case implies a duty to protect (Kopels & Kagle, 1993). There are many concerns about the implications of the Tarasoff case, especially around the confidentiality of the client-social worker relationship and violent clients avoiding treatment.

Since the second Tarasoff decision in 1976, there has been argument and debate as to the applicability of this judgment to the client-social worker relationship. The environment has changed for social work and confidentiality, as social workers now divulge confidential information to third-party payers. Tarasoff is an important decision with legal implications, and only 13 states in the U.S. lacked Tarasoff-like provisions at the time of Herbert's report in 2002.

*Duty to warn* means that the social worker must verbally tell the intended victim that there is a foreseeable danger of violence. *Duty to protect* implies a therapist determining that his or her patient presents a serious danger of violence to another and an obligation to use reasonable care to protect the intended victim against danger (Harvard Mental Health Letter, 2008, January). This may entail a warning, police notification, or other necessary steps.

Duty to warn and duty to protect have implications for social work practitioners in the fields of mental health, HIV/AIDS, domestic violence, and medical social work. There are also serious implications for malpractice and unethical behavior. What began as a mental health issue has been expanded to other fields of social work practice.

## Duty to Warn and Duty to Protect in Mental Health

In the field of mental health, it is difficult to actually make predictions of client violence. The *Harvard Mental Health Letter* (2006, January) makes recommendations for handling duty to protect with homicidal and suicidal patients.

*The principles for managing a threat of violence are generally the same as those for dealing with a suicidal threat. Therapists should find out whether a patient has ever seriously injured or thought about seriously injuring another person. Especially with new patients or any patients whose symptoms are becoming worse, it is important to know whether they are dangerous to others and whether the danger is due to mental illness. Is the patient losing the capacity to control violent impulses? (p.4)*

Duty to protect can involve warning the potential victim, notifying the police, starting a commitment hearing, informing mental health evaluators of the threat, and utilizing professional supervision. Duty to protect involves working with homicidal and suicidal clients. The obligation of duty to protect varies from state to state (Dolgoff, Loewenberg, & Harrington, 2009).

Failure to protect potential victims of violence can result in losing one's job at an agency. Consider the following hypothetical example.

*A professional social worker conducted an intake interview with a client with a history of mental health problems and violence toward his father. The client was somewhat delusional and stated that he might hurt his father that evening. The social worker made no effort to commit the patient for hospitalization. That evening, the patient became violent and broke his father's leg. The next day, the social worker was fired for negligence.*

Protecting the well being of homicidal and suicidal clients is the obligation of professional social workers. Social workers should frequently utilize supervision and consultation when working on this issue of duty to protect, because it has ethical and malpractice considerations.

## Duty to Warn and Protect in HIV/AIDS Cases

Social workers often work with clients who are HIV-positive or have AIDS. Confidentiality is very important to such clients, because of the stigma attached. Huprich, Fuller, and Schneider (2003) consider the question as to whether the therapist has the obligation to warn a third party of risk of transmission of HIV if his or her client is actually putting another party at risk. Stanard and Hazler (1995) report a case in which duty to protect seems important.

*Brian is a 24-year-old married bisexual man entering counseling to deal with grief and depression associated with a recent diagnosis of HIV infection. During the course of counseling, Brian discloses that he continues to be sexually active with his wife and also occasionally with anonymous male partners. Brian has not disclosed his diagnosis to anyone and maintains that it is not necessary to do so because he practices "safe sex." (p. 397)*

Melchert and Patterson (1999) discuss how being HIV-positive may pose a different situation from that of the Tarasoff case. Mental health professionals do not have the legal right to disclose that a person is HIV-positive to another person. This is at the discretion of physicians in many states. However, social workers and mental health professionals must struggle with this legal situation if a client insists on potentially harming another person through risk of transmission of HIV.

## Domestic Violence

In domestic violence situations, there can be an identified threat of harm to a victim. Domestic violence is a cross cutting issue that affects the daily lives of many people receiving social services (Danis, 2003). People who commit domestic violence will often commit criminal acts such as homicide, assault and battery, criminal trespass, terroristic threats, stalking, and sexual assault. Depending on the state, social workers have a legal obligation to report threats of violence and to warn the potential victims. Attorneys sometimes play a similar role to that of social workers and are privy to information about potential violence. Different states have varying levels of obligation to report specific threats of violence or intention to act (Buel & Drew, 2007).

In working with clients who have a history of domestic violence, it is important to do a risk assessment of the situation to determine if there is a potential for harm. Also, the social worker needs to make every effort to try to defuse any potentially violent situation. Good clinical practice encourages social workers to send battering partners to groups to work on issues of anger management. Social workers also need to protect potential victims by referring them to safe places where they are not exposed to violence.

Couples therapy can work when each person has contracted for no further incidents of violence.

Consider this hypothetical case vignette, in which duty to warn a potential domestic violence victim presents a dilemma for a social worker.

*A social worker is counseling a couple around issues of domestic violence. The husband reports that he has made threatening comments to his wife in the past. The wife has threatened to divorce her husband. The husband has stated that he would hurt his wife if they divorced.*

The social worker must make a decision. Should she report the case to the police as a threat? Is this threat serious? How is she going to assess the situation to possibly carry out a duty to warn?

## Duty to Warn and Protect in Medical Social Work

Social workers practice in the medical field, where many ethical dilemmas may arise with respect to duty to warn and duty to protect. With an increasing population of older clients in the United States, there are issues around caring for the frail elderly. Their children may not be willing to accept the recommendations that social workers make for their parents' care. Following is a hypothetical vignette of just such a situation.

*A social worker has recommended that an 88-year-old woman receive home health care. The family refuses this request, feeling that the 88-year-old woman can care for herself in her home. There is extreme danger of falling, missing meals, and not remembering to take medication at scheduled times. The social worker considers reporting this situation to Adult Protective Services.*

Social workers may be consulted by medical personnel to help resolve issues in genetic counseling. Issues of duty to warn and duty to protect may come into play, for example, if a patient refuses to disclose genetic information or test results to a relative. A physician may need to consult a medical social worker to work with the family on this critical issue, because sharing the information may save the relative's life.

Following is a hypothetical situation:

*A 34-year-old woman receives the results of testing for cystic fibrosis, showing the probability of transmission of the disease through genetics. She wants to become pregnant but does not want to tell her husband about the test results. This presents a dilemma for the social worker who is counseling her.*

Pullman and Hodgkinson (2006) discuss the issue of whether duty to warn in situations of genetics overrides considerations of confidentiality. In the United States, case law is expanding the responsibility of clinicians beyond patients to include family members.

## Ethical Concerns and the Duty to Warn and Duty to Protect

Since the first Tarasoff decision in 1974, there has been an expansion of the debate around duty to warn and duty to protect, in that the social work literature has expanded to include mental health, HIV/AIDS, domestic violence, and medical issues. Social workers are confronted every day with difficult ethical concerns around duty to warn and duty to protect beyond the mental health field. Social work educators, practitioners, and students need to become knowledgeable about these concepts and their application in various specialties of social work.

A social worker must assess whether and when to apply duty to warn or protect and when to protect confidentiality, and this is not an easy decision. Appelbaum (1985) states that since the time of Tarasoff, mental health professionals have been concerned about confidentiality and the prediction of dangerousness. He sees three stages to making this decision: (1) gather relevant data to evaluate dangerousness and make a determination based on this data, (2) once determining a situation to be dangerous a course of action must be taken, and (3) the therapist must implement this decision.

Borum and Reddy (2001) believe that a fact-based deductive approach is effective in dealing with the issue of duty to warn and duty to protect. They posit that the challenges to making a decision about duty to warn and to protect are based on whether the client poses a serious risk of violence to another and what steps are necessary to protect an intended victim. The question for the clinician

is whether in this situation something should be done and then what to do. The ethical obligation of confidentiality may conflict with the objective of preventing harm to others. To make this determination, Borum and Reddy (2001) state that the clinician must distinguish between making a threat and posing a threat, inquire into attack-related behavior, and conceptualize and gauge the client's risk as a dynamic pathway to action.

Two hypothetical cases illustrate the duty to warn and duty to protect as they relate to confidentiality.

### Case 1

*John is a 35-year-old delusional mental health client who has been hospitalized numerous times. He states that he does not like his brother who lives in California and states that he has threatened him in the past. Today, the client has made a phone call to his brother again and threatened to beat him up. The social worker in assessing the dangerousness of the situation decides that there is no duty to protect or warn. The social worker determines that the threat posed is not serious. The social worker refers him to his psychiatrist for a medication check.*

### Case 2

*David is a 35-year-old male who has a history of domestic violence toward his wife. Both David and his wife are in counseling separately for David's violence toward his wife. In the counseling session, David insists that he is going to hurt his wife tonight at the house. He says that he is going to use a club or hurt her if she does not straighten up. The social worker questions further and determines that this threat is very serious. David has hurt his wife three times with moderate injury each time. The social worker decides that there is a duty to warn based on the threat posed to David's wife.*

A social worker failing to become knowledgeable about these critical issues can be subject to ethical and legal problems, including malpractice and ethical complaints before licensing boards. Social workers need to seek out knowledge in this area to be effective practitioners and educators. NASW provides a valuable Web site (http://www.naswdc.org/ldf/legal_issue/2008/200802.asp?back=yes) on duty to warn laws in different states (NASW, 2011).

# References

Appelbaum, P. S. (1985) Tarasoff and the clinician: Problems in fulfilling the duty to protect. *American Journal of Psychiatry. 142,* 425-429.

Borum, R., & Reddy, M. (2001) Assessing violence risk in Tarasoff situations: A fact based inquiry. *Behavioral Sciences and the Law, 19,* 375-385.

Buel, S., & Drew, M. (2007). Do ask and do tell: Rethinking the lawyer's duty to warn in domestic violence cases. *University of Cincinnati Law Review, 175,* 447-496.

Danis, F. (2003). The criminalization of domestic violence: What social workers need to know. *Social Work, 48* (2), 237-246.

Dolgoff, R., Loewenberg, F. M., & Harrington, D. (2009). *Ethical decisions for social work practice* (8th Ed.) Belmont, CA: Thomson.

Harvard Mental Health Letter, 2006, January, 22, (7), 4-5.

Harvard Mental Health Letter, 2008, January, 24, (7)4-5.

Herbert, P. B. (2002). The duty to warn: A reconsideration and critique. *Journal of the American Academy of Psychiatry and the Law, 30,* 417-424.

Huprich, S., Fuller, K., & Schneider, R. B. (2003). Divergent ethical perspective on duty-to-warn principles with HIV patients. *Ethics and Behavior, 13* (3), 263-278.

Kopels, S., & Kagle, J. D. (1993). Do social workers have a duty to warn? *Social Service Review, 67* (1), 101-126.

Melchert, T., & Patterson, M. (1999). Duty to warn and interventions with HIV-positive clients. *Professional Psychology Research and Practice, 30* (2), 180-186.

NASW (2011). *Social workers and "Duty to Warn" state laws.* Retrieved http://www.naswdc.org/ldf/legal_issue/2008/200802.asp?back=yes

Pullman, D., & Hodgkinson, K. (2006). Genetic knowledge and moral responsibility: Ambiguity at the interface of genetic research and clinical practice. *Clinical Genetics, 69,* 199-203.

Stanard, R., & Hazler, R. (1995). Legal and ethical implications of HIV and duty to warn for counselors: Does Tarasoff apply? *Journal of Counseling and Development, 73* (4), 397-400.

*Tarasoff v. Regents of the University of California* (Cal. 1976) 5551.p.2d 334.

Walcott, D. M., Cerundolo, P., & Beck, J. C. (2001). Current analysis of the Tarasoff duty: An evolution towards the limitation of the duty to protect. *Behavioral Sciences and the Law 19,* 325-343.

*Steven Granich, LCSW, MPA, DSW, is Assistant Professor of Social Work at Lock Haven University. He has 30 years of experience as a licensed clinical social worker and licensed marriage and family therapist in mental health and substance abuse practice. He has research interests in social work clinical practice, drug courts, and international social work.*

## Letter to the Editor

Dear Editor:

In the wake of the Jerry Sandusky sexual abuse allegations, this is a time to raise awareness about the potential of sexual abuse in our communities. Children are sexually abused at alarmingly high rates in our country. The FBI estimates 1 in 3 girls and 1 in 7 boys will be sexually abused before they turn 18. While strangers do abduct children, the rate of stranger abductions is only about .0017 per 1,000 children. The real danger for children comes from neighbors, relatives, coaches, priests, and teachers. Sexual abuse knows no socio-economic, racial, religious, or cultural limitations. White, wealthy, heterosexual men with families and wives sexually abuse more than any other group of people. Sex offenders are charming, skilled deviants who groom their victims into submission or at least silence.

Our society sexualizes everything from toothpaste to soda in advertising. But we fail to prepare children to respond to the sexually abusive acts. Victims, who are children, are made to feel responsible for the acts of adults. Childhood abuse does immeasurable damage to self-esteem and one's ability to trust. Sex is everywhere, but our children have limited understanding, knowledge, or empowerment about their own bodies. Sexual abuse is the silent epidemic that is damaging generation after generation of our children. It is time we stop allowing our fears about discussing sexuality and criminal behavior to create fertile ground for sex offenders to prey on the trust of our children.

This latest case, like every case of child sexual abuse, deserves an immense public outcry. Listening to the news accounts, this story seems almost as much about Penn State and its football program as it is about a child or children being raped by a grown man. In fact, the media is coding rape in nice words like "sexual abuse" or "sexual assault" or "inappropriate touching." These are violent acts. There may not be gory pictures of blood soaked walls like traditional crime scene photos, but don't fool yourself into thinking that nobody was hurt too badly by a little touching. The sexual abuse of a child, any child, is a violent act. Offenders have often groomed their victims so well that the offender thinks the abuse is a consensual act. This delusional justification is part of the pathology that allows sex offenders to continue preying on children.

The most important lesson we can take from this case has nothing to do with football or coaching, but is simply that adults can prevent child sexual abuse. We in fact have a collective moral responsibility to prevent, stop, and report suspected abuse. It is law enforcement and child welfare's responsibility to determine what legal actions to take, but it is your responsibility to make that call. Step up and do what is right. Send a message that you will not tolerate child abuse in your community.

*Jenna Mehnert, MSW, ACSW*
*Executive Director, NASW, Pennsylvania Chapter*

*Editor's Note:* Read more about mandatory reporting of suspected child abuse at: http://www.childwelfare.gov/systemwide/laws_policies/statutes/manda.cfm.

# How My Field Placement Showed Me Why I Wanted To Be a Social Worker

*by Katie Ullman*

People often ask, "Why social work?" It is almost inevitable that a social work student will be asked to answer this question multiple times during his or her social work education. Of course, many people will answer with something along the lines of "wanting to help people." Personally, I have always hated this question. I knew I wanted a career in social work, but I could never find the words to fully explain why. Becoming a social worker was something that just seemed right, an unexplainable feeling that this is what I am supposed to do. Having a feeling is great (especially in this field), but I needed a more definite answer. I needed a universal answer I could tell to salesclerks, my 80-year-old grandfather, and potential employers. So how do you capture your passion for social work in words? I struggled with this question for a long time, and it wasn't until the end of my field placement that I finally understood what social work actually means to me.

My first official field placement was at Families Moving Forward, a supportive program to assist families experiencing homelessness. This field placement was everything I could have hoped for: an amazing field instructor, friendly staff, meaningful work, support, independence, and my very own caseload. The abundance of knowledge I obtained during my placement was something for which I will forever be grateful.

As my hours were coming to an end, I began to invest less of myself at my internship. As many social work students understand, I was juggling far too many things to finish school. Papers, tests, work, field placement, family, friends were taking a toll on me. I was on a race to the finish line, counting hours until I could breathe again. It was in the midst of this chaos that I finally began to answer the infamous question, "Why social work?"

My last case started out seeming ordinary. Little did I know Mary would have such an influence me. Mary was a hardworking single mother who came to Families Moving Forward seeking shelter. She was a delight to be around and was a breath of fresh air to the emergency shelter program. Mary had an associate's degree and was considered highly employable. I would often find her diligently working on the computer to find housing programs and applying to new jobs.

In one of our case management meetings, Mary shared with me the

> **Social work is acting out of love for strangers in tangible ways. We are made to represent love so that all people we encounter have a more profound sense of hope and faith within themselves.**

devastating news–she had been diagnosed with cancer and needed to be treated with chemotherapy and radiation immediately. My heart broke for this woman; being homeless is one thing, but having to go through a serious illness while being in a shelter seemed like cruel and unusual punishment. As social workers know, when it rains it pours. A series of unfortunate events followed as Mary began treatment. As her case manager, I felt completely powerless. What could a social work student such as myself have to offer someone facing cancer in a homeless shelter?

My internship was coming to an end. I only had a few more appointments scheduled with Mary, and I did the average things that needed to be done. Mostly, I just listened to Mary share her experience. I felt bad for not having any profound resources for her and didn't think she would bat an eyelash when

I told her a new case manager would be taking over for me because my field placement was coming to an end.

The day I told Mary I was leaving completely shocked me. She cried hysterically and disclosed that I was the only person who had taken the time to just let her talk about the cancer. She didn't want me to go, because in the midst of all the pain, our weekly meetings were what held her together. Knowing that someone would just be sad with her made the week bearable. All of these weeks, I had been feeling bad about myself for not knowing what to do, and in the end just sitting with her was the most influential thing I was able to do for her.

Mary's response to my leaving was sadness and anger. This makes perfect sense when I look back on the situation, but in the moment I truly thought Mary barely even knew my name, let alone would be angry at me for leaving (oh the joy of being a student!). I felt horrible that I had to leave her and hated that I had to add another piece of sadness to her already fragile plate.

This experience hit something inside me, and for the first time, I finally understood what being a social worker looks like to me. In all of my scrambling to get to the finish line, I finally knew in a logical way, not just an "it feels right" way, why social work is the right profession for me. Social work is acting out of love for strangers in tangible ways. We are made to represent love so that all people we encounter have a more profound sense of hope and faith within themselves. We do the hard, intimate, sometimes painful work, and in return bring a little more of the divine into daily life. We get to remind one another about the bigger, more beautiful picture that we can't always see from where we are.

Sometimes the bottom just falls out, and nobody is exempt. Everything is not okay. And one of the most profound gifts we can give to our clients is the willingness to hunt down tissues or offer a safe place to be upset. Because in the end, what else is there to do? I can't take away the cancer, although I would if I could. I can't buy my client a house, although I would if I could. I can't say that it's never going to happen again and everything will be okay. But I can be there, and I can listen to their stories, of funny things the doctors said, and the strange and annoying things that people think are helpful to say in these situations. I can sit in silence in the moments of rage, knowing that everything is not okay, but that this tiny moment is.

Thanks to my field placement, I now feel confident as to why I am dedicating my career to social work, and I couldn't be more grateful for the amazing people who allowed me to be a part of their journey.

*Katie Ullman is a student in the University of St. Thomas/St Catherine University School of Social Work. Her field placement for 2010-2011 was at Families Moving Forward, a faith-based program in Minneapolis that provides temporary housing and supportive services to children and families. Katie recently became a volunteer at the Angel Foundation where she provides support to adults facing cancer. Her favorite activities are yoga and watching movies with friends. She plans on attending graduate school next year to become an LICSW.*

# I Am Not Sure How To Tell You This:
## Delivering Unwelcome News
### by Misty L. Wall, Ph.D., MSSW, LCSW

Many times, social workers are called upon to deliver unpleasant news to clients and families. Some of the most difficult discussions have to do with death, dying, long-term care placement of a loved one, loss of custody or removal of children, and placement in foster care. There are a few simple steps you can take to facilitate the conversations that no one really wants to have.

Let's look at an all-too-common experience for social workers specializing in child protection. Consider this: As a social worker, you have been working with a family for several months to alleviate risk of injury to their child while living in a home that is full of safety and sanitation hazards. To date, the family has been unable, or unwilling, to make the necessary changes that will allow their child to safely remain in the home. No suitable family members have been located who can provide care for the child while the family makes the necessary changes, so the child will be removed from her biological parents and placed into a foster home.

## PREPing for the Conversation

If you are entering the field of social work, you can safely assume that at some point you will have to deliver news that is not going to be easily received, like the situation mentioned above, when you must tell a family that their child will be placed in foster care. A great deal of work happens before you actually meet with the client to deliver the bad news, and you can use four simple steps (pause, react, evaluate, plan—or PREP) to prepare to deliver challenging news.

*Pause.* It is important to pause before the delivery of unwelcome news, because the focus of the delivery should be the client(s) rather than the social worker. New social workers may feel overwhelmed with feelings surrounding self-doubt, including mistrusting their ability to convey the unwanted news, being unsure of their ability to stay in the moment, fear of the client's reaction, or alarm about their personal safety. Pausing allows you, the social worker, to take a personal inventory of your fears, emotional triggers, and physical reactions before you meet with the client.

*React.* Taking inventory of your fear, emotional triggers, and physical reactions is not enough to ensure you are able to stay present and focused on the client during the delivery of unwelcome news. After taking a breath, social workers should give themselves permission to react emotionally or physically, consciously allowing whatever physical and emotional reaction simmers to the surface to happen. Stuffing or refusing to acknowledge emotional and physical reactions can lead to burnout, compassion fatigue, or somatic complaints. Everyone's reactions will be different—it may mean crying, screaming, venting to a trusted peer, or any number of things. Only after you allow this initial reaction can you refocus yourself on your goals.

*Evaluate.* Evaluation while PREPing to deliver unwelcome news includes consideration of the client's perspective and planning to reduce the impact of trauma resulting from negative news to the greatest extent possible. Considering the task before the child protection social worker described earlier, we may feel limited in our ability to empathize with the parents who have been unable, or unwilling, to make the necessary changes to allow their child to remain in their care. However, many of us can imagine a time that we have received painful news that changed our lives forever.

Reflect on the setting where you first learned there had been an attack on the Twin Towers on September 11, 2001. Chances are that when you think about that time, you can remember everything about where you were, what the room looked like, who was with you, what they were wearing, what you heard, and how you felt.

When preparing to deliver unwanted news to a client, it can be beneficial to acknowledge the pain associated with receiving such news. Potential ways in which social workers may be able to reduce the stress caused by receiving hurtful news may include considering location and physical setting, ensuring there are adequate chairs for everyone, and providing for small comforts such as water or tissues. Also, it is important to take into consideration who will be present, who will be excluded, and timing.

Reflect on the chore before our child protection worker. Although there is likely never a good time to convey the decision to remove a child from his/her parents, there are times when such information may be received with less difficulty. Contemplate the difference between delivering the news of a foster

## Steps in Delivering Unwelcome News

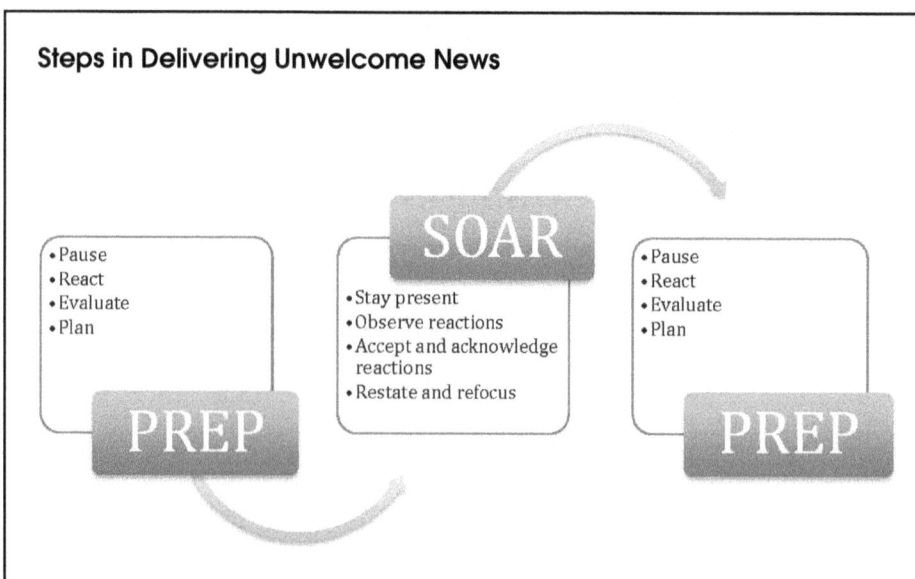

- Pause
- React
- Evaluate
- Plan

**PREP**

**SOAR**
- Stay present
- Observe reactions
- Accept and acknowledge reactions
- Restate and refocus

- Pause
- React
- Evaluate
- Plan

**PREP**

care placement at the client's place of employment and delivering the same news at the client's home or trusted family member's home. Likewise, imagine that you are delivering the decision to remove a child from the parents in the lobby of your office versus in a visiting room with a bottle of water, a chair, and tissues available for the client. Your empathy for the client's experience will be evident in the setting you choose for the delivery of undesirable information.

*Plan.* After you have paused, reacted, and evaluated the situation objectively, it is time to actively plan your delivery. At the least, you should know the reasons leading up to the "news" and be able to respond concisely to your client's concerns and questions. This is not a time to have to review the file or ask someone else.

Again, remember where you were when you heard of the first and second attacks on the Twin Towers. Remember the agony you experienced, as so many questions remained unanswered? Imagine the agony of the mother who has been told she is unable to provide a safe home for her child and the questions that would swirl through your mind after hearing such news. What can I do to have my child returned? What about a relative? How long will she be gone? Can I see her? Imagine a social worker retorting to your concerns with uncertainty, ambiguity, or disinterest.

Additionally, consciously determine your goal for the delivery. Take a deep breath and think about what you want your client to remember at the end of this conversation. This is the goal. It should be short, specific, and clear.

## SOARing Through the Delivery

The actual delivery of a hard-hitting announcement is generally over very quickly. In fact, when you have prepared yourself thoroughly as described above, the actual delivery of bad news should not take more than a few minutes. Many beginning practitioners feel they must stay with the client while he or she processes the worrisome information. This is not true. The actual processing and making meaning of bad news is the responsibility of the client. If we stay, we can actually prevent the client from beginning this important work. Consider

the following suggestions to SOAR (stay present, observe reactions, acknowledge reactions, restate and refocus) through the actual delivery of difficult news.

*Stay present.* Stay present in the room with your client and help the client stay present. Remember that you have taken considerable time to plan for this moment. You have a solid plan that is client-focused. If you feel the conversation is getting beyond your control, take a break, refocus on your goal, and trust in your ability.

*Observe reactions.* Your client will undoubtedly give you the clues you need. Pay attention. If someone appears lightheaded, offer water or a place to sit. If your client appears to need some time alone, offer to step away for a moment. Your reaction to your client is important to maintaining your working relationship, because the delivery of unwanted news is often the beginning of a social worker's relationship with a client.

*Accept reactions.* It does not matter if your client should have seen this coming; his or her initial reactions will be genuine and emotion-focused. Think about our child protection social worker once again. Comments from the social worker such as, "You have had several warnings and could have prevented this if you wanted to," put your client in a defensive stance and make you the enemy rather than a teammate. Validate immediate emotional reactions without judgment. Another way our child protection social worker may respond, this time with the focus being on acceptance and empathy, may be, "I can see you are extremely upset by this news. I imagine you have questions." This is not the time to make connections between behavior and consequences.

*Restate and refocus.* After you paraphrase the news and the client's reactions, point out any strengths you have seen in your client, and convey that you will work with the client to sort out the pieces and that you are confident that you and the client will be able to work together to find a path of action. Our child protection social worker may close with something such as, "You seem very upset and tearful at the thought of your child being in foster care tonight. I have seen you face many difficult situations during our work together, and I am confident we will make a plan that will help keep your child safe."

## PREPing For Next Time

Remember again your reaction when you found out about the terrorist attack on New York City. Just hearing the story and subsequent news coverage was simply the beginning. The real processing or sorting out of the events happened later. The same is often true of delivering bad news to a client. We may relive or replay the scenario in our heads, have difficulty sleeping, doubt or second-guess our decisions, or have other physical or psychological reactions.

Understanding that your work does not end with the actual delivery of arduous information is critical to your ability to provide the best services to your client, remain healthy, and avoid burnout or compassion fatigue. When you finish delivering the bad news, it is time to revisit the original PREP (pause, react, evaluate, plan) process previously discussed, this time with an eye toward

> **Understanding that your work does not end with the actual delivery of arduous information is critical to your ability to provide the best services to your client, remain healthy, and avoid burnout or compassion fatigue.**

your future work with this client and many more to come. The following are a few suggestions for managing your reactions to delivering bad news and preparing for the inevitable time when you find yourself in a position to deliver trying news again.

*Pause.* As quickly after the delivery as possible, pause. Take a few deep breaths.

*React and refocus.* Allow whatever physical and emotional reaction simmers to the surface to happen. Only after you allow this initial reaction can you refocus yourself on your goal.

*Evaluate.* After you have given yourself the opportunity to feel the emotions that simmer up, it is time to start sorting out your professional performance. Is there something that seemed to help the client? Is there something you think was ineffective or even unhelpful? How can you improve next time?

*Plan.* After you have given yourself time to pause, react, and evaluate, it is time to plan for next time. Respect the fact that you are an important vehicle for effecting change for your client. Take the reactions of you and your client and plan to increase the positive experiences next time and reduce the negative impacts when possible.

*Misty L. Wall, Ph.D., MSSW, LCSW, is an assistant professor in the School of Social Work at Boise State University.*

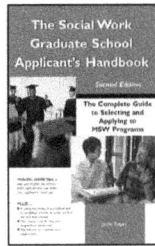

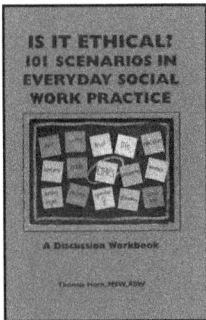

# When To Surrender: A New Definition for Veterans in Substance Abuse Treatment

## by Heidi Peck, LCSW

Substance abuse counselors often find clients unsure about sobriety. There are many ways to process ambivalence in the therapeutic setting. Achieving a strong foundation to support sobriety calls for a firm commitment and steadfast willingness to adapt former thinking patterns. Addressing ambivalence is an integral part of the treatment process, and not addressing it can welcome the likelihood of returning to active using in the future.

Chronic relapse plagues many substance abusing veterans. Trying over and over to walk the same path of treatment while aspiring to acquire new insight into one's own addiction can be tedious and frustrating. One area in which ambivalence habitually runs rampant is with the concept of "surrender," a term that is used in treatment centers universally. Among the veteran substance abusing population, this struggle seems to be further complicated by the intellectual track-work laid down early in their military careers.

### Surrender—What Does It Mean?

The word "surrender" can evoke fear and resistance from anyone trying to recover from the devastating grips of addiction. For veterans, this is not only an uphill battle, but they can stay paralyzed for years, even decades, by applying consciously or unconsciously an old definition of the word. Witnessing this cycle of confusion led me to recognize the benefits of taking a more comprehensive look into the word "surrender."

When I mention surrender and ask what this means from their understanding of a recovery-based or 12-Step Model perception, many veterans report they think of the following: admitting powerlessness or unmanageability in life, taking a suggestion, or accepting help. When I ask what they think of when hearing the term "surrender" from a military standpoint, many often reply: Give up, fail, quit, or retreat. They express a strong fixed notion to "Never surrender!" Originally this was taught, probably in basic training, as a military tactic. And throughout the time they served, this evolved into a belief that holding to this steadfast decree would preserve their

unit's honor. This was often portrayed to be a last resort strategic move. Years later, many veterans continue to abide by this mantra as translated to become true devotion to their comrades and country, believing that surrender is for the weak. This attitude adopted in the past can be at the root of their ambivalence today. Not reconciling this, I believe, contributes greatly to the vast recidivism rate of veterans returning to treatment.

### Does Surrender Equal Defeat?

"Who cares to admit complete defeat? Practically no one, of course." These are the first words of the chapter on Step One in the book AA often uses, *Twelve Steps and Twelve Traditions*. There are some similarities associated with both terms. For instance, in the military, surrender is a tactic that can be used if death seems more than likely but probable. Similarly, people often come voluntarily to treatment when death seems close. Both are tactics that preserve life when terror evoked by the sudden awareness that death is near becomes present.

"Historical references have shown that even though the troops were trained one way, triumphant military commanders were trained another—they knew how to surrender. Or at least we know that the successful ones did," says Joe McQ. in *The Steps We Took*. Throughout history, the names Custer and MacArthur are often brought up when referencing this topic. Not only was surrendering an option, but the act of deciding when to deploy this approach was crucial. MacArthur exemplified the belief that choosing to surrender didn't mean to quit. In fact, unlike Custer, MacArthur's choice kept his troops in the battle only to finish victoriously.

Often, resistance toward surrender remains in the unconscious mind of the veteran, and old notions of "Never surrender!" turn into fixed behavior. So how do we help them reconcile this conflict?

### A Group Intervention

The group intervention I developed while working with outpatient veterans

in abstinence-based substance abuse treatment can be utilized in various treatment modalities. I begin this intervention in a psychodynamic group, by dividing the members into two teams. I assign one team to represent the concept of surrender from a military standpoint, and the other to represent surrender from a recovery standpoint. I ask each team to pull their chairs together, appoint a recording secretary, nominate a spokesperson, and answer the following questions: *What is a definition of the word "surrender" from your team's perspective? What are similarities between both standpoints? And what are the differences?*

Once these have been answered, I ask the group members to move their chairs back into the usual formation, and I set up two chairs next to each other toward the front of the room. I ask the two spokespersons to sit in these two chairs. Then, using answers the teams recorded, I have each spokesperson represent the team's perspective in a mock trial.

As we go through their answers, I am mindful to ask the team members whether they have anything to add, and whether their spokesperson is accurately representing the work of the team. This facilitates maintaining everyone's attention and also prevents the spokesperson from giving impromptu answers. In the trial, I pose the question, "Which is the correct definition of the word surrender?" I then have the group members engage in a debate representing their respective teams.

After we finish the debate, we start to process the activity. I ask if there were either any barriers or an additional level of comfort when they were asked to break down the larger group. Together, we speak about changes in communication patterns that occurred by moving chairs, working in smaller groups, and being assigned a task. Working with the camaraderie of the teams, I give the group members an opportunity to advocate for each other by asking, "Did any team member offer an answer you were surprised by, changed your opinion, or provided new insight?" This is usually an opportunity for some of the more vocal members to highlight work of the less talkative members in the group. Often, certain individuals experience intimidation and/or social anxiety in the large therapeutic group setting, but when charged with a specific task in a smaller group, they emerge as leaders. It is important to acknowledge this strength. This often helps these individuals feel more comfortable actively participating in the larger group setting, and it encourages their peers to elicit future participation from them based on their meaningful past contributions in the smaller group setting.

Next, I ask each of the members to share when they were discharged from the military. We point out how many years each group member has held the military, or "old," definition of this word. And for those veterans in active duty or recently discharged, it's likely they are still actively functioning by this military mindset. In my experience, these members have the greatest struggle with adapting a new concept. At this point, I turn to the group members for confirmation that they have been associating with the military definition since the time of their service. Asking if they agree with this statement provides an opportunity for breakthrough. Members commonly become enlightened and share that they have not thought about this conflict before.

I ask the group members to speak about how their definition of surrender has changed as a result of this activity. As a facilitator, I remain open to both positive and oppositional feedback, understanding that some may not agree with adapting a new connotation. I ask the group members to explain struggles that not embracing the recovery concept of surrender have posed in past treatment episodes.

## Associations and the Brain

Also, I provide a psychoeducational component regarding how associations work in the brain. We speak about the definition of Hebbian Theory (see *http://tinywiki.org/Hebbian_theory.html* ) and the statement, "Cells that fire together, wire together." I provide the following example: "Have you ever passed kids playing on a playground and suddenly wanted ice cream?" When people see a child on a playground, they may consciously or unconsciously recall their own childhood, playing in the playground, and buying a snack from the ice cream truck. Although these activities are

different, they become related through the power of association. At the point when someone wants ice cream, or even in the present as I am illustrating in this example, they may picture the ice cream, see an ice cream cone melting in the sun, have the illusion of how the ice cream would taste in their mouth, and so forth. Associations are common in addiction. Often, addicts and professionals refer to them as "relapse triggers." For example, this is why an alcohol dependent person may experience an intense craving to drink a beer on a hot summer day. Even though he is sober and alcohol is nowhere in sight, the person associates the beer with the weather, and consequently is increasingly triggered to drink.

Finally, I ask the group to remain mindful and share feelings of comfort or tension release that they experienced during this activity. Often, bringing this conflict from the unconscious to the conscious results in tension release. When trying to permanently reconcile this conflict, first we must begin by talking about it. Then we can point out disparities to break this association. For example, I might say, "In the military, you surrender as a unit, while in recovery this is an individual action. In the military, surrender is the last line of defense, whereas in recovery, we learn this is the first line of defense. Surrender and the rest shall follow."

As we prepare to end this activity, I bring to mind embracing a gradual change. I tell the group if they are aware that something has changed slightly, remain confused, or still feel ambivalent toward fully embracing this new concept, that's okay. I remind them of how many years they were abiding by one strongly ingrained military definition of surrender. Changing this word's meaning will be a personal process, but becoming aware of this conflict is the mission of this intervention.

I encourage the group members to continue to think about this concept, allowing time for the process of accepting the recovery definition to gently unfold into the conscious and unconscious mind. Ultimately, if veterans remain in isolation still grappling with this concept, they fail to avail themselves of many benefits of group cohesion. However, once the veterans are able to accept this term into their recovery process, they are welcomed by others who have also chosen to do so. Many veterans will share that the bonds formed with sober

peers in treatment are reminiscent of their time in the service. Depending on their comrades in matters of life and death once again creates a unique level of trust. Encouraging feelings of inclusiveness can promote a healthy social network through the common bonds of both military service and addiction, which fosters a supportive environment in which veterans can be successful in attaining long-term sobriety.

Learning new perspectives and utilizing different terminologies or word meanings can be uncomfortable at first. Breaking old associations and forming new ones can open the door toward acceptance of concepts that ultimately will provide the cornerstones of one's recovery. For many, working to resolve internal conflicts and gain acceptance of a new perspective is vital to successful treatment. And for the veteran, not changing the word "surrender," but adapting its connotation, may just cut off the central lifeline fueling ambivalence toward sustaining long-term sobriety.

## References

Anonymous. (2007). *Twelve steps and twelve traditions.* New York: Alcoholics Anonymous World Services, Inc. (Original work published 1952).

McQ, J. (1990). *The steps we took.* Little Rock, AR: August House Publishers, Inc.

Doidge, N. (2007). *The brain that changes itself.* United States: Viking Press. pp. 427.

*Heidi Peck, LCSW, graduated from New York University with her MSW in 2005. She has worked for the VA Medical Center in New York since 2007. Prior to that, she held the position of Senior Counselor in the Intake Department at Realization Center, Inc. She has provided clinical services for the Su Casa Methadone-to-Abstinence Therapeutic Community's Pregnant Women and Infants Program, Lower Eastside Services Center's Mental Health Clinic, and Somerset Youth Services Commission for Juvenile Justice in New Jersey. Heidi completed a fellowship at Eagleton Institute. She would like to dedicate this article to the memory of her father.*

# Sexualization of Young Girls in Entertainment
## by Heather Dawley-McClendon

Concerns exist today among parents, particular social groups, and the government that girls as young as seven are being introduced to sexual material, and this is affecting their psychological well-being in many different ways (Grabe & Shibley-Hyde, 2009). Adolescent girls are dealing with poor body image, eating disorder symptoms, depression, and anxiety, as well as reduced mathematical ability, logical reasoning, and spatial orientation (Grabe & Shibley-Hyde, 2009).

In 2007, the American Psychological Association (APA) authorized a task force to investigate the connection of entertainment with the sexual objectification of youth. Sexual objectification, according to Grabe and Hyde's essay *Body Objectification, MTV, and Psychological Outcomes Among Female Adolescents*, is defined as "instances in which a person is made into a thing for others' sexual use, rather than being seen as a person with the capacity for independent action and decision making" (Grabe & Shibley-Hyde, 2009). According to the article *That Swimsuit Becomes You: Sex Differences in Self-Objectification, Restrained Eating, and Math Performance*, self-objectification occurs when individuals take on the perspective of another when viewing their own body, rather than an internal view (Fredrickson, 1998). In other words, they focus on what others see rather than what they are personally feeling or experiencing. The APA determined that the following factors distinguish sexual objectification from a healthy sexual identity:

- *a person's value comes only from his or her sexual appeal or behavior, to the exclusion of other characteristics;*
- *a person is held to a standard that equates physical attractiveness (narrowly defined) with being sexy;*
- *a person is sexually objectified; and/or*
- *sexuality is inappropriately imposed on a person* (American Psychological Association, 2011).

Only one of these needs to be present for it to be considered sexual objectification, and naturally, the final factor is the one that most characterizes adolescent girls. According to *Body Objectification and Depression in Adolescents: The Role of Gender, Shame, and Rumination,* self-evaluation is "characterized by vigilant monitoring or self-surveillance" (Grabe, Shibley-Hyde, & Lindberg, 2007). Self-objectification, self-surveillance, body objectification, and sexualization are often used interchangeably, although Grabe and co-authors (2007) argue that self-objectification is the result of extensive self-surveillance.

## Data

A bill was introduced in the Senate by Kay Hagan (D-NC) and Robert Menendez (D-NJ) that requests funding for research to examine the role that media play in sexual objectification and for programs that would educate and empower young girls combatting the harmful effects of sexual objectification. This bill states that most 8- to 18-year-olds use some form of recreational media for around ten hours a day. It also tells us that only 34% of girls report being very satisfied with their bodies, and that 60% compare their bodies to fashion models. Almost 90% of girls feel pressured by the fashion industry to be thin, 55% diet, 42% know someone who has purged after eating, 37% know someone diagnosed with an eating disorder and 31% acknowledged that they have starved themselves or refused food to lose weight. Fifty-five percent of third through fifth grade girls worry about their appearance, with 37% of those specifically about their weight (Hagan & Menendez, 2010). These numbers are concerning, to say the least. There has been little research to determine if there is a difference between races, socio-economic status, and gender in regard to the impact of entertainment on early sexualization.

## Legislation

The bill introduced by Hagan and Menendez, known as the "Healthy Media for Youth Act," primarily addresses research and education. Both are highly necessary to give girls the tools they need to grow with a sense of security, value, and empowerment. The bill would give funds to research the impact the entertainment industry has on the development of youth, focusing on how girls are depicted and the effect that has on their cognitive, physical, and social behavior. It would also fund research that would focus on how perceptions and attitudes regarding the abilities, equality, appearances, and leadership potential of girls and boys are affected by entertainment depictions of women. The funds would also provide education to provide critical thinking skills, promote a balanced depiction of women in media, and counter the damaging effects already widespread.

The biggest concern about the bill was the provision that "the applicant will abide by any limitations deemed appropriate by the Secretary on any charges to individuals receiving services pursu-

ant to the grant. As deemed appropriate by the Secretary, such limitations on charges may vary based on the financial circumstances of the individual receiving services" (Hagan & Menendez, 2010). In other words, programs that receive funds would be subject to limitations that the Secretary would impose in regard to how much they would be able to charge for educating youth. There is no definition of what is appropriate and what would constitute the need for limitations to be put in place. The solution to this ambiguity would be to make it more specific, yet open enough to benefit girls from all socio-economic backgrounds. Something like a sliding scale based on income might work, with a single cap limit set by the Secretary. That would allow for low-income families to utilize the services while also allowing girls from a higher income bracket family to receive services without either being turned away because of income restrictions.

The current version of this bill, introduced July 13, 2011, by Rep. Tammy Baldwin, can be found at *http://www.govtrack.us/congress/bill.xpd?bill=h112-2513*.

## Recommendations

Although there has been research demonstrating self-surveillance and objectification in college-age students, studies need to be conducted that sample adolescent girls and boys to determine if gender differentiates the objectification of oneself (Grabe, Shibley-Hyde, & Lindberg, 2007).

Psychologists, social workers, counselors, and other mental health workers need to be educated on the role that self-objectification takes in the development of young girls and armed with material and activities to counter the effects that entertainment has on girls at vulnerable stages (Grabe, Shibley-Hyde, & Lindberg, 2007).

Mentoring programs could be established to give adolescent girls a safe place to voice their concerns, fears, and desires and allow someone equipped with the knowledge, insight, and compassion to help them through difficult times relating to the prevalence of sexual objectification that they are exposed to on a daily basis.

Finally, programs ought to be put into place to educate parents. As L. Z. Ganderson aptly points out in his editorial, *Parents, Don't Dress Your Girls Like Tramps*, children are not the ones with

the money to spend on clothing that sexualizes them. It is the parents who are spending the money so that their young girls become objects of sexualization (Granderson, 2011). This is an area in which many parents seem to be in need of help in raising and educating their children.

Something has also been lost along the way with such a separation of generations that has come around with technology. Many children are very tech-savvy and have grandparents and parents who do not use much of the technology available. The differences over the last several decades have affected the inter-relations of the generations (Thornton, 2001).

Because of this gap, youth are losing out on important, relevant information from their elders. A program to promote inter-generational relations and utilizing available family members of different generations to teach them to communicate and educate one another would be beneficial to youth. It would allow children to teach their elders how to use technology, and would encourage respect for others while broadening the knowledge base of youth with regard to communication, diversity, and personal character traits.

## References

American Psychological Association. (2011). *Sexualization of girls*. Retrieved April 22, 2011, from American Psychological Association: http://www.apa.org/pi/women/programs/girls/report.aspx#

Baldwin, T. (2011, July 13). *H.R. 2513 Healthy Media for Youth Act*. Retrieved December 14, 2011, from http://www.gov-track.us/congress/bill.xpd?bill=h112-2513.

Fredrickson, B. R. (1998). That swimsuit becomes you: Sex differences in self-objectification, restrained eating, and math performance. *Journal of Personality and Social Psychology*, 269-284.

Grabe, S., & Shibley-Hyde, J. (2009). Body objectification, MTV, and psychological outcomes among female adolescents. *Journal of Applied Social Psychology*, 2840-2858.

Grabe, S., Shibley-Hyde, J., & Lindberg, S. M. (2007). Body objectification and depression in adolescents: The role of gender, shame, and rumination. *Psychology of Women Quarterly*, 164-175.

Granderson, L. Z. (2011, April 19). *Parents, don't dress your girls like tramps*. Retrieved April 20, 2011, from CNN.com: http://www.cnn.com/2011/OPINION/04/19/granderson.children.dress/index.html

Hagan, K., & Menendez, R. (2010, September 28). *S.3852 Healthy Media for Youth Act*. Retrieved April 22, 2011, from http://www.govtrack.us/congress/bill.xpd?bill=s111-3852

Thornton, A., & Young-Demarco, L. (2001). Four decades of trends in attitudes toward family issues in the United States: The 1960s through the 1990s. *Journal of Marriage and Family*, 1009-1037.

*Heather Dawley-McClendon is a non-traditional student at Syracuse University in the School of Social Work. She is a member of Social Workers United on the campus and works with teen mothers through the Young Lives program in Syracuse, New York. She has three children from age 7 to 15—one son and two daughters.*

# 3 Components of Turning Passion Into a Successful Social Work Career

## *by Sonya O. Hunte, MSW*

It is no secret that social workers are often described as passionate. The question becomes: *How can one turn that passion into a successful and fulfilling career?* Many social workers desire a career that is not characterized with "burnout" but with true joy. Personal passion has to be defined, directed, and cultivated to have career success. The three major components of building a successful career–defining vision, seeking mentorship, and participating in professional development–can assist in building a career that fuels your passion or help sustain you!

## 1. Define your vision.

Defining your vision can be a challenging task. Vision forces us to think about the life we want and its components. The keys in creating a vision are to have goals, steps, and timelines. Most of us have done this with our clients when creating family and treatment plans. A fun way of creating goals is to create a vision board. Vision boards are usually large poster boards containing a collage of words and pictures that come together to create a story in future tense. For example, a vision board can include a picture of your dream home, the words of an inspirational song that provide you with motivation, the names of two countries that you plan to visit within the next two years, and a picture of the building that houses the agency for which you aspire to work. Vision boards are not permanent, in that they can be edited and updated as often as you see fit. The vision board should be placed in an area where you can view it daily. I usually create a new vision board every other year. For me, 24 months allows room to work toward my goals at a reasonable pace.

Some people may find that a detailed checklist works better. Checklists can be divided into categories such as entrepreneurship, professional learning, work objectives, special projects, volunteerism, debt management, and family. The checklist should include reasonable timelines for each goal listed. If you are saying to yourself, *I need help to even break down what I visualize for my life,* there are books available on this phenomenon. Those books are usually located in the self help section of most bookstores.

An experienced mentor will also aide in the creation of reasonable aspiration setting and attainment.

## 2. Seek mentorship.

Mentorship is an opportunity for the mentee to be developed professionally and personally. After creating a physical display of your vision, you should seek a mentor who is currently occupying your dream job. Many people are open to having at minimum one meeting with an aspiring professional. Do not be afraid to ask those you admire to coffee or lunch to "pick their brains" for ideas and suggestions on professional development and growth.

Mentorship does not always have to be one-on-one but can take place in a group setting. The mentor can share his or her experience with a group of aspiring professionals. Conferences that are geared toward personal and professional development may provide the information you need.

Personal growth is very much a part of this process, especially for young professionals. It makes no sense to work hard at career goals but lack the interpersonal skills needed for success. Personal attributes like interpersonal and communication skills can be worked through in a mentoring relationship.

Mentorship can also take the form of patterning. This can be initiated by reading the biographies of those you admire. A great way to pattern is to take note of the mentor's organizational affiliations, educational background, and skill sets. In the age of social networking, it is easy to locate information about those we admire. Many people have LinkedIn

## Sonya's Vision Board

*This is my vision board. It reflects various aspects of my life and changes about every two years.*

accounts where their résumé is made available to the public. The résumé, as opposed to the bio, may provide insight as to the work completed and the timing. I once heard Oprah state that she often mimicked Barbara Walters' interviewing style and wanted to dress like many veteran television personalities. It appeared that without meeting these people, Oprah was able to mimic some of their characteristics until she could develop her own style. In the same way, we should glean from those we admire until we are able to find our own path and what works for us.

## 3. Participate in professional development.

Skill and professional development takes on many forms. They can range from classroom-based courses to volunteer work. It will be helpful to look at the trends in your social work specialty to get a sense of what degrees and certifications are needed for you to flourish. There are social workers who work with public health agencies who have found it beneficial to return to school for a public health degree. Other social workers who work in the nonprofit arena have obtained certifications in nonprofit management. Social workers who work in school systems often return to school to enter doctoral programs in educational policy.

By developing new skills, you are adding features that polish you as a job candidate. Find out what skills you need to occupy your dream job. Skill development-based organizations like Toastmasters International provide free or low cost opportunities for public speaking development. Many volunteer based organizations provide leadership development as a part of the volunteer experience.

On a personal note, I have benefitted from leadership and brand development courses offered at the Junior League of Atlanta, where I am a member. I have also taken a writing workshop given by the National Association of Social Workers, Georgia Chapter. Many local Chambers of Commerce offer leadership courses that promote leadership in local communities. The leadership program model spans economic, social, governmental, and cultural segments. The skills developed in volunteer leadership roles, programs, and on-the-job commit-

tees can be used as résumé builders. Dr. Lois Frankel, author of *101 Unconscious Mistakes Women Make That Sabotage Their Careers,* advises us to volunteer for special projects in the workplace to increase skills and to gain recognition.

Skill and professional development also occurs in networking. In 2010, I was a part of a women's networking group. The objective of the group was to provide a diverse group of women an opportunity to create a New Year plan, share it with the group, and for the group to utilize its networks and influences to aid fellow group members in achieving their goals. The diversity of the group members also provided additional insight and considerations in my goal setting and life planning. This may be a great idea for some workplaces, as well as social and other groups. Some of the women in the group desired to go back to school, and the group read and edited each personal statement. One of the women is now completing her master's in business administration at Cornell University.

Many of you may be taking some of these steps now. It is important to organize your vision for positive outcomes. Mentorship will be a key factor in your organization of goals. As social workers, we tend to be resourceful for others. Research opportunities to fine tune *your* goals. Take advantage of low- and no-cost trainings and leadership opportunities. Skill and professional development are important in becoming the ideal you. As you take this journey of turning your passion into a successful career, your clarity will increase with every step and goal accomplished. Much success to you on your journey!

*Sonya O. Hunte, MSW, is a Homeless Education Liaison with the Atlanta Public Schools. She is also the CEO of Hunte Community Development Consulting LLC, a company specializing in nonprofit strategic program development, training, and community partnership planning.*

## STUDENT SOCIAL WORK ORGANIZATIONS

Please send us a short **news** article about your group's activities. Also, send us **photos** of your club in action–we may even feature you on our front cover!

It's easy to share your club's activities with our readers. Send your news/photos to:

Linda Grobman, ACSW, LSW, Editor/Publisher
THE NEW SOCIAL WORKER
P.O. Box 5390, Harrisburg, PA 17110-0390
or to *lindagrobman@socialworker.com*

### National Day of Silence at Mississippi State University

*Social work students at Mississippi State University participated in the National Day of Silence on April 15, 2011. On the National Day of Silence, hundreds of thousands of students from middle school through the university level took a vow of silence to bring attention to anti-LGBT name-calling, bullying and harassment in their schools.*

## Mansfield University Introduction to Social Work Students Help in Flood Relief Efforts

Students in a Fall 2011 Mansfield University Introduction to Social Work class were encouraged to assist in flood relief activities following Hurricane Irene and Tropical Storm Lee. In bus trips organized by the Mansfield University admissions office, students volunteered full days to travel to flooded communities in Athens and Towanda, Pennsylvania, to help in the flood relief. Students donned their waterproof boots, gloves, and facemasks to help families clear their homes of mud soaked items. Other options for students to get involved included participation in campus organized flood relief fundraisers, such as collecting community donations at Walmart and staffing a campus fundraising concert. Since this was a project of an Introduction to Social Work class, students learned first hand that giving their time to others in need helps to foster the social work values of service to the community.

*Mansfield University Intro to Social Work students provide flood relief.*

### Social Work Association of Tomorrow Day Without Violence

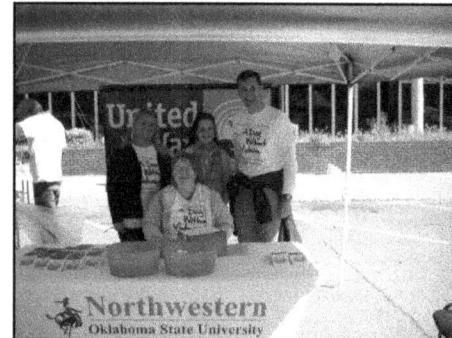

*Northwestern Oklahoma State University social work students represent the Social Work Association of Tomorrow (SWAT) "manning" the booth during the Garfield County DV Task Force Second Annual Day Without Violence event on April 16, 2011. Seated: Connie Stevens. Standing from left to right: Kaimi Botts; Jennifer Ghigna; and Mike Fields, Garfield County District Attorney.*

FOLLOW ME ON TWITTER

**The New Social Worker is on Twitter! Follow us at:** *http://www.twitter.com/newsocialworker*

# Social Work Students in Action

*Dominican College (NY) BSW students advocate for human rights and social justice, locally and globally.*

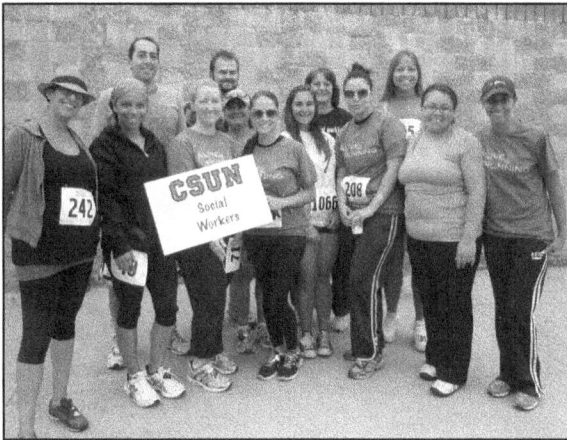

*MSW students from the California State University-Northridge Social Work Society participated in the Didi Hirsch Alive and Running 5k to raise awareness for suicide prevention.*

*Some of the 21 seniors in the Siena College BSW Program participated in the Annual Walk to End Alzheimer's in Saratoga Springs, NY, on September 24, 2011. Students raised more than $1,300 for the Walk and conducted on-campus public awareness activities about the disease. The flowers were a part of the Walk this year, with purple flowers representing knowing someone with Alzheimer's and the orange flowers representing supporters.*

*Gilberto—continued from page 3*

both. But the influence goes in both directions, she insists. "To me, a good leader can both lead and take direction from others, and I feel I have a good balance between the two. It is really important to listen to what the people you are leading have to say, and I feel I do that, as well."

Gilberto attended her first NASW meeting recently, and found herself the youngest person in the room. "Everyone else was well into their careers, in their 40s," she says. But Gilberto found the other members welcoming.

At this point, she's just observing, feeling comfortable speaking with her fellow members outside the meeting rooms, but less so during the meeting itself. By the time the next in-person meeting takes place in April—in between there are two virtual ones—the self-defined extrovert expects she'll have more to say.

"I want to be an advocate for other BSW students," she comments. "A lot of them don't know about NASW and about its *Code of Ethics*. The organization can help with their social work careers and futures. They don't know how much."

In an age that values Renaissance people, Gilberto is very career-oriented. Even her volunteer work is centered around her career. She dates casually, but isn't ready for anything serious yet.

"Social work and volunteering are what I like to do," she says. "I like talking to people, and I like reading books about addiction and journeys, like the book *Beautiful Boy: A Father's Journey Through His Son's Addiction* (by David Sheff).

Still, if she had a block of time to do whatever she wanted and no responsibilities, Gilberto said she'd travel. "Different cultures really fascinate me, and I really hope to go to Africa, India, and Greece some day," she says. "But with just a week, I'd definitely go to Italy to see my family. And since I'd be in Italy, I would go to the Island of Capri to soak up the sun."

But she doesn't mind too much—not at all, in fact—being immersed in social work and volunteerism, with an occasional weekend at home.

*Barbara Trainin Blank is a freelance writer based in Harrisburg, PA.*

# Poetry

## We Are Social Workers
### by Tammie Knick, MSW

We are
Social workers
Action takers
Change agents
Policy makers.

We are
Social justice pursuers
Impression makers
Vulnerability protectors
Barrier breakers.

We are
Good listeners
Task organizers
Self-determination promoters
Empathizers.

We are
Thought provokers
Community organizers
Cultural responders
Story summarizers.

We are
Informed consent disclosers
Confidentiality keepers
Code of Ethics followers
Risk takers and leapers.

We are
Global explorers
Soul searchers
Passionate helpers.

We are Social workers!

*Dedicated to the MSW Class of 2010
Minnesota State University, Mankato*

*Tammie has been the Gibbon-Fairfax-Win-
throp Middle School Social Worker in Fair-
fax, Minnesota for the past 10 years. Tammie
obtained her master's degree in social work
from Minnesota State University in Mankato,
Minnesota and is currently working toward
becoming a Licensed Independent Clinical
Social Worker. Tammie wrote this poem as
part of the speech she gave at her MSW class
graduation ceremony in July of 2010. Tammie is also the President of the Minnesota
School Social Workers Association.*

## Be a Fan of *The New Social Worker* on Facebook!

As of December 16, 2011, we have reached 12,967 fans (or "likers") of our page on Facebook at *http://www.facebook.com/newsocialworker*.

Besides providing information about *The New Social Worker* magazine, the page has some of the features of a typical Facebook profile—a "wall" where you can exchange messages, a discussion board, and a place for photos and videos.

We also list upcoming events, such as the online chats we co-spon-sor with the National Association of Social Workers (NASW) at *http://www.socialworkchat.org*. And we send updates to our fans when there is something interesting happening!

Are you on Facebook? Do you love *The New Social Worker?* Show us how much you care! Be one of our Facebook "likers" and help us reach 15,000 (and beyond)!

We also have a Facebook page for our SocialWorkJobBank.com site! Go to *http://www.facebook.com/socialworkjobbank* to "like" this page. New job postings at *http://www.socialworkjobbank.com* are now automatically posted to the Facebook page, as well.

Finally, stay up-to-date on our latest books at *http://www.facebook.com/whitehatcommunications*.

In addition, we'd like to know how *you* are using Facebook. Have you found it a useful tool for networking with social work colleagues, searching for a job, or fundraising for your agency? Write to lindagrobman@socialworker.com and let us know.

**Facebook address:** *http://www.facebook.com/newsocialworker*
*Also check out our other pages:*
http://www.facebook.com/socialworkjobbank
http://www.facebook.com/newsocialworkerbookclub
http://www.facebook.com/whitehatcommunications
**AND...look for The New Social Worker's group on LinkedIn.com.**

# Phi Alpha Poster Contest at CSWE 2011 Annual Program Meeting

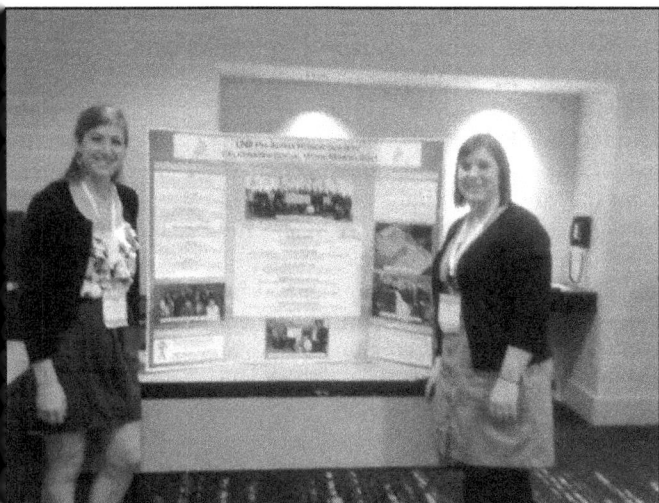

*University of North Dakota presenters, Kathy Scholl-Schommer and Holly Williams, presented "Believe in Change," emphasizing "Social Justice Advocacy Day" at the State Capitol in Bismarck along with other service project activities.*

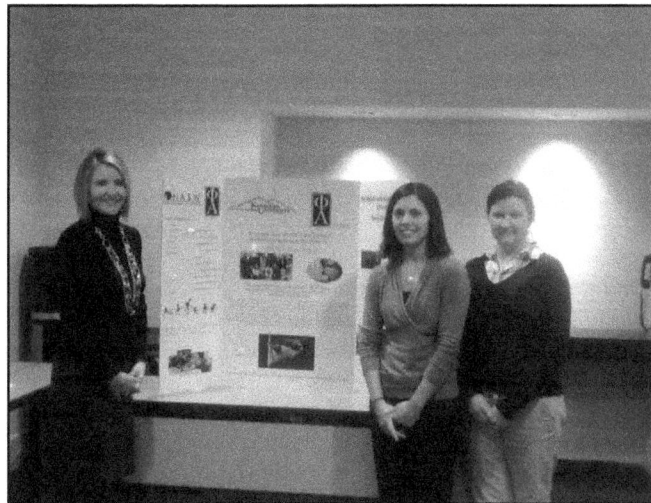

## Happy New Year from the Phi Alpha International Office

Phi Alpha hosted a poster board presentation in conjunction with the Council on Social Work Education Annual Program Meeting (CSWE-APM) in Atlanta, GA, in October 2011. Various chapters across the region presented at the national conference and were awarded monetary funds to use toward future Chapter Service Projects. The next poster board presentation will be held in Washington, DC, in 2012 at CSWE-APM. Please join Phi Alpha on Facebook and on the Phi Alpha Web site at *http://www.phialpha.org*.

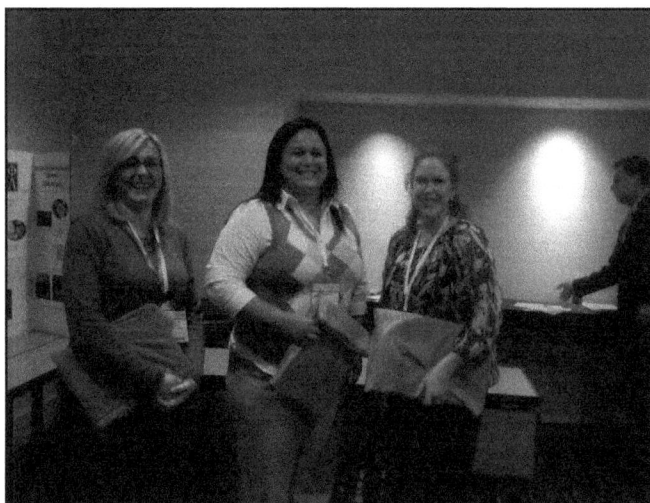

*Kennesaw State University presenters Jessica Alexander, Courtney Eichelberger, and Denise Thibaudeau presented on reaching out to several community programs, such as hospice and a child abuse prevention program.*

*Poster board judges (left to right): Dr. Laurel Hitchcock, University of Montevallo; Marian Ascencio, University of Texas at Austin; and Sandra Gonzales, University of Tennessee at Nashville.*

*Wichita State University presenter Maggie Green presented on the Hygiene Bag Volunteer Project, focusing on hygiene needs for the homeless.*

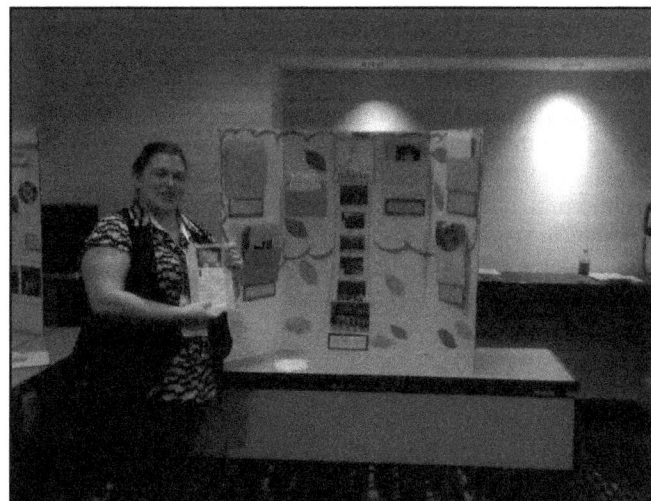

*Buffalo State College presenter Paula Madrigal presented on a "Pay it Forward" theme that focused on several community projects.*

*Little Victim: The Real Story of Britain's Vulnerable Children and the People Who Rescue Them, by Harry Keeble with Kris Hollington, Simon and Schuster, London, 2011, 274 pages, $7.23.*

*Little Victim* is a collection of narratives illustrating one year in the life of Hackley Child Protection in the United Kingdom, as told by Harry Keeble, a once drug task police officer turned child protection agent. In 27 chapters, Harry exposes an assortment of child protection investigations involving physical and sexual abuse, endurance punishment, drug abuse, mental illness, neglect, and cultural incongruity. Harry describes each one of these cases from beginning to end—receiving a referral, components of the investigation, and the outcome of the case. In illuminating these narratives, Harry brings to light the vulnerability and resiliency of children along with his own inner conflict concerning what he thinks is best for children and the unfortunate and painful limitations of child protection services. Harry aims to dissolve common misconceptions as he praises social workers for fighting the war against systemic problems that adversely affect children with minimal resources and negative perceptions of their work. The book concludes purposefully as Harry promotes positive change by challenging funding cuts to prevention services, encouraging readers to get involved as advocates for children, and diagramming a treatment team model that he feels will be safer and more productive for other social service agencies that are underfunded and understaffed.

Although this book centers on one borough in the United Kingdom, the messages and implications transcend to child protection by and large. The accounts in this book may seem graphic and upsetting to the general public, but individuals working in child protection know them all too well, and for that reason, social work students considering a career in child protection could benefit from the content about why some individuals feel called to the profession and why some choose against it. Novice social workers could benefit from the subject matter presented in each case, as well as the facts, advice, and insight pro-

vided by an experienced child protection worker. This book could be utilized by experienced social workers and social work educators as an update on current trends in child protection. This book could also be informative for social work clients involved with child protection services, because it may facilitate an understanding of the decisions that are made by the child protection agencies.

Overall, *Little Victim* is an honestly descriptive, sometimes gritty, compilation of narratives that accurately depict the ups and downs, as well as successes and failures, of child protection while still imparting the reader with a sense of optimism.

*Reviewed by Angie Chisholm, LLMSW, Clinical Social Worker at Hope Network Behavioral Health.*

---

*Angels of Mercy: White Women and the History of New York's Colored Orphan Asylum, by William Seraile, Fordham University Press, New York, 2011, 220 pages, $27.95.*

Over the course of their careers, many social workers will find themselves working directly in the child welfare profession or working in conjunction with child welfare professionals. William Seraile's book, *Angels of Mercy: White Women and the History of New York's Colored Orphan Asylum,* provides a detailed account of the history of New York City's first orphanage for African American children from its establishment in the early nineteenth century to its transition to the more modern child welfare agency in the mid-twentieth century.

Seraile opens his book with an interesting take on the driving forces that led white women in the 1830s to take up the cause of the "colored" orphans. These forces were two-fold; the first was a paternalistic attitude in which these women hoped to save the orphans' souls by instilling a strict Protestant moral code they felt was missing in the "colored" race. The founders made a point to avoid any talk of social equality or amalgamation and fostered an "us vs. them" mentality by refusing to turn to the black community for guidance and support.

The second was the desire of the founding women to pursue work outside the home that would not upset the strict gender roles of the time. Their race deemed them superior to the children they were serving, so they were able to

take on an empowered and authoritative role that would otherwise have been forbidden without de-feminizing themselves.

Seraile then follows the Colored Orphan Asylum over a century, as it grows in size by opening itself up to half-orphans, abused and neglected children, and delinquent children. He continues to analyze the recurrent issues the Asylum faces over time. These include the need for a trained and professional staff to meet the demands of a challenging population, the budget constraints that make it difficult to retain qualified staff, and the movement from an agency whose responsibility is to provide placement to an agency whose responsibility is to provide safety and permanence.

Whereas it is clear that Seraile was meticulous in his research of the Asylum's finances, management, and individual cases, he has difficulty integrating the research data into a cohesive discussion of the topic at hand so that the reader becomes focused on the data rather than on the storyline. Nonetheless, *Angels of Mercy* presents a fascinating history of one agency's journey and perseverance over more than a century.

*Angels of Mercy* is relevant to all social workers as a reminder of the importance of cultural competency in social work practice and is of particular relevance to any social worker in the child welfare field, as well as social work students and teachers in the areas of both direct service and administration. Many current social workers can no doubt draw parallels between the difficulties experienced by the Asylum staff and the issues faced by child welfare staff of today.

*Reviewed by Alexandra Kline, LGSW, Social Worker, D.C. Child and Family Services Agency.*

---

*The Whole-Brain Child: Revolutionary Strategies To Nurture Your Child's Developing Mind, by Daniel J. Siegel, M.D., and Tina Payne Bryson, Ph.D., Delacorte Press, New York, 2011, 168 pages, $24.00 USD/$27.00 CDN.*

World renowned author and neuropsychiatrist Daniel Siegel and pediatric and adolescent psychotherapist and parent consultant Tina Payne Bryson form a dynamic duo in this "must have" volume. It was written to help parents understand their children using information gleaned from neuroscience. The genius of this book is its clear and simple delivery of theory and practice. Finally, neuroscience made easy!

Siegel and Bryson set out to give 12 strategies for understanding children with the brain in mind. The right brain and its emotions dominate the logic of the left brain in young children. They remind us that the brain undergoes significant changes during the first few years of life and then again during the teen years into adulthood. The human brain is not fully developed until the mid-twenties. This would explain why parents think it can take so long for reason and good decision-making to prevail in the lives of their children.

The six chapters are structured to provide real life situations that parents of younger children typically deal with: temper tantrums, irrational fears, lack of consideration for others, anxiety, disappointment. Each chapter includes illustrated (comic style) examples of how to intervene with children and ends with an invitation for parents to reflect on their own experiences. All of these elements are woven together with strands of information about the developing brain of a child.

Siegel and Bryson's brilliance is shown in their unique descriptions of the brain. Some examples are: the upstairs (middle pre-frontal cortex) and downstairs brain (primitive), building a staircase to integrate the upstairs and downstairs brain, understanding the difference between upstairs and downstairs tantrums. Their use of simple phrases such as: "connect and redirect," "name it to tame it," "engage, don't enrage," "use it or lose it," "move it or lose it," "let the clouds of emotion roll by," "use the remote of the mind," "connect through conflict," and "argue with a 'we' in mind," make learning new brain facts interesting and easy to remember. The book is complete with a "Refrigerator Sheet," which summarizes the basics of *The Whole-Brain Child*. In addition, the authors include a reference guide that outlines the stages of child development, types of brain integration, whole-brain strategies, and applications.

Siegel and Bryson state that the focus in *The Whole-Brain Child* is from birth to pre-teens. I was disappointed that this book didn't include adolescents, although many ideas can be modified for use with teens. It would be ideal if the authors would write another volume to address the whole-brain teenager and young adult, thereby assisting parents who struggle to navigate the latter stages of parenting. That being said, this material is a wonderful primer for any parent-to-be, early childhood educators, teachers, and medical and helping professionals. For those who would like a simple explanation of neuroscience, this is a good place to start. This book will help any professional grasp the basics of brain science and how it intersects with the developmental stages of childhood.

*The Whole-Brain Child* is another one of Siegel's masterpieces and a great debut for Bryson. Their combined effort to integrate practical applications of neuroscience to the most important job in the world, parenting, is long overdue. I would highly recommend this work to anyone who works with, lives with, or engages with children. You won't be disappointed!

*Reviewed by Patricia Berendsen RMFT, RSW, SEP, OAMFT/AAMFT-approved supervisor, clinician with the Clinical Supports program of the Centre for Children and Families in the Justice System of the London Family Court Clinic in London, Ontario.*

# A Social Worker's Resolutions
## by Kristen Marie (Kryss) Shane, MSW, LMSW

As this is the time of year when it is customary to make resolutions, I've decided to share mine with you.

This year:

## 1. I will be better at utilizing the amazing network of social workers who are willing to guide a newer member of the group.

I will participate in social work chats, I will attend webinars, I will be more active at NASW chapter meetings. I will be less afraid of "bothering" someone and more afraid that not asking will cause me to miss out on knowledge others want to share.

## 2. I will encourage others to become more active in the politics happening around them.

With everything from our next President to same-sex marriage to teachers' unions to a woman's right to choose being debated on, it is important that open-minded people stand together in our votes, so that the folks at the top don't create laws that will further hinder our clients.

## 3. I will put myself and my needs first more often.

Although this field so often causes me to feel that there is always more I could be doing–more I could be giving–I will keep in mind that burning myself out benefits no one. I will check massage schools for discount offers, I will buy myself flowers every so often, and I will not feel guilty for using the vacation/sick/personal time off that I have earned.

## 4. I will become more educated in financial matters.

In a field where most don't make much, where new laws and aid are coming up every day, it is more important than ever that we each take the time to understand our companies' retirement options, our flexible spending account opportunities, and what's changing within the laws of student loan repayment.

## 5. In addition, I will remember that I vote with every dollar I spend.

I refuse to spend my money at stores that promote inequality, child labor, or political beliefs I disagree with. Even though low prices are great, I will not allow saving a few dollars to

mean I am using my money to contribute to the very things my clients battle daily.

## 6. I will give at least two complements per day.

These may come when someone is especially helpful or when I notice how great the color of someone's sweater looks when she sits next to me on the subway. The reasons aren't so important. What is important is that I take a minimum of two moments each day to acknowledge how much better a minute or even a split second was simply because of others' involvement, and that I perhaps create a chain of kindness that will continue long after I've finished the task or left the subway platform.

## 7. I will branch out.

I will learn both about the topics related to my current client population and about other populations, because the biopsychosocial perspective teaches us that everything is interrelated. As the saying goes, "Well read is well said!"

## 8. More than anything else, though, I will be happier more often.

I will learn to wake up and see the sunshine before the early time on the clock. I will surround myself with things and people that make me happy and rid myself of everything else. I will be grateful for all I have and put more effort into showing the people I love how much I appreciate their presence in my life.

**Happy 2012, Everyone!**

*Kristen Marie (Kryss) Shane, LMSW, earned her B.S. at The Ohio State University and her MSW at Barry University. She currently resides in the New York City area. Her professional foci are in the areas of LGBTQI issues and in the elder population. She is a regular guest speaker at Columbia University, where she gives professional trainings on making professionals, agencies, and companies more inclusive. She has aided in the introduction of Gay Straight Alliances in numerous high schools; marched in the National Equality March in Washington, D.C.; rallied for non-discrimination laws in numerous states; and she continues to advocate for LGBTQI and elder rights on the local, state, and federal levels. In addition, she is on staff at socialworkchat.org and is a columnist and the 2011 blogger for The New Social Worker, where her weekly thoughts can found at: http://blog.socialworker.com/search/label/Kryss.*

# Land a Career in Social Work

The U.S. Bureau of Labor Statistics sees blue skies ahead for social workers. Especially in specialized areas like military social work. Now you can earn your Master of Social Work from the University of Southern California on campus or online. Take classes at one of our local academic centers in Los Angeles, Irvine or San Diego or through our new web-based Virtual Academic Center. A bright future is on the horizon.

**Visit our website at** http://msw.usc.edu/NewSocialWorkerMag **today to learn more.**

## USC School of Social Work

**Shape your future**
Reshape the world

# Infusing Social Work and Reproductive Justice To Advocate for Women's Sexual Health

## by Nicole Clark, MSW

*Nicole Clark*

Since the United States Supreme Court ruled in Roe v. Wade in 1973, there has been a war on women's sexual and reproductive health. From the most recent Amendment 26 (also known as the "personhood" bill) vote in Mississippi, the Department of Health and Human Service's (HHS) mandate that health insurance companies cover birth control without co-pay, to the Food and Drug Administration's recommendation that Plan B (also known as emergency contraception) be sold over the counter (and HHS' subsequent veto of that recommendation), countless legislation has been introduced on the state and federal levels to limit women's access to adequate and much needed medical services, including birth control options and abortion. More than ever, social workers are needed in the fight to make sure that women's sexual health and reproductive justice is not compromised.

I'm new to social work, but have been involved in various aspects of the sexual and reproductive justice movement for nearly 10 years. What drew me to social work were the limitless possibilities to help others, from working one-on-one in a counseling session to being an executive director of a nonprofit. I have found social workers in a variety of positions, and it always amazes me. Reproductive justice recognizes the intersections of social, political, and economic structures that work to empower women to make healthy decisions about our bodies, sexuality, our families, and our communities. Social work compliments this, because we advocate for our clients within these structures, and bringing more social workers into the reproductive justice framework will further bring women's reproductive rights to the forefront, as well as highlight social work as a whole.

In 2010, we saw the beginning of efforts to restrict access to medical and social services, including much needed services such as breast exams, cancer screenings, abortion, and birth control. Instead of focusing on more obvious matters, such as job creation and the economy, lawmakers across the country introduced 1,000 bills, including the Stupak Amendment, which sought to undermine women's health. The year 2011 also saw some awful bills focused on women's sexual and reproductive health, and with the 2012 election season underway, so much is at stake. How we collectively advocate for women can have a positive or negative impact on the future of women's sexual and reproductive health.

The National Association of Social Workers has provided several recommendations, including defining our role as social workers within women's health, educating more social workers on women's health and how discrimination affects how women access sexual and reproductive health services, supporting policies that advocate for positive women's health objectives, and advocating for federal and state funding for research that can better connect social work with women's health. We can use the NASW's recommendations to advocate for sound policies that help women to make knowledgeable decisions regarding their sexual and reproductive health. We can go out into our communities and into the communities of the populations we serve to bring awareness to the importance of healthcare and the importance of being informed about policies that are set to derail a woman's right to make the best decisions for her health. We can make lobby visits and speak with legislators on key policies that affect women's health (as well as thank those legislators who support legislation that

makes sexual and reproductive health care accessible for all women). We can develop programs and interventions in our agencies and practices to provide women and girls with strategies to keep their sexual health safe, as well as educate our staff on sexuality, sex education, and advocacy.

As social workers, we often are on the frontline, combining our responsibility to social justice and the ethics of what social work stands for to advocate for a wide array of causes for an even bigger array of populations. It is especially evident in underrepresented communities, where poverty, inadequate access to healthcare services, discrimination, and the "isms" (racism, sexism, and heterosexism, among others) create multiple barriers to having an adequate quality of life.

In 2012, we have to hold fast to our ethics and vision for a better country for women to live in. Women deserve to live in a country where our sexual and reproductive rights are no longer trampled on, where young women receive the best and medically accurate information in order to make the best decisions for their health and lives, and legislators are not constantly finding ways to limit women's choices. As social workers, we are in a perfect position to be the best advocates for women's sexual and reproductive health.

*Nicole Clark, MSW, lends her expertise as a consultant with nonprofits and community groups who want to improve their approach to developing culturally relevant and youth and/or gender-positive programming, campaigns, and initiatives. She has a B.A. in psychology from Spelman College and a Master of Social Work degree from the Columbia University School of Social Work. Based in New York City, her Web site is http://www.nicole-clark.com.*

# Facebook and Suicide Prevention

*by Linda May Grobman, MSW, LSW, ACSW*

Facebook announced in December 2011 a new partnership with the Substance Abuse and Mental Health Services Administration (SAMHSA) and the National Suicide Prevention Lifeline 1-800-273-TALK. Through the new service, Facebook users who see a suicidal comment posted by a friend can report this to Facebook using the "Report Suicidal Content" link or the report links found throughout Facebook. Facebook will then send an e-mail to the person who posted the suicidal comment, encouraging him or her to call the National Suicide Prevention Lifeline or to click on a link to begin a confidential chat session with a crisis worker.

With 800 million active users, Facebook has the potential to make an enormous impact with this new service.

"Facebook and the Lifeline are to be commended for addressing one of this nation's most tragic public health problems," says Surgeon General Regina M. Benjamin, MD, MBA. "Nearly 100 Americans die by suicide every day—36,035 lives every year. These deaths are even more tragic because they are preventable."

Social worker Brad A. Palmertree, BSW, who is co-chair of the Gay, Lesbian, and Straight Education Network (GLSEN) of Middle Tennessee, says of the partnership, "[It] is a natural progression of social service professionals meeting the clients where they are. Social media has become a place where individuality and personal expression is not just accepted but expected and embraced. So it's only natural that life's troubles show up alongside its triumphs."

He adds, "I think it's a wonderful step in the right direction. As someone who works daily on creating and maintaining safe spaces for lesbian, gay, bisexual, transgender, or questioning (LGBTQ) youth, social media has been a double-edged sword. It allows young people to freely express themselves while building community with others who are navigating the murky waters of adolescence with an identity that is not always easily accepted or understood. But it also allows for a space where the bullies come at full force, often anonymously. Those who self-identify as LGBTQ, or even those who do not but are labeled as such because of preconceived gender norms, are bullied and harassed at a rate much higher than

their heterosexual and cisgender counterparts. When school is not a safe haven and neither is home, LGBTQ youth turn to the Internet to seek answers, counseling, or simply validation."

The Lifeline has actually partnered with Facebook since 2006, but the new partnership adds the option of chatting online with a crisis counselor. John Draper, Ph.D., the Lifeline's project director, says, "We have heard from our Facebook fans and others that there are many people in crisis who don't feel comfortable picking up the phone. This... provides a way for them to get the help they need in the way they want it."

Ellen Fink-Samnick, MSW, ACSW, LCSW, of EFS Supervision Strategies LLC, believes the new collaboration, "on face value alone...is a promising means to enhance suicide intervention." However, like others, she thinks that related ethical concerns warrant equal attention. "Courtesy of rapidly emerging technology innovation, the framing of professional ethics has changed from 'what one does while nobody watches,' to 'what one does while everyone watches, 24/7 in cyberspace,'" she points out.

For social workers and other clinical professionals who may be involved in these efforts, Fink-Samnick says ethical concerns include:

- *State-to-state licensure: It would seem there is a high likelihood that professionals will find themselves practicing across state lines as they assess clients in cyberspace. Will the professionals be appropriately licensed, credentialed in all jurisdictions?*
- *With respect to "duty to warn," what will the turn-around time be from identification to assessment to intervention?*
- *How will professional liability be addressed?*

Others have brought up concerns about privacy and "Big Brother"-like worries. What happens when Facebook sends an e-mail to a suicidal user, and that e-mail address is a shared address with the user's spouse, parents, children, or co-workers? Is this a violation of the person's health information privacy? And if so, is it excusable, given that it is for the purpose of saving the person's life? Does the answer to this question depend on

who is employed by Facebook to perform this task? And while we're at it, what is a social worker's responsibility when he or she comes across suicidal content, on Facebook or elsewhere online?

Any effort to prevent suicide is commendable. At the same time, the best way to implement this plan is yet to be seen. The suicide reporting tool may be hard to find. There is no obvious "Report Suicidal Content" button in big red letters. (See *http://idealab.talkingpointsmemo.com/2011/12/facebook-explains-report-suicidal-content-tool.php* for an explanation of how it works and where it is located.)

"I am eager to see how Facebook and its partners increase awareness of this new suicidal behavior flagging tool, how they continue to streamline the...process, which at the present time seems difficult to find and cumbersome to use, how the partnership develops, and how they roll out pertinent information to their users in a timely manner," comments Karen Zgoda, MSW, LCSW, ABD, a social work doctoral candidate at Boston College and former technology columnist for *THE NEW SOCIAL WORKER.*

She points out that typing "suicide" into Facebook's search box takes users to a page *(https://www.facebook.com/help/search/?q=suicide&ref=ts)* that may help someone directly, adding, "I wonder how someone who is in crisis or who is trying to help a friend in crisis would get to this information via Facebook as quickly as possible."

Despite questions during this early stage of implementation, Palmertree is hopeful that the new partnership can help save the lives of people like Jacob Rogers, a young man in Ashland City, TN, who took his own life in early December 2011 after reaching out on Facebook, just days before the partnership was announced.

"When they reach out, it's our responsibility as friends, family members, neighbors, and community members to take notice," says Palmertree. "Friends and family say that Jacob Rogers was bullied and harassed daily because he identified as gay. Like most teenagers, Jacob had a Facebook profile. The day of his death, Jacob reached out to his Facebook friends several times. It's hard to say that Jacob would still be alive if this tool had been available (and utilized), but it's nice to know that it's there to help prevent other similar tragedies from occurring."

# Choosing Civility
## by Patti Sabla

Is civility dead? It has been said that chivalry is dead, but have we lost civility, too? Do we live in such a fast-paced world that we no longer have the time to be considerate toward others? Are we so wrapped up in technology that we have lost our connection with and compassion for social interaction? If we think about our recent experiences at the DMV, the airport, a crowded mall, or even the parking lot at our local grocery store, we may begin to believe that civility may be dead, or a least in need of resuscitation. Graciousness and common courtesy seem only to be concepts from a by-gone era. Random acts of kindness seem to be less common, while random acts of violence appear on the rise. Do we live in a society where respect and consideration for others is going by the wayside? Dr. P. M. Forni believes we may be headed in that direction and has penned a book, *Choosing Civility: The Twenty-Five Rules of Considerate Conduct* (St. Martin's Griffin, 2003, ISBN: 978-0-312-30250-4), to help guide us back on track.

Before reading Forni's enlightening and thought-provoking book, I wondered how so many of us, including myself, had gotten so far off course. After reading this book, I realized that it has been a slow and steady decline. We have fallen prey to a slippery slope resulting from a lack of empathy and personal restraint. Without being consciously aware of our behavior or fully engaged in our actions, we tend to make minor social faux pas. As these faux pas become more widely accepted, or at least tolerated, they slowly become the norm.

## What I Have Learned

In Part I of the book, Forni highlights the importance of going beyond our Selves in order to see our everyday encounters as a We mentality, rather than an Us versus Them outlook. How we operate affects more than just ourselves. Our behavior is impressionable upon everyone around us. Knowing this, we need to use our words and actions with a great deal of responsibility and reserve. We also need to remain accountable for those words and actions, should we use them unjustly.

The author covers this nicely in Part II with his twenty-five rules. Rule Number Seven, "Don't Speak Ill," speaks to the sentiment noted above. In addition, it touches on a relatively modern form of unjust discourse that is due to the anonymity of Internet chat rooms, online message boards, and blogs. At this point, it looks as if civility does not stand a chance when one hides behind a screen name.

Furthermore, he explains that simply not speaking ill of someone is not enough. To be civil, we must also "Speak Kindly" (Rule Number Six). He points out that this includes communicating with both words and body language. Besides speaking kindly, he reminds us that "Listening" (Rule Number Four) is a critical element of civility, as well. Obviously, one should know that listening and speaking go together. However, the author clarifies that listening is more than just hearing what the other person is saying. It is about "listening with no other intention than that of listening" (p. 51). How often do we really commit ourselves to the other person's needs and not just "disregard (their exchange) and proceed" (p. 51)? I internalized this detail, as I know I am guilty of this gaffe myself. Too often, I am thinking about how I am going to respond or what I can say to turn the conversation in a different direction. As a future social worker, I am aware that this is a bad habit that may cause me to miss the underlying messages my clients may be conveying.

## What I Thought I Knew

I do not think Forni has taught us anything we do not already know about ourselves. For the most part, we have been trained, at a very young age, how to conduct ourselves in a socially appropriate manner. In Part III, he has shown me that although I have these abilities, I do not always exercise them. He has not asked anything of me that I do not have the power to accomplish. Instead, he has raised my awareness to the fact that I take these important rules for granted. I am guilty of getting caught up in everyday life and not paying close attention to my actions. In turn, I act in a manner in which many of the 25 rules are not followed.

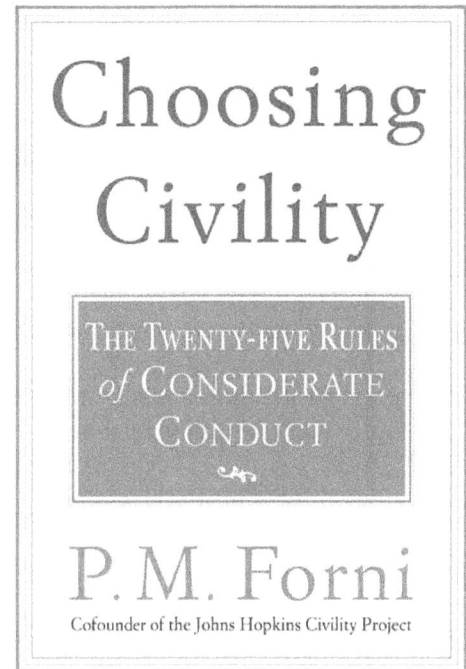

I believe that everyone could benefit from reading this text. The author discusses such basic, yet extremely important, concepts. This book could certainly enrich the lives of anyone, including those working in the social work field.

As a social work student, I witnessed a great deal of adherence to the Rules of Civility in my fieldwork setting. This gives me great hope, not only for the social work profession I will soon be entering, but also for the young children of today. Positive role models who demonstrate a disciplined use of self are a great asset to those involved in social services. Maybe some of them have already read this book and are making a conscious effort. Maybe it just comes naturally for some. I believe I am a more mindful person after reading this book. Perhaps social work professionals would all become more cognizant if this book became as secondary as the DSM-IV? One may never know...but one can hope.

*Patti Sabla is an MSW candidate at Widener University in Chester, PA. She is currently an intern therapist at the South Jersey Healthcare Behavioral Wellness Center in Vineland, NJ. She wrote this article as a student in the Richard Stockton College social work program.*

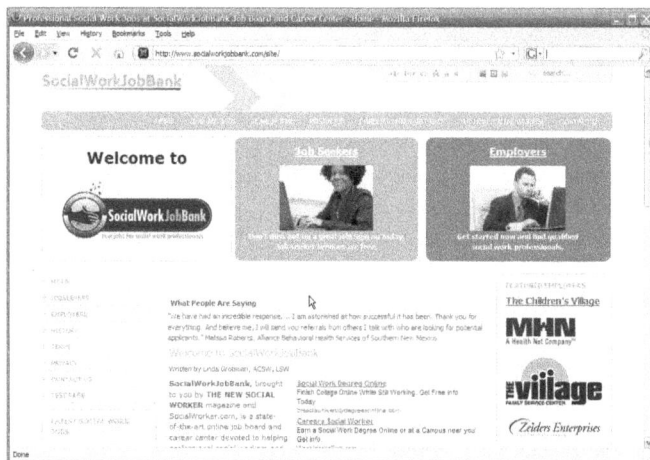

# CONTENTS

THE NEW SOCIAL WORKER®
Spring 2012
Volume 19, Number 2

## FEATURES

## DEPARTMENTS

# Publisher's Thoughts

Dear Reader,

We have just completed another Social Work Month in March, with the theme "Social Work Matters!" Yes, social work *and* social workers matter, as you can see from the topics represented in this issue.

We talk a lot about ethics and knowing the Code, but do you really know what an ethical *dilemma* is? The concept of a true ethical dilemma, a situation in which two ethical principles compete with each other, is spelled out in Karen Allen's article on page 4.

Next we turn to the issue of conflict in the workplace, which includes field placement. It is inevitable that you will face such conflict at some point. Are you prepared to make the most of the situation, learn from it, and grow from it?

*The publisher/editor*

The social work licensing exam. Is there any social work student or new graduate out there who is NOT thinking about it? Ammu had every intention of taking the exam and becoming licensed immediately after graduation. Then life took over! Four years later, she is licensed and ready to share her tips with you.

The historic Hull House Association in Chicago filed for bankruptcy and closed its doors earlier this year. Laura Gale takes a look at lessons to be learned from the Hull House experience.

Kryss Shane is ending her tenure as columnist with this issue. She shares some very personal thoughts about social work, words, the Internet, and her precious Nikko. I want to thank Kryss for sharing her insights, enthusiasm, and experiences over the past year and a half. It has been a pleasure to have her on board as our columnist in 2011-2012. And she is not going away completely...I won't let her! She will still write reviews and other occasional pieces.

Have you experienced The Social Work Podcast? You can find it on our site at *http://www.socialworker.com/home/menu/Social_Work_Podcast/*. Jonathan Singer, the podcast's founder, is interviewed on page 25.

Social workers and social work students are on the forefront when it comes to social justice. On the front cover of this issue, you will find a photo of students marching against institutional racism in response to the shooting of Trayvon Martin in Florida. You can find more news of students in action on pages 20 and 21.

I am busy at work on a couple of new book projects! I will share more as the publication dates get closer. One is a book on group work, and the other is on finding your niche in clinical social work.

Do you have ideas or experiences you would like to share with our readers? Perhaps you would like to write an article or serve as an expert interviewee for a future issue! Let me know.

Until next time–happy reading!

*Linda M. Grobman*

## Write for The New Social Worker

We are looking for articles from social work practitioners, students, and educators.

Some areas of particular interest are: social work ethics; student field placement; practice specialties; technology; "what every new social worker needs to know," and news of unusual, creative, or nontraditional social work.

Feature articles run 1,500-2,000 words in length. News articles are typically 100-150 words. Our style is conversational, practical, and educational. Write as if you are having a conversation with a student or colleague. What do you want him or her to know about the topic? What would you want to know? Use examples.

The best articles have a specific focus. If you are writing an ethics article, focus on a particular aspect of ethics. For example, analyze a specific portion of the NASW *Code of Ethics* (including examples), or talk about ethical issues unique to a particular practice setting. When possible, include one or two resources at the end of your article–books, additional reading materials, and/or Web sites.

We also want photos of social workers and social work students "in action" for our cover, and photos to accompany your news articles!

Send submissions to lindagrobman@socialworker.com.

## The New Social Worker

**Spring 2012
Vol. 19, Number 2**

*Publisher/Editor*
Linda May Grobman, MSW, ACSW, LSW

*Contributing Writers*
Barbara Trainin Blank
Kristen Marie (Kryss) Shane, MSW, LMSW

THE NEW SOCIAL WORKER® (ISSN 1073-7871) is published four times a year by White Hat Communications, P.O. Box 5390, Harrisburg, PA 17110-0390. Phone: (717) 238-3787. Fax: (717) 238-2090. Send address corrections to: lindagrobman@socialworker.com

Advertising rates available on request.

Photo/art credits: Image from BigStockPhoto.com © Elena Elisseeva (page 8).

*The New Social Worker* is indexed/abstracted in *Social Work Abstracts*.

Send all editorial, advertising, subscription, and other correspondence to:

**THE NEW SOCIAL WORKER**

**White Hat Communications**
**P.O. Box 5390**
**Harrisburg, PA 17110-0390**
**(717) 238-3787 Phone**
**(717) 238-2090 Fax**

lindagrobman@socialworker.com

http://www.socialworker.com
http://www.facebook.com/newsocialworker
http://www.twitter.com/newsocialworker

**Print Edition:**
http://newsocialworker.magcloud.com

# Stephanie Maldonado

*by Barbara Trainin Blank*

Her life the past few years has been one of firsts. Stephanie Maldonado is in the first class of BSW candidates at the University of Illinois at Urbana-Champaign. She is a founding member and president of the Bachelor of Social Work Student Organization and the first U. of I. student in nine years to win the prestigious Truman Scholarship.

Established by an Act of Congress in 1975 in honor of the late President Harry S. Truman, the Truman Scholarship Foundation gives merit-based scholarships of $30,000 each to college juniors seeking to attend graduate school in preparation for careers in public service. Maldonado is one of about 60 students chosen from a total of 602 nominated by U.S. colleges and universities.

When Brenda Coble Lindsey, director of the BSW program at U. of I., put a booklet about the scholarship in Maldonado's mailbox, the student had never heard of it. Her career goals were newly emerging. David Schug, co-director of the university's National and International Scholarships Program, asked her to elaborate on them. Maldonado could only say: "I don't know [exactly]. I just decided to be a social worker."

Now she does. After obtaining her MSW, Maldonado aims to be a school social worker and to eventually direct an advocacy agency serving the Latino community in Chicago. She is especially interested in the root causes of random violence–such as the lack of educational opportunities and parental involvement.

"I know I'll be hungry for direct practice," Maldonado says. "But I'd also like to do macro practice, such as youth development or community engagement. I'd like to work on community-school relationships, which now are such a disconnect."

Applying to the Truman Scholarship was a time-consuming and, in some ways, stressful process. Although she believes herself articulate, and indeed, speaks freely, the BSW student was a lot less confident about her writing abilities. It wasn't easy to come up with what she wanted to write about for the scholarship, either.

When she stopped and thought, though, it wasn't hard. Maldonado's father is from the Dominican Republic, and she was born in Puerto Rico, where their mother still resides. Her younger siblings had some language-adjustment difficulties. Maldonado is intensely aware of what it's like to be in a society with little tolerance for language differences and what the risks are to children's well-being when they face these and other cultural barriers.

In the end, Maldonado wrote about college preparation starting in pre-school for Latino immigrants and their children. "I had a grand plan to target more pre-school slots toward them, since one in four pre-school kids are Latinos," she says. "They will be the majority of the work force, and they're not qualified."

That Maldonado would equip herself well in the scholarship process did not surprise Lisette Piedra, who taught her in the course "Hispanics in the United States: Building a Social Policy Agenda."

Stephanie "combines considerable academic gifts with great intellectual courage," Piedra wrote to Schug and his co-director, Laura Hastings. "From the

*Stephanie Maldonado*

first day of class, she sought to question commonly held beliefs and to challenge traditional stereotypes."

Maldonado's qualities and insights enriched the experience for other students, and her "palpable energy" motivated her peers," Piedra added. "She will pursue an issue until she is satisfied, and her relentless questioning and insatiable curiosity distinguish her."

According to Piedra, assistant professor in the School of Social Work, Stephanie also exhibits empathy and a willingness to express it through action.

"Stephanie represents the new face of social work," Piedra says. "She's technologically savvy, forward thinking, and can play an essential role in finding innovative, real solutions for problems."

But Maldonado almost didn't make it to, or through, the interview part of the scholarship process. A cousin had been shot in the head by a "gang banger" and was in serious condition in the hospital that day. Maldonado didn't want to leave his side. In fact, she had even made up her mind not to return to school. "I have no words to describe what my family means to me," she says. "My cousin is alive, but he lost his vision completely.

*Maldonado–continued on page 21*

# What Is an Ethical Dilemma?
*by Karen Allen, Ph.D., LMSW*

Social workers are routinely confronted with ethical dilemmas in practice, and social work programs infuse their courses with professional ethics and values to help students prepare for this eventuality. The Council on Social Work Education (2008) requires that students learn how to "apply social work ethical principles to guide practice, engage in ethical decision making, recognize and manage personal values in a way that allows professional values to guide practice, and tolerate ambiguity in resolving ethical conflicts" (EPAS 2.1.2). Social work students become familiar with the *Code of Ethics,* learn one of the various models on ethical decision making (Congress, 1999; Dolgoff, Loewenberg, & Harrington, 2009; Reamer, 1995) and, at some point in their education, are typically required to write a paper on an ethical dilemma. However, students are not routinely taught how to recognize what an ethical dilemma is. Correctly identifying an ethical dilemma is the first step in resolving it.

## What Is an Ethical Dilemma?

There are three conditions that must be present for a situation to be considered an ethical dilemma. The *first condition* occurs in situations when an individual, called the "agent," must make a decision about which course of action is best. Situations that are uncomfortable but that don't require a choice, are not ethical dilemmas. For example, students in their internships are required to be under the supervision of an appropriately credentialed social work field instructor. Therefore, because there is no choice in the matter, there is no ethical violation or breach of confidentiality when a student discusses a case with the supervisor. The *second condition* for ethical dilemma is that there must be different courses of action to choose from. *Third,* in an ethical dilemma, no matter what course of action is taken, some ethical principle is compromised. In other words, there is no perfect solution.

In determining what constitutes an ethical dilemma, it is necessary to make a distinction between ethics, values, morals, and laws and policies. *Ethics* are prepositional statements (standards) that

are used by members of a profession or group to determine what the right course of action in a situation is. Ethics rely on logical and rational criteria to reach a decision, an essentially cognitive process (Congress, 1999; Dolgoff, Loewenberg, & Harrington, 2009; Reamer, 1995; Robison & Reeser, 2002). *Values,* on the other hand, describe ideas that we value or prize. To value something means that we hold it dear and feel it has worth to us. As such, there is often a feeling or affective component associated with values (Allen & Friedman, 2010). Often, values are ideas that we aspire to achieve, like equality and social justice. *Morals* describe a behavioral code of conduct to which an individual ascribes. They are used to negotiate, support, and strength-

en our relationships with others (Dolgoff, Loewenberg, & Harrington, 2009). Finally, *laws and agency policies* are often involved in complex cases, and social workers are often legally obligated to take a particular course of action. Standard 1.07j of the *Code of Ethics* (NASW, 1996) recognizes that legal obligations may require social workers to share confidential information (such as in cases of reporting child abuse) but requires that we protect confidentiality to the "extent permitted by law." Although our profession ultimately recognizes the rule of law, we are also obligated to work to change unfair and discriminatory laws. There is considerably less recognition of the supremacy of agency policy in the *Code,* and Ethical Standard 3.09d states

## Table 1. Personal and Professional Ethics, Values, and Morals

| Professional | Personal |
|---|---|
| **Ethics** | **Values** |
| What relevant standards and expectations are outlined by my profession in its Code of Ethics?<br><br>How do ethical principles conflict in this case?<br><br>• If ethical principles conflict, use an ethical decision making process to resolve. | What relevant personal values apply in this case and where did they originate?<br><br>What professional values are outlined in the Code of Ethics and do any of them apply in this case?<br><br>• If there is conflict between personal and professional values, how can I manage my personal values so that I allow my professional ethics to guide me?<br>• Seek supervision, use self-reflection and values clarification process. |
| **Laws and Policy** | **Morals** |
| Are there any legal obligations in this case?<br><br>How do my agency's policies direct me?<br><br>Are there any conflicts between my profession's ethics and my legal obligations or my agency's policies?<br><br>• Legal obligations usually supersede professional ethics.<br>• Agency policies should not prevent the ethical practice of social work.<br>• Seek supervision in both cases. | How does my behavior affect my relationship with others?<br><br>What would I like to do and/or what would I want done to me in a situation like this?<br><br>• Distinguish between personal and professional behavior and obligations. |

that we must not allow agency policies to interfere with our ethical practice of social work.

It is also essential that the distinction be made between personal and professional ethics and values (Congress, 1999; Wilshere, 1997). Conflicts between personal and professional values should not be considered ethical dilemmas for a number of reasons. Because values involve feelings and are personal, the rational process used for resolving ethical dilemmas cannot be applied to values conflicts. Further, when an individual elects to become a member of a profession, he or she is agreeing to comply with the standards of the profession, including its *Code of Ethics* and values. Recent court cases have supported a profession's right to expect its members to adhere to professional values and ethics. (See, for example, the Jennifer Keeton case at Augusta State University and the Julea Ward case at Eastern Michigan University.) The Council on Social Work Education states that students should "recognize and manage personal values in a way that allows professional values to guide practice" (EPAS 1.1). Therefore, although they can be difficult and uncomfortable, conflicts involving personal values should not be considered ethical dilemmas.

## Two Types of Dilemmas

An "absolute" or "pure" ethical dilemma only occurs when two (or more) ethical standards apply to a situation but are in conflict with each other. For example, a social worker in a rural community with limited mental health care services is consulted on a client with agoraphobia, an anxiety disorder involving a fear of open and public spaces. Although this problem is outside of the clinician's general competence, the limited options for treatment, coupled with the client's discomfort in being too far from home, would likely mean the client might not receive any services if the clinician declined on the basis of a lack of competence (Ethical Standard 1.04). Denying to see the patient then would be potentially in conflict with our commitment to promote the well-being of clients (Ethical Standard 1.01). This is a pure ethical dilemma because two ethical standards conflict. It can be resolved by looking at Ethical Standard 4.01, which states that social workers should only accept employment (or in this case, a client) on

the basis of existing competence or with "the intention to acquire the necessary competence." The social worker can accept the case, discussing the present limits of her expertise with the client and following through on her obligation to seek training or supervision in this area.

However, there are some complicated situations that require a decision but may also involve conflicts between values, laws, and policies. Although these are not absolute ethical dilemmas, we can think of them as "approximate" dilemmas. For example, an approximate dilemma occurs when a social worker is legally obligated to make a report of child or domestic abuse and has concerns about the releasing of information. The social worker may experience tension between the legal requirement to report and the desire to respect confidentiality. However, because the NASW *Code of Ethics* acknowledges our obligation to follow legal requirements and to intervene to protect the vulnerable, technically, there is no absolute ethical dilemma present. However, the social worker experiences this as a dilemma of some kind and needs to reach some kind of resolution. Breaking the situation down and identifying the ethics, morals, values, legal issues, and policies involved as well as distinguishing between personal and professional dimensions can help with the decision-making process in approximate dilemmas. Table 1 (see page 4) is an illustration of how these factors might be considered.

## Conclusion

When writing an ethical dilemma paper or when attempting to resolve an ethical dilemma in practice, social workers should determine if it is an absolute or approximate dilemma; distinguish between personal and professional dimensions; and identify the ethical, moral, legal, and values considerations in the situation. After conducting this preliminary analysis, an ethical decision-making model can then be appropriately applied.

## References

Allen, K. N., & Friedman, B. (2010). Affective learning: A taxonomy for teaching social work values. *Journal of Social Work Values and Ethics, 7* (2). Retrieved from http://www.socialworker.com/jswve.

Council on Social Work Education. (2008). *Education policy and accreditation standards*

*(EPAS)*. Retrieved from http://www.cswe.org/NR/rdonlyres/2A81732E-1776-4175-AC42-65974E96BE66/0/2008EducationalPolicyand AccreditationStandards.pdf.

Dolgoff, R., Lowenberg, F. M., & Harrington, D. (2009). *Ethical decisions for social work practice* (8th Ed.). Belmont, CA: Brooks/Cole.

Congress, E. P. (1999). *Social work values and ethics: Identifying and resolving professional dilemmas.* Belmont, CA: Wadsworth Group/Thompson Learning.

National Association of Social Workers. (1996, revised 1999). *Code of Ethics of the National Association of Social Workers.* Washington, DC: Author.

Reamer, F. (1995). *Social work values and ethics.* New York: Columbia University Press.

Robison, W., & Reeser, L. C. (2002). *Ethical decision making for social workers.* New York: Allyn & Bacon.

Wilshere, P. J. (1997). Personal values: professional questions. *The New Social Worker, 4* (1), 13.

*Karen Allen, Ph.D., LMSW, is an associate professor at Oakland University's Social Work Program.*

# Professional Growth—Flourish or Wither in the Face of Conflict
## by Patty Hunter, MSW, LCSW, Chris Sims, MSW, LCSW, and Kimberley Davis, MSW

During the first week of placement, an MSW student finds herself face-to-face with an agitated agency staff member expressing strong feelings that he believes the intern is there to take his job. The employee is very confrontational and seems to hold irrational fears toward the student, refusing to teach the student anything involving the program where they work. As a first time intern with this agency, the student now finds herself dealing with a hostile staff member and unsure how to handle the conflict. Relying on her engagement skills and focusing on the issue the worker is presenting, the student attempts to tune in to the worker's feelings. She listens to the worker's concerns and attempts to reassure the worker that she is there to learn and that any attempt on her part to take the worker's job would be unethical. The student leaves this confrontation feeling awkward, confused, and unsure of how to proceed. She wonders if other workers in the agency hold the same fears toward her. Are these uncommon feelings for social work students in the placement setting? Maybe not.

Conflict is a common occurrence in the workplace and can occur for a variety of reasons, including differences in personal values, professional values, gender, race, culture, or competition for scarce resources (De Dreu, 2007). Social service settings are not immune to these conflicts, which often relate to tasks, how the work is being done, or relationship issues (De Dreu, 2007). Given the demanding nature of social work and the stress that often accompanies various practice situations, social work organizations are often ripe for conflict. The scenario at the beginning of this article reflects a need to educate social work students on how to deal with conflict in the workplace.

The student in this scenario viewed the conflict as a platform from which her personal and professional growth would either flourish or wither according to the decisions she made in response to the angry employee. By choosing to build relationships with individuals who were open and willing to teach her and by respecting the disgruntled worker's feelings, the student came to understand that the actions by the worker were not personal in nature. As a result, the student was able to remain empathetic toward the worker by acknowledging the fear behind the actions. With this, the experience became a catalyst for creating a solid foundation for building her career as a social worker.

The student in this scenario was left with two choices in relation to how she would incorporate the event into her

> A social worker's ability to recognize his or her needs and perspectives as legitimate is a critical step in developing professional integrity.

professional and personal identity. First, she could conclude that she was wrong as evidenced simply by the manner in which a more seasoned worker had identified her. Second, she could use the incident to develop her skills as a social worker and better recognize her worth.

The learning process in this scenario was provoked by the student, instructor, and school working to develop a genuinely supportive relationship and the provision of open and honest feedback. Although the workplace might not have presented as a safe place initially, a safe place was created for the student to recognize her feelings, personal observations, experience, and to have these normalized and validated. The internship site itself was also active in supporting both the student and the school as they worked simultaneously with the disgruntled worker and the student to insure the worker's reaction did not have a negative impact on the placement.

Through this process of mutual support and consultation, the student was able to practice being in an uncomfortable space without letting the opportunity for growth pass. In this way, an internship experience that might have been easily repudiated became an internship experience that was made significantly more meaningful.

Conflict can occur in any setting. Teaching students that "constructive conflict management fosters effective communication and clarifies appropriate boundaries" (Koch & Keefe, 1999) is a critical component of professional development in the field of social work. Helping students understand the various factors that can both contribute to and alleviate conflict in the workplace provides a context for students to develop a constructive approach to such experiences with colleagues. Additionally, helping them identify tools that they can use to clarify feelings and thoughts they may experience around the conflict will contribute to their professional and personal growth.

The opportunity for students to observe the negative impact that an angry co-worker can have on an organization's culture and then reflect on their own professional and personal response to the conflict provides a unique window for students to examine the type of co-workers they will choose to be. Supporting students during this process may be the best approach to insuring that as practitioners they extend the professional practices of self-reflection and healthy communication beyond their work with clients and into their interactions with professionals. Both of these practices will contribute to a work environment that promotes respect and empowerment for social workers, as well as the clients they serve.

The process that field agencies use to facilitate the introduction of students to their agency staff and socialization to organizational goals, role expectations, and services is critical to the development of the learning environment. What information is agency staff provided about incoming social work students? Are the employees who are not directly involved in training students included in the preparation for students? Are agency staff clear what role, if any, they will have with students and what role the student will have in serving clients? A lack of communication around such issues can result in students having to deal with scenarios similar to the one described. Helping students view these conflicts from a systems perspective and reframing these conflicts as normal reactions to change presents an opportunity for students to grow and enhance their confidence in their ability to deal with conflict.

The parallel process of personal and professional growth is one of the true treasures of social work practice. This developmental course demands the application of practical approaches and strategies discussed in the classroom and the recognition of self in situation. No aspect of social work education presents these opportunities more clearly or consistently than internships in the field. Through the appropriate use of available supports, the student was provided the tools needed to create self-awareness, which allowed her to implement a proactive approach to dealing with the conflict. Whereas the hope might be that opportunities for such growth be limited to our work with clients, our profession necessitates that our work is not restricted to those we seek to assist. Instead, such prospects of self-development routinely extend into our professional relationships with other workers.

A social worker's ability to recognize his or her needs and perspectives as legitimate is a critical step in developing professional integrity. Helping social workers understand strategies, tools, and approaches they can use in dealing with potential conflicts further enhances their ability to function in a professional manner. Although conflict in the field can be commonplace, such experiences hold the potential for significant benefit to the student both personally and professionally and ultimately the field of social work as a whole.

## References

De Dreu, C. (2007, April). The virtue and vice of workplace conflict: food for (pessimistic) thought. *Journal of Organizational Behavior, 29,* 5-18.

Koch, S., & Keefe, T. (1999, Spring). Teaching conflict management in social work, *Journal of Teaching in Social Work, 18,* 1 & 2, 33-52.

*Patty Hunter, MSW, LCSW, is the Director of Field Education for the School of Social Work at California State University, Chico. She has also previously served as an agency field instructor and faculty field liaison. Her current research interests include supervision, leadership, and the impact of cultural humility on social work practice.*

*Christopher Sims, MSW, LCSW, is a graduate of California State University, Chico's Master of Social Work program. He has served as both an agency field instructor and faculty field liaison. He enjoys practicing with a variety of populations in both agency and private practice settings.*

*Kimberley N. Davis, MSW, earned her BS in sociology at California State University, Sacramento and her MSW at California State University, Chico. She is currently working with disadvantaged foster youth in a therapeutic setting and is exploring opportunities to further her interest in advocating for and working with older adults.*

# School Social Work Group Benefits High School Students Living in Non-Traditional Families

## *by Pam Ladetto, MSW*

Teenagers involved in the foster care system are far more likely to drop out of high school, get pregnant, get arrested, and become homeless. These are the same kids who do not have the benefit of a stable home environment or positive role models. This group of teenagers have the common bond of being abandoned, let down, and rejected by their parents and other adults who were entrusted with providing care for them. They have typically been shuffled through several foster homes, schools, therapists, and friends. They don't understand trust or the basic principle of permanency. They do have

each other, though. These kids can benefit greatly from social work services.

These are the thoughts and concerns I had when working on an individual basis with three high school students living in foster care at my last MSW field placement through Michigan State University. My research determined that there were even more students than I was aware of residing in kinship care or adopted through the foster care system. My investigations further revealed additional students living with other non-related adults.

I was able to identify eleven students who were being cared for by adults other than their parents. I found these students by getting a list of "homeless students" from the high school administrative staff. I also identified students by coordinating with teachers. All of these students were attending the same high school. They had similar experiences and a common bond.

My clinical social work practice classes were teaching me about the power of social work groups, and I wondered about the advantages of a group for this demographic. It seemed that creating a social work group could prove beneficial for these students.

When considering the possibility of a group, I was concerned with taking students out of the classroom, confidentiality, and whether or not they would be interested in participating. The school could provide a safe environment for this unique group of students by giving them a place to talk freely about their past without judgment. They could identify and relate to each other's struggles, offer support, and share knowledge. This particular minority had difficulty relating to the general high school population. Their life experiences were not comparable to those of the typical teenager. They would be given the opportunity to grieve about their losses, including death, drug abuse, sexual abuse, prostitution, neglect, and homelessness. Most of these kids understand what it feels like to be unloved and unwanted.

My field placement supervisor, Terry P. Reen, LMSW, gave me permission to approach the students and determine their interest. I invited each of the eleven students individually to be a part of the group. I presented it to them as a trial experience, and we would have the opportunity to create this group together. I wanted their help to make this a positive experience not only for them, but for the students who would be entering the high school in the following years. I expected that some would decline based on privacy concerns and the risk of sharing personal information. None of the students declined the offer, and all were very interested and even excited about becoming members.

Under supervision, I was able to produce a rough outline for a group. I reached out to the social work community by asking for advice, direction, and assistance. Initially, I was searching for a standardized curriculum, because I was under the assumption that there were high schools all over the country providing this service. After weeks of contacts and research, I did not find any program that offered group social work services to students living in non-traditional families. However, there were two curricula that were designed for similar groups through different agencies. Both were attempting to prepare foster care youth for permanency placement. I was able to adapt several of their activities for our group.

Another MSW intern and I developed and co-facilitated the group under the direction of our field placement supervisor. Our group met on a weekly basis for one hour during the school day. We met every Wednesday, but rotated hours each week to avoid having students miss the same class regularly. The sessions were held in a private conference room that was in an isolated area of the school. The purpose of the group was to offer support and a safe place for kids living in non-traditional families. Focus was placed on normalization and advocacy. The objectives of the group were to:

- provide information regarding independent living, emancipation, and the Department of Human Services
- educate about maneuvering through the foster care system
- instill self-esteem and self-confidence
- offer advocacy for the students and teach them to advocate for themselves
- link them to supportive adults and assist with permanency planning
- improve independent living skills and prepare for aging out
- connect students with others with similar experiences
- create an alliance with the new local service providing shelter to girls when they age out of the system and become homeless.

The Foster and Kinship Care Support Group started with eleven students. Four were actively residing in foster care, two in kinship care, and one recently aged out of the system. One student resided with her boyfriend's family. Another member was residing with her father's ex-wife. One was living in a semi-independent living facility, and one student had aged out of the foster care system and was living on her own. One member was adopted through the foster care system. There were only two male members of the group. The group was operational for approximately eight weeks. We had one member who transitioned into a new foster home, but did return to the school and the group. She reported that this group was very helpful to her during this transition. We had another member who moved to another foster home and did not stay at the school.

The first sessions were spent establishing rapport and creating the group rules. We clearly explained to the students that this would be their group and they had complete control over what content was focused on. We asked the students to think about their needs and expectations to direct our content. The foster care students wanted information about emancipation and how "the system" operates. Other members were primarily concerned with independent living skills. All of them wanted to be able to talk about their feelings regarding their past and current living environments. Additional concerns consisted of resources, understanding their rights, and being able to express themselves.

The official curriculum for the group included an activity for each session. Typical topics included personal history, trust, self esteem, identity issues, independent living skills, job interview information, education benefits, and emancipation. However, each session started by giving each member the opportunity to share or discuss anything that the group could help with. Sometimes students shared journal entries, discussed concerns about their foster parents or biological parents, or shared information about something they learned. Typically, this lasted for about half of the session, and the remaining half hour was devoted to an activity aimed at the group objectives.

In our third session, we gave each participant a binder to help them organize themselves. I bought a binder specifically for foster care kids from a Web site. Each participant was given category dividers,

paper, pens, calendars, and logs to make their own binders. Binders included sections for journals, notes, court papers, education, contacts, resources, and other materials. We taught them how to use this tool to their advantage. This activity was received well, and they enjoyed the opportunity to start taking some control and ownership over their lives. It was a good resource for them, and in every meeting, someone shared how the binder had assisted them in some way.

In one of the following meetings, a foster care student reported that she was having a really rough week and asked to share her journal entry with the group. She read about two pages of emotional purging, but one sentence really summed it up for me. "When I wake up in the morning and go downstairs for breakfast, I don't see family. I see strangers." Every single student in the group validated her emotions with words of understanding, support, and encouragement. I really believe that this group has made a positive impact on each member.

The group received approval to continue on an on-going basis. The intention is that next year's graduate student interns will continue to facilitate and further develop this group. Hopefully, they will be able to start meeting earlier in the year.

Students reported that they enjoyed coming to group and felt secure in their confidentiality. Students also said the group was a positive experience. Several members reported that they appreciated the

resources, independent living information, and tools they obtained. All of the members told me that our support group was comforting and that it felt good to have a place to talk about being sold by their mother for drugs, being homeless, having drug addicted parents, and not being wanted. The support and validation offered and received by each participant was absolutely valuable to every student. They could talk freely about their worst experiences safely and without judgment, because in this group, that is what is "normal."

Through these weekly group therapy sessions, I witnessed the members offering each other support, understanding, friendship, advice, and knowledge. I noticed that they were building friendships with a potential for lasting bonds. They appeared to trust each other more than any other adults and most of their general student population peers. I believe that we gave them a positive experience, and I feel good about the tools and information we provided to them. I am hopeful that this group will continue in my absence, and I look forward to the opportunity to start similar groups in the future.

*Pam Ladetto earned her MSW from Michigan State University, her BS from Northern Michigan University, and her MOM degree from Sophia and Alexis. Pam is an adoptee and proud adoptive parent. She has dedicated herself personally and professionally to non-traditional family issues. She can be reached at psladetto@yahoo.com.*

# First Impressions of Social Work: An Honors Introductory Class

*by Gary L. Villereal, Ph.D., Beth Avis, Alicia Beach, Kayla Carter, Melinda Dearing, Cassie Ernstes, Ashley Fitzsimons, Sabrina Heinrich, Mary Katherine Higginson, Rebekah Huffman, Alex Kimura, Matthew Martin, Mackenzie Perkins, Courtney Rymer, Angela Stethen, and Kevin Worthy*

Students were asked to submit their first impressions and thoughts of what social work meant to them. The Foundations of Human Services class is a required course for social work pre-majors and the Honors section requires that a student be eligible for the Honors College. The students that made up this section were social work majors as well as other disciplines, and the majority were undeclared with no major. The students in this class provided some expected responses, as well as some unexpected ones. For the most part, there were favorable comments that ranged from the stereotypical to the unique.

Beth Avis stated, "I thought social work entailed helping victims of abuse and children without parents. Before even the first class period began, as I was reading through my textbook, I discovered what I believe is the most important aspect of social work that I have learned thus far: it affects everyone in America. Social workers do things like help the elderly, provide all types of rehabilitation services, work to end discrimination, care for those with diseases and their families, provide recreational services, house the homeless, and many other services. It was extremely surprising to me that it is such a broad field of study. Overall, my first impressions of social work are positive ones. If social work in the United States didn't exist, many more people would be in need of support and help. My first impressions of social work made me believe that it is a positive aspect of our country, because every single person should be given the best chance they have at a good life."

Alicia Beach offered that "a social worker covers many aspects of life. My first impression of a social worker was a very professional person, usually a woman, who stepped in when families became unsafe for children or a child went through adoption. I thought a social worker only dealt with tragic and unstable situations. A social worker works within numerous situations. They are beneficial people to life and are there to better the communities in which we live, always lending a hand."

Kayla Carter's reaction was that "a large segment of social work is dedicated to dealing with people who have developmental disabilities. One of these programs is the Special Olympics—an international program of year-round sports training and athletic competition for more than one million children and adults with intellectual disabilities. Until people with disabilities are given an opportunity, not only legally but also socially, to be treated and respected as peers, social services will be only partially effective."

Melinda Dearing expressed, "My first impression of social work focused solely on the profession of a clinical social worker. I have learned that social work encompasses a diverse realm in our society. Social work includes an overlapping of many fields that all work together.... Social work deals with creating a positive environment so that each individual can reach his or her full potential. Social inequality encompasses income, race, gender, and education. Social work provides the means to help individuals overcome various risk factors, enabling them to reach their full potential. Society can only benefit. It is my belief that compassion for others and a desire to enhance social justice produce a better world."

Cassie Ernstes stated that "social work is a unique career that contains many aspects of joy, happiness, and self-gratification, as well as defeat, sadness, and tribulations. Social workers are often given the most difficult situations to deal with on a long-term basis, ranging from problems concerning education, family matters, drug or alcohol abuse, juvenile discipline, or government roles. Social workers identify with their clients on a more personal level than any other profession. Social workers provide a voice for the people, allowing a sense of empowerment to fulfill those they serve."

Ashley Fitzsimons expressed, "So when considering my first ideas on social work, and what it means, I have come to view it not only as something I am learning about and working toward, but also as community based action, which I do not have to put off until after I graduate. I've come to learn that there are cycles of poverty, there are systems that exist which are hard to escape from, and there are situations that are difficult to overcome. There is, furthermore, discrimination, political disagreement, inequality, inadequate homes and schooling, and any myriad of things to contend with in American society."

Sabrina Heinrich stated, "When I think of a social worker, I think of someone with a huge heart and a strong soul. The heartache social workers must feel when they are too late, or a child ends up displaced and lost in the system, must be tremendous. I also feel like they must find their work very rewarding, when their efforts lead to a happy ending. It must be one of the most rewarding careers out there. I think most people associate social work as women's work; only women could be compassionate enough to deal with certain kinds of domestic issues. On the contrary, I feel like men and women are equally qualified for the job; personality and emotional stability trumps gender."

Mary Katherine Higginson felt that "The field of social work is oftentimes perceived very incorrectly. Being from a family that in many cases could be considered privileged, I previously assumed that social work was an area of study that only affected those in underdeveloped or less privileged areas. However, now that I have become more educated in the subject, it is clear that social work, and the effects that people in the field make, affects every person's life in some

> The most prevalent theme throughout was that social workers are caring people who have joined the profession to make a difference in the lives of those they serve.

facet. Social work is as diverse a field as the people it affects. Social workers help individuals cope with family and relational problems, domestic violence issues, unemployment, substance abuse, and even work in policy development. Social workers are many times seen as the 'bad guys,' but in reality, all people who decide to become social workers do so because of an innate and persistent desire to help people."

Rebekah Huffman stated, "My first impression of social work focused mainly on professionals who dealt with the poor or underprivileged on a daily basis. Unfortunately, I had a stereotype already formed in my mind because of where I have been raised. After learning more about social welfare and social work, I have gained a new appreciation for the system and the social workers who provide social welfare services to the poor. My eyes have been opened to all the positive things that come from the system of social welfare."

Alex Kimura related that "I used to only think of the people who helped orphans as those who did social work. I have come to realize that it is a very broad field and one that I am very interested in knowing more about. Social work to me now basically means work with the purpose of people–helping people. For that reason, this is probably one of the most pivotal and crucial lines of work we can discuss for our world. Social work addresses all qualities and levels of life. Domestic violence, rape, pregnancy, abortion, and all other issues dealing with women and children are things that social workers address. Issues involving oppression of human rights, racism, discrimination...are also involved in social work. Social work is something I can see myself doing."

Matthew Martin believes that "social work is 'the practice to improve the quality of life for a community and all those in the community.' It deals with life's everyday problems, which are complicated, and there's not always a right or wrong answer. Getting into this field of work is saying that you want to help improve the quality of life for those in your community."

Mackenzie Perkins said, "My initial thoughts on social work include an idea of a type of charity. A group of individuals attempting to better the world without thinking of themselves and how it could affect them. Social workers are strong and motivated individuals that have a passion for others. The participation in social work activities is more solely based on the individual that is in need of service. The individual must be understood on many different levels of need and psychological development. Individuals working in this field must be equipped with the knowledge of how to deal with people during a very stressful situation and be able to uphold a trust with each individual they come into contact with."

Courtney Rymer stated, "Before I knew anything about social work, my initial ideas of what it entailed were a bit off. I thought that social work was simply dealing with old people and poor people and trying to make their lives a little better. I thought it was just people who sit at a desk all day and answer phones and help kids when something has happened to their parents or situations like that. Little did I know it was so much more. As I became more informed about social work, I learned it is working to a goal to actually make changes in the world and try and reverse the problems in the world, rather than just pacify them like I had previously thought. I have learned that some of my original thoughts about social work were right, but for the most part I was very uneducated about what it truly was. I have learned it is much more complex than I originally thought it was."

Angela Stethen thinks that "when social workers are involved, I used to immediately think that there was an abusive, drug related, or other horrible scenario surrounding a child. I used to believe that social workers could only be found within a school system to help protect needy children in the schools. However, because of the nature of their work, I do believe that often kids, especially kids in need of some sort, are their priority...however, not their only purpose. I now understand that along with helping kids recover or be removed from dangerous and unhealthy situations, social work is a profession that also helps the general community. I still consider social work to be a very selfless career. To be a social worker, the primary aspect of your job, is to care for others in the community."

Kevin Worthy concludes, "I began my courses in social work at Western Kentucky University and immediately knew that I made the right decision in choosing social work. Even though I have many more classes to complete and much more to learn about social work, my impression of social work has already changed drastically. One of the most important aspects of social work, in my opinion, is that anyone working in the social work field is an advocate for [his or her] clients. Social workers are there to help people, especially those who really need an extra boost in life. Social workers are in a place of power, and as such, they have the duty to fight for the rights and needs of the people."

All the students remarked favorably about their impressions of social work as a profession. Most of the students learned through the class that social work is much more than working with children and the needy. The most prevalent theme throughout was that social workers are caring people who have joined the profession to make a difference in the lives of those they serve.

*Gary Villereal, Ph.D., associate professor, teaches a social work honors 101 Foundations of Human Services course at Western Kentucky University. Students engage in lively debate and write in a critical manner to enhance their learning. This article was co-authored by members of one such class.*

# How I Passed the Licensing Exam: 10 Tips
## by Ammu Kowolik, LMSW

Four years ago, I graduated with my MSW degree from what is now known as the Silberman School of Social Work at Hunter College. My method was in Community Organizing and Planning, and after two wonderful years in grad school, I was ready to enter this world as a professional.

I planned to get my license first, especially since I was told it's easiest to get it right out of school.

So, immediately after graduating, I took the review course offered to alumni and purchased study material from a commercial licensure prep service. I decided to study and register with NYSED and ASWB. But a month after graduation, I wanted to give my brain a chance to rest. Then reality slowly crept in, and I realized I *really* needed a job! So, let's fast forward through a few months of job hunting and landing a position at NASW, the New York City Chapter.

Diving into the first real job of my adult life, I consumed myself with work and used the little extra time I had to "veg." I had the books, but I didn't study. And so this was put off for another four years.

The year 2011 was different for me. In planning my wedding, I had somehow made a promise to my fiancé that he would marry an LMSW, and so in May 2011, I took the NASW LMSW Test Prep class with Dr. Dawn Hall Apgar. I sat in on this class a few years ago, but this time something else clicked, and I got it. Dawn gave us the tools we needed to take the exam, and after having passed, let me tell you *she was on point!* Not only did Dawn cover the content areas we need to focus in on, but she also showed us how to *read* the questions on the exam. It can be tricky (and if you've taken the exam, you know what I mean!).

This last summer, I made a decision that greatly affected my study ethic–I got a study partner! My friend, a recent graduate from NYU Silver School of Social Work, and I planned to meet weekly, for about a month, to study and take the exam in September. This actually ended up taking nearly three months for us. We were diligent, met weekly, and went over the content areas in depth. When we weren't together, we made up flash cards

and read up on areas that needed more of our attention. By the beginning of October, we both realized we needed to schedule our exam and be done with it. And so we did! I am happy to report that as of November 1, 2011, we both passed our licensing exams!

If you are worried about taking the exam, here are 10 suggestions:

### 1. First thing to do, and the thing you must consistently do throughout your studying and testing process: Find a way to battle your ANXIETY!

I have spoken to many NASW members on the phone who have taken the exam multiple times but did not pass. I have spoken to social workers who need to pass this exam to hold onto their jobs. That is a *lot* of pressure. And in this economy, I hear that and feel that. No matter your situation in getting licensed, you must find a way to relax your mind and slow your racing heart, so you can focus on the exam.

I have been meaning to meditate for a long time, but haven't quite mastered a routine. But what works best for me is taking seven (why seven? I have no idea) long *deep* breaths and exhaling slowly. Whenever I am anxious (in any setting), doing this relaxes me. Try it. Most of us don't breathe enough.

### 2. Find a study partner.

I am usually a loner when it comes to doing something I need to focus my energy on. But the *main* thing that helped me with this process was finding a study partner I could trust and rely on. Meeting with my friend held me accountable–and without that, I could have easily put this off longer. Meeting together kept us focused, had us talk out content ("What does projective identification actually mean?"), and find ways to remember things that we would need to know on the exam. I owe so much to having her be a partner in this with me.

### 3. Register and schedule your exam.

When you set an exam date, it *really* helps you focus.

### 4. Consider what helps you with recall.

For me, it's the act of writing things down. I made flash cards, and seldom used them, but the mere act of writing down the various stages of development or what the side effects of MAOIs are helped me retain this knowledge for the long run. The test is tricky, yes, but you must know your content.

### 5. The exam is not "all clinical" stuff.

Trust me, I was a CO student. I took core classes on human behavior in the social environment and a casework class, but I did not necessarily apply these subject areas into my direct work. Are there questions on clinical diagnosis and medication use? Yes. Do these outweigh direct practice questions? No. So if you are not a clinical social worker (like me), you can still pass this exam. Review your content and know the basics.

### 6. Take a review course to help you know what you need to know.

For example, I cannot recommend the test prep course offered by NASW-NYC enough. You get a study guide with material to focus in on, and practice questions at the end, to test your recall, as well as the full NASW Code of Ethics. As an alum, I took the test prep offered by Hunter, which was also helpful. I got some great tips there and used those in my exam, four years later. Either way, take a review course–even if you know your content, you may not be completely prepared for what is ahead.

### 7. Know the NASW Code of Ethics.

We all should know this, but you definitely *need* to know this for the exam. Review it and understand it. Know what you are legally being held to, as a professional social worker.

### 8. Find supplemental study materials.

A few weeks before the exam, I found an array of resources online for *free*. There is the Social Work Podcast, by

Jonathan B. Singer, a great resource for social workers in general, not only for the exam. There are also podcasts from Dr. Linton Hutchinson that you can find on iTunes called "Social Work Exam Review." I signed up for daily questions via e-mail from Harvey Norris, LCSW (they were helpful to test my knowledge "on the go"). And lastly, I paid $75 to take the ASWB practice exam online. The main purpose in this was to give an idea of what it will feel like to take the exam. Please keep in mind that the test you take online is a replica of the actual exam and the questions may not reflect those that will actually be on the exam. If you think that might help with your anxiety, do it. You even get a breakdown of the content areas in the end. I found it valuable, even if I had to pay extra for it.

## 9. Think positively.

I know you may be under a lot of pressure to get this license; remember, give yourself some time to breathe, find other stress-reducing activities, and keep a positive energy around this exam. I used some visualization techniques that truly helped with my anxiety. (Silly me took this exam two weeks before my wedding!) Do not let the exam rule you–you must rule the exam. And with enough preparation, you will!

## 10. And lastly, TRUST YOUR GUT.

More often than not, our first instincts are always correct. Do not second guess yourself. If you flag questions on the exam and review them, remember what made you choose the answer in the first place. Don't think too much into it and trust in your knowledge.

*Ammu Kowolik, LMSW, is Program and Administrative Associate, NASW-NYC Chapter. Ammu is a lifelong resident of New York City, new to Brooklyn, and was married in November 2011.*

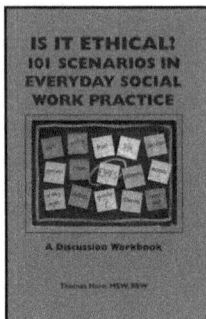

# Students at Earlham College Work to Change Perception of Mental Health

Despite its relatively short time in existence, Earlham College's chapter of "Active Minds On Campus" has already made great strides toward the goal of ending the stigma that surrounds mental health treatment. Earlham College counselor Jessica Sanford, founder and advisor for the chapter, explained, "My goal at Earlham is to encourage students to talk openly about mental health and seek help right away any time it is needed." Sanford described Active Minds as "an effective way to help the campus talk about mental health issues openly. It's the only nonprofit organization in the U.S. that uses student voices to raise mental health awareness among their peers. The organization supports student-run chapters on college campuses that help educate the entire student body about resources in the community."

In the last two years, the Active Minds chapter at Earlham has done a number of things to increase awareness and end the stigma that surrounds mental illness and prevents people from speaking up and seeking treatment. The group participated in National Day Without Stigma and sponsored the nationally known speaker, Eric Ostendorf, who has appeared on CNN and the Dr. Phil TV show,

*Jessica Sanford and a student talk about Active Minds on Campus.*

to speak about his own battle with an eating disorder and his journey to recovery. During "Get the Stress Out Week," Active Minds offers stress relieving activities on campus like cupcake decorating, chair massages, music, and films.

Jessica Sanford, advisor for Active Minds at Earlham and editor of the student mental health publication *Stall Stories,* is a licensed social worker with a Master of Social Work from Indiana University. In her work as an Earlham counselor, her eclectic, problem-solving therapeutic approach blends supportive, behavioral, cognitive, and psychodynamic therapies to help students make changes in their lives. Sanford has taught Earlham College workshops on sexual assault, and is frequently requested as a speaker for her presentations on sexual assault, eating disorders, obsessive compulsive disorder, attention deficit hyperactivity disorder, and proven strategies for addressing student stress.

Earlham College is a private liberal arts college in Richmond, Indiana. For more information about Active Minds on Campus, please contact Jessica Sanford at Earlham College at (765) 983-1449.

# Reflections of a Child Welfare Social Worker

## *by Sonya O. Hunte, MSW*

Natosha walked into her supervisor's office on her first day back from Child Welfare Foundations training and was told that she was inheriting twenty cases. Panic started to set in. She immediately ran to her desk to rummage through the cases in an attempt to make telephone contact with each caretaker of the child(ren) listed on her new caseload. Anxiety started to take over. After all, Natosha had heard some horror stories about children dying or becoming seriously injured while a child welfare agency was involved with the family. Natosha began to manage her caseload from a crisis stance instead of taking the time to strategically approach the work. Kimberly, a veteran social worker and staff mentor, observed Natosha's frustration over the following weeks in trying to visit children, call collateral contacts, attend court hearings, and return phone calls. Kimberly offered Natosha several tips for successful case management.

**1. Review each case that is inherited and write a summary paragraph.**

The summary should include the date the child(ren) were last seen by a social worker, any recommendations given by a professional, any services placed in the home or for a particular household member, the family's response to service intervention, and any court action or other pertinent information. This will help in developing a strategy for serving the family and serve as a quick review for each case.

**2. Staff each case with an immediate supervisor for an outside view and directive measures.**

Utilize the supervisor as an agency and policy expert. Follow all suggestions and directives.

**3. Ensure that all critical issues are managed by the family.**

If the family is not capable of moving to autonomy, utilize in-home services to ensure that they are headed in that direction.

**4. Be concise but descriptive in writing about the visit with the family.**

The person reading your notes should be able to envision what was observed. This will allow the supervisor to give better supervision in that he or she will be able to capture solid information about the family. For example, if a child had a bruise, the shape, color, size, location, and story behind the mark/bruise should be documented.

**5. Allow the family to take the lead in creating the goals and steps of their treatment plan.**

This creates a solid level of family buy-in. The family is more familiar than any outside party on its functioning and needs. As a social worker, do help in redirecting the goals and steps to remedy the issue that led to child welfare involvement.

**6. If needed, refer the family to services that meet their needs.**

Cookie cutter services not need apply! Each family needs tailored services for growth and successful autonomy to occur.

**7. If there is still access to the prior social worker on the case, conference with that social worker to gain additional insight.**

There may be information that was not captured fully in the case notes that may be communicated verbally.

**8. Always provide the family with a community resource listing.**

This information will enable the family to locate resources on their own and equip them to move forward without agency dependency.

Kimberly gave Natosha the eight tips that would lead to a reduction in frustration and better case management. Whenever Natosha inherited a case, her case log reflected her summary of prior intervention, staffing with her supervisor, descriptive yet concise family interaction and observations, family-led goals and steps for the treatment plan, referral to tailored services and family responsiveness, case conferences, and a summary of resources provided. She used the tips and was able to watch her families thrive.

Natosha also had the lowest amount of recidivism in her unit of five social workers. Natosha shared her tips when she became a social work mentor after five years of service at her county child welfare agency.

*Sonya O. Hunte, MSW, is a Homeless Education Liaison with the Atlanta Public Schools. She is also the CEO of Hunte Community Development Consulting LLC, a company specializing in nonprofit strategic program development, training, and community partnership planning.*

# Your Community
# Needs You

## Make a Difference at Home

Earn a Master of Social Work
Online from the Top-Ranked
USC School of Social Work

**USC**School
of Social Work

http://msw.usc.edu/NewSocialWorkerMag

# Lessons From Hull House

## *by Laura Gale, LCSW*

My staff member knocks tentatively on my half open office door, and I invite her in. I notice immediately the wide eyes and how she is twisting a strand of long brown hair around her finger.

"Is it true?" She asks.

"Will I lose my job? What about my clients? Sergio can't go without his medication, and Nancy just started with the behavioral aide it took us four months to line up. What would happen to them?"

I settle back in my chair. I've had this conversation before. Despite my best efforts to maintain an environment of safety for both my clients and my staff, rumors once again emerged. News stories of county and state budget cuts make their way into lunchtime conversations. Fears arise, and conversations like the one I am about to have must take place.

I have been fortunate. My organization has not had to shut down programs, pulling through each year by reducing costs and managing staff reductions through attrition rather than lay offs. We are the exception rather than the rule. Even established, respected institutions are having to make hard economic choices regarding which services to continue to offer and which to abandon to keep their doors open, as the recent closing and subsequent filing for bankruptcy of the Hull House Association in Chicago illustrates.

Founded by Jane Addams in 1889, Hull House provided social services to residents of Chicago for 122 years. In recent years, the agency focused services in the areas of foster care, domestic violence, and job training. At the time of closure, it employed more than 300 workers, and served 60,000+ clients in 50 programs at 40 sites throughout Chicago (Jane Addams Hull House Association, n. d.).

While rumors about mismanagement of funds began to circulate and fingers began to point regarding the agency's over-reliance on government funds, there is another lesson to be learned from this tragedy. The social work profession has forgotten about our role in advocating for social justice at the policy level.

It has been reported that 85% of Hull House funding came from various federal, state, and local grants and contracts, whereas only 10% came from unrestricted private donations. As a result, when government money dried up, the agency's revenues decreased by almost half, from a high of $40 million in the 1990s to $23 million (Wisniewski, 2012). The management of Hull House is being criticized for not diversifying its funding streams more effectively, and for not putting more emphasis on private donations.

But is reliance on unrestricted private funds and foundation grants any more reliable in tough economic times? Would Hull House have realistically been able to raise an additional $17 million to cover existing programs? Perhaps, but individuals and foundations are also struggling with limited funds. What is available is being stretched over the increased need for services that a poor economy stimulates, resulting in difficult dilemmas about who should receive services. When economic times become difficult and government money seems to be unavailable, it is easy to throw up our hands and blame the now struggling nonprofit for not seeing that the good times would end. Perhaps an additional approach would be to put pressure on local, state, and federal governments to increase commitment to social welfare programs in times of economic challenge.

When Jane Addams began her work at Hull House, she was an active fundraiser for her organization. However, she also involved herself heavily in the areas of political and social reform. She sat on the Chicago Board of Education, was a founding member of the American Civil Liberties Union (ACLU), and was a charter member of the National Association for the Advancement of Colored People (NAACP). She also campaigned heavily for Theodore Roosevelt and the Progressive Party, contributing to the eventual passage of the Social Security Act, the foundation for many of our government welfare programs today ("Women in History," n. d.).

Jane Addams understood the vital role that government funding needed to play in the provision of social services and was committed to engaging in policy advocacy work toward this end. It has been the habit of the social work field to shy away from macro practice in times of political conservatism and to focus heavily on micro work, waiting passively for the political and economic times to change before becoming involved in policy work once again. However, it is exactly in times of greatest economic and political challenge that social workers need to grab the public attention and

---

## Pioneering U.S. Social Worker Lillian Wald Featured in NYC Museum Exhibitions

Two new exhibitions highlight the trailblazing social worker Lillian Wald (1867-1940), also famed as the "mother of public health nursing." In the 1890s, Wald founded the Henry Street Settlement and the Visiting Nurse Service of New York (VNSNY), two institutions that are still going strong today. In fact, more than 500 social workers are employed by VNSNY, the nation's largest not-for-profit home health care organization.

On view until August 12 at Yeshiva University Museum near Union Square in Manhattan, a show entitled "Trail of the Magic Bullet: The Jewish Encounter with Modern Medicine" devotes considerable attention to Wald's life and work, including archival photographs and artifacts. This museum, located in the Center for Jewish History, at 15 West 16th Street, is open free on Mondays and Wednesdays from 5 to 8 p.m. Admission at other times is $8 for adults and $6 for students. This exhibition will be of interest to all who are interested in learning more about the history of social work in the United States.

*Photo of Lillian Wald: Courtesy of Visiting Nurse Service of New York*

Starting May 4, a permanent exhibition featuring Wald and her work will open in the Puffin Gallery for Social Activism at the Museum of the City of New York, at 1220 Fifth Ave and 103rd Street in Manhattan. This exhibition will remain on view for at least two years.

– *Susan Rita Ruel*

work to focus our political systems on the needs of our most disadvantaged citizens.

Through involvement in political campaigns, social workers can help insure that progressive candidates who share our values of social justice and equality are voted into office. We can use the many easily accessible media outlets available today to educate the public about how the provision and funding of quality social services positively affects all of society. We can become aware of the policies that are being proposed in Congress every day that affect our clients both positively and negatively, and work to ensure the passage of those that support our clients' best interests, including those that appropriate funds to important social issues.

So, perhaps the greatest lesson from the closure of Hull House is that the field of social work needs to recommit itself to macro policy work. Yes, private money and the diversification of funding will always play a vital role in the sustainability of social service agencies, as will the sophisticated and skillful management of boards of directors and nonprofit administrators. However, without government commitment to adequate and timely payments to nonprofits, long-term sustainability will be difficult to achieve for many organizations. It is time to recommit to the work that Jane Addams so clearly understood–that social work is not just about meeting individual client needs; it is also about creating changes within systems that will have a radical impact on the quantity and quality of services our clients receive.

## References

Jane Addams Hull House Association. *Who we serve*. Retrieved from http://hullhouse.org/aboutus/whoweserve.html.

Wisniewski, M. (2012, January 19). *Chicago Hull House closing for lack of funds*. Reuters. Retrieved from http://www.reuters.com/article/2012/01/19/us-hullhouse-closing-idUS-TRE80I2IQ20120119.

*Women in history. Jane Addams biography*. Retrieved from http://www.lkwdpl.org/wihohio/adda-jan.htm.

*Laura Gale, LCSW, is an adjunct lecturer for the University of Southern California School of Social Work Virtual Academic Center. She has 20 years of experience in the areas of nonprofit administration, clinical supervision, and social welfare policy.*

## Poetry

# Blackbirds
### by Johanna Slivinske, MSW, LSW

Through your window
    the blackbirds banter as they surreptitiously swoop
    as a flock from limb to limb.
We both eye them through blurred vision
    as we cannot bear to watch each other;
    we are glad they are there to comfort us.
They blur together as surreal winged licorice,
    jellybean ovals engulfed by the smog of our unspoken emoticons
    sadness, sweetness, sentimentality
    swept away in the silentness of our bellowing blackbirds;
    simultaneously beckoning yet balking our own reserve.
 Our blackbird teardrops cried in the sky for both of us,
    melding into the trees in fluid motion
    shifting and swooping
    then lifting and soaring
    into the unknown, undefined beyond
A point of focus for our nonverbal, mute discussion of undetermined, inevitable things to come. Where will they fly tomorrow, we wonder?

*Johanna Slivinske, MSW, LSW, is an author, educator and social worker. She is the author of the book* Storytelling and Other Activities for Children in Therapy *and has also written professional journal articles.*

## STUDENT SOCIAL WORK ORGANIZATIONS

Please send us a short **news** article about your group's activities. Also, send us **photos** of your club in action–we may even feature you on our front cover!

It's easy to share your club's activities with our readers. Send your news/photos to:

Linda Grobman, ACSW, LSW, Editor/Publisher
THE NEW SOCIAL WORKER
P.O. Box 5390, Harrisburg, PA 17110-0390
or to *lindagrobman@socialworker.com*

## University of Alabama School of Social Work Students Help in Storm Relief

In the aftermath of the storm of April 27, 2011, Bess Dulaney and Shelley Rawlings, University of Alabama School of Social Work MSW graduates, assisted children with toys and school supplies in the devastated Rosedale Court housing community of Tuscaloosa, Alabama. The toys and school supplies were gathered and donated by nonprofit organizations.

## Methodist University Social Work Students Attend Conference

*On March 1, 2012, some of the social work students from Methodist University attended the NASW Ethics Conference in Raleigh, NC. It was an amazing day of learning about ethical dilemmas while also socializing with many social work professionals. Speakers talked about ethical considerations when working with victims and survivors of human trafficking and also with undocumented immigrants who have been deported and whose children are left in the care of the United States forster care system. The students enjoyed and learned a lot from this conference and encourage other social work students to attend these types of functions.*

## Boise State Social Work Students Participate in PRIDE Rally

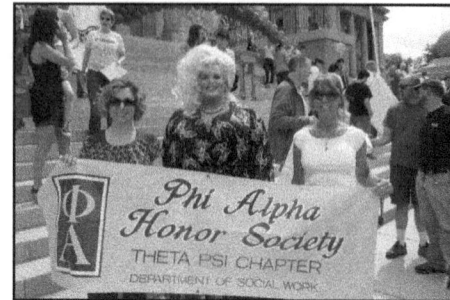

*Students in the Phi Alpha Honor Society of Social Work–Theta Psi Chapter, Boise State University, are shown adding their voices and presence to the underrepresented populations both on and off campus by participating in the PRIDE Rally at the State Capitol. Shown (left to right): Tami Bishop, BSW student; Minerva Jane, community member and activist; and Lisa West, BSW student.*

## FAU Students Attend Lobby Day in Tallahassee

*Each year, the Florida Atlantic University School of Social Work drives to Tallahassee, FL, and meets with legislators to advocate for specific bills to be passed or not. FAU students are shown here in the old Capitol Building on the stairs, during their April 2011 trip. The building is now a museum.*

FOLLOW ME ON TWITTER

**The New Social Worker is on Twitter! Follow us at:** *http://www.twitter.com/newsocialworker*

*Maldonado—continued from page 3*

# Phi Alpha Director's Message

*by Paul Baggett, Ph.D., Executive Director*

Phi Alpha began in 1962 with six chapters. Today, we are approaching 400 chapters. As Phi Alpha enters its 50th year, the Executive Council thanks students and faculty who have contributed time and energy to their chapters. Chapters are recognizing scholarship and engaging in service activities across the country.

The Phi Alpha business meeting was held in Atlanta during the CSWE APM. Robin Walters Powell from the University of Findlay was the first recipient of the Outstanding Advisor of the Year. The students who nominated her commented on her commitment to student success. An exceptional group of students participated in the Poster Presentation Program. They shared service activities that positively affected their universities and communities. Also, Chapter Service Award winners received their awards.

Phi Alpha has partnered with BPD to launch a scholarship program for BSW students. Six thousand dollars will be awarded this year. Applications are on the Phi Alpha Web site and are due May 31, 2012. Phi Alpha will have a new listserv through the Web site for students to communicate with one another. The International Office is working on new initiatives, including a Chapter Grants Program and an Outstanding Student Leader Program. We are in need of advisors to serve as reviewers. We look forward to serving students for the next 50 years.

## Social Work Day Celebration at Northern Caribbean University

*A captivated audience at NCU's Social Work Day*

a panel discussion moderated by Mr. Tani Gray,MSW; and an interesting empowerment session led by Mrs. Lita Allen, MA, Ed., who is a life coach and social work counselor. The group was also treated to a creative and wide display of talents by the social work students ranging from poetry to dramatizations. The day ended with a campaign for male social workers and a pledge to serve our country and abide by the code of ethics of the Jamaica Association of Social Workers (JASW) and our profession at large.
*—Shanniel Shakespare*

Social Work Day was celebrated under the theme "Social Work Matters" at the Northern Caribbean University (NCU) in Manchester, Jamaica. Social work students and facilitators of the behavioral sciences department orchestrated the event. The main thrust was to highlight and emphasize the necessity of social workers in our country in light of the various social ills that plague the majority of the population. The key features of the day included discussions on social work entrepreneurship facilitated by Mrs. M. Higgins and Ms. Eva Forde,MSW;

*NCU students' handiwork shows why social work matters.*

He's doing amazingly well, though. His shooter was convicted a year ago and pled guilty to attempted murder. He was sentenced to 16 years."

It was only at the insistence of her cousin Giancarlo, his mother, and other relatives that Maldonado agreed to go to the interview. "Even he started yelling, 'Get the ____ out,' " she recalls, "even though it hurt him to talk."

Maldonado hadn't studied and thought she had done horribly, until an e-mail came indicating she had been nominated for the scholarship. During the second part of the competition, she began to cry, until her father told her to "put away Giancarlo" and focus on the people she was meeting. They included the niece of Chicago Mayor Rahm Emanuel.

"It was very intense," Maldonado says. "One of the people on the committee was a Truman—the President's eldest grandson."

"Intense" describes her school/work schedule. Since August, Maldonado has been a program assistant with the Mahomet Area Youth Club, where she teaches conversational Spanish; promotes multiculturalism, diversity, inclusivity and tolerance; and collaborates with staff in addressing personal and family dilemmas and creating youth-development programs. Last year, she was a multicultural advocate for residential life at the university. Maldonado's community service has included tutoring at the SOAR Youth Development Program.

The two research projects with Piedra—who recommended her for the Truman Scholarship—involve the extra tasks human service workers do outside their professional expertise, and an analysis of service providers who work with Latinos in a new-growth community.

It's hard for Maldonado to find time for after school/after work activities. "I work a lot," she admits. She spends as much time as possible with her four siblings (although one is in Puerto Rico, with her son) and other family, as well as with friends. "I love food and used to dance," she says. "I also love to eat."

Not surprisingly, Maldonado loves children. The family she lives with off-campus has four of them.

*Barbara Trainin Blank is a freelance writer based in Harrisburg, PA.*

# Kryss Meets Career

## Words Matter
### by Kristen Marie (Kryss) Shane, MSW, LMSW

A few months ago, when I began to think about what I'd like to write in my last piece under "Kryss Meets Career," I'd planned some light-hearted words or some type of summary, hoping to convey how much I have enjoyed authoring this column. Instead, I've decided to leave you with this.

Those who know me best, who have known me longest, would tell you that I've never been very good at asking for help or leaning on others. I've mostly tried to ignore that about myself, to be honest. Instead, I've focused on the things I am good at–baking, activism, being the mother to an adorable pup.

Nikko was a Maltese I rescued from an abusive family who placed an ad to "get rid of him" on the Internet about seven years ago. When we met, he didn't trust humans, wasn't housebroken, and had hair that stuck out at every angle. Over the years, we conquered undergrad graduation (me), potty training (him), and bad haircuts (both). We lived in three states, we survived the long hours of graduate school, and we learned to appreciate each other's quirks. For example, he learned not to get upset when I shouted at the television during Ohio State football games or political debates, and I learned to accept that the last piece of pepperoni on a slice of pizza eaten at home always belongs to him.

This past December, Nikko got sick. The emergency room vets tell me they'd never seen someone act so quickly, but I just sensed that something was wrong. He spent four days in the ICU, in an incubator, IVs in both paws. During those days, I was too busy waiting for vets' phone calls to take care of myself. It was here when I began to experience the real power of social networking.

For years, I'd been a member of Facebook, of a Web site dedicated to professional women, and to one meant for Maltese owners. I posted in each what was going on with Nikko and of how horrible the waiting was. Some nights, while I was too worried to sleep and the world felt a little too quiet, I would just sit and read the pages of comments and

*Kryss, with Nikko. Photo credit: Sidnei Beal at Clique Photography.*

well-wishes on these sites. And it kept me going until I got to take Nikko home.

In the six weeks that followed, I truly appreciated the silver lining of having been laid off, as it meant spending almost every hour with Nikko. He was weaker now, rested more, but I'd take a pillow and lie with him on the floor and he'd put his paw on my hand.

And then he got sick again. Back to the emergency room, the ICU, and the incubator. And I went back to the Internet. Comments and hopeful words from people I'd never laid eyes on kept me somewhat sane while I waited to see whether the medications would be enough.

On Super Bowl Sunday, while the rest of NYC was rooting on the Giants, I found myself sitting in front of his

incubator, trying to decide how I could ever make the choice the vet needed me to make. I sat for a long time there, my hand through the slot in the incubation window. After a few hours, he stopped looking me in the eye and, much like feeling a wave when you're already underwater, I knew. Nikko spent his last moments with a belly full of treats, lying in my lap, with my hand on his back, wrapped in his favorite blanket (one I'd had since my own birth). While NYC celebrated the National Championship win, I was beside myself with grief. On autopilot, I returned to the computer and shared the outcome, gave my personal e-mail address, and signed off.

In the days that followed, I received more than 150 e-mails from people all over the world. Some were real friends who'd learned of the news through Facebook, some were people I'd chatted with on one of the networking sites, and some were complete strangers who read my words and felt compelled to tell me their stories of loss and how they healed. One woman sent me a fruit basket, giving me the store information and asking me to call to give them my personal information. Another sent me e-mailed reminders a few times each day to eat. Different friends took turns staying up on instant messenger to keep me company in the middle of the night when I was far too grief-stricken to sleep. And I, someone who has never been any good at asking for help, in my most devastated moment, was gifted with the love I needed but wouldn't have been able to ask for.

This magazine, research studies, and so many anecdotal stories have spent the past few years looking at social networking Web sites and discussing the ways in which the Internet has had an impact on people, and most often, we hear about the ways in which so many separate themselves from the "real" world now that there are so many ways to communicate virtually. Although that is certainly a concern, this experience has reminded me that social media can also be an opportunity for us to help each other, to share with each other, and to feel far less alone, even when no one else is standing in the room.

A few months ago, I'd envisioned my final column here to impart some mind-altering words of wisdom that you'd never have thought of on your own. I wanted to leave you with something unique or to find some surprisingly eloquent way to close a column that has meant so much to me to have written. Now though, all I have to offer is this: *words matter*. Intentions matter. As social workers, we are taught about the DSM and therapeutic treatment models, theorists, long-term success rates, huge overarching plans for our clients and our field in a way that sometimes feels a bit overwhelming to take in. While I don't at all discount the importance of those, I've come to learn that sometimes the smallest moments matter most. A moment of your time, a hug, a kind sentiment, a Facebook or Web site forum acknowledgement, cutting someone a little slack, showing up. *It all matters*.

For those with love to give, please do so when you see someone in need. For those who, like me, aren't so good at

asking, trust that those folks are out there when you're the one who needs. Thank you to all who have been reading and commenting here and on my blog posts for allowing me into your lives and for giving me such guidance and encouragement along the way.

*Note: I won't be disappearing. You will still find me reviewing books and writing anything else the incredible editor allows...so keep an eye out!*

*Kristen Marie (Kryss) Shane, LMSW, earned her B.S. at The Ohio State University and her MSW at Barry University. She currently resides in the Miami area, where she is always open to new professional opportunities. Her professional foci are in the areas of LGBTQI issues and in the elder population. She is a regular guest speaker at Columbia University, where she gives professional trainings on making professionals, agencies, and companies more inclusive. She has aided in the introduction of Gay Straight Alliances in numerous high schools; marched in the National Equality March in Washington, D.C.; rallied for non-discrimination laws in numerous states; and she continues to advocate for LGBTQI and elder rights on the local, state, and federal levels. In addition, she is on staff at socialworkchat.org and was the 2011 blogger for The New Social Worker, where her weekly thoughts can found at: http://blog.socialworker.com/search/label/Kryss.*

*The Life and Thought of Louis Lowy: Social Work Through the Holocaust, by Lorrie Greenhouse Gardella, Syracuse University Press, Syracuse, NY, 2011, 213 pages, $24.95 hardcover.*

Louis Lowy (1920-1991) was a survivor of the Holocaust and a professor for 28 years. This biography of his life was based heavily on more than 16 hours of oral narratives he recorded in the last year of his life. Structured chronologically, these narratives end in the early 1950s, so we have only the briefest of sketches about his professional life in America after that time. Accordingly, this biography might be best categorized as a Holocaust memoir rather than a complete life story.

Born into a Jewish family in Munich, Germany, Lowy was sent to school in England at 13 years of age after it became clear that the Nazis were rising to power in Germany. When his father passed away two years later, he returned to Munich to help his family relocate to Prague, Czechoslovakia, which was considered a safer place than Germany for a Jewish family. Less than three years later, Lowy—who was now a college student—was arrested by Nazi stormtroopers in Prague. Two years later, he and his family were in Theresienstadt, a transit concentration camp that served briefly as a Potemkin-like "model" camp for propaganda purposes.

Gardella makes much of Lowy's experiences in Theresienstadt, where he worked as a residence hall leader for thirty or so adolescents. Education was prohibited, and no educational materials were available. Despite these obstacles, however, Lowy organized educational programs. He viewed "education as the source of personal and social fulfillment and as the means of instilling hope for a future" (p. 33).

He nearly lost hope himself after his deportation to the Auschwitz death camp, but through an amazing series of events, he managed to survive Auschwitz and ended up leading the Deggendorf Displaced Persons Camp after the war. Jewish survivors were less than 5% of the displaced persons returning home in the summer of 1945, but unlike the rest, Jewish survivors had nowhere to go. They were dispossessed, stripped of their national citizenship, and largely unwanted by the rest of the world.

At Deggendorf, Lowy addressed the challenges of returning—"to create conditions for people that allow them to fulfill themselves optimally, find their place in tomorrow's world, and participate constructively and actively in the society as part of a larger world order" (p. 91). He was elected twice to chair the Deggendorf Jewish Committee and worked tirelessly in that role, but he also emigrated to the United States at the first opportunity, arriving in New York in May 1946. He was 26 years old.

There are only 35 pages about Lowy's life in the United States, during which he completed his education, practiced as a social worker, and joined the faculty of the School of Social Work at Boston University. His academic work focused on gerontology, adult education, international social work, and intergenerational relationships.

Gardella augments Lowy's narratives with personal interviews with his wife and closest friends who were also Holocaust survivors, and she makes extensive use of quotations from the narrative, interviews, and Lowy's written material. It has been said that "if social work did not exist, it would have to be created" (pp. 152-153). Lowy's life story gives shape to the adage in a way that is both powerful and persuasive. I believe that Lowy's life story may be an effective antidote to incipient professionalism in today's students. I recommend it highly as an example and reminder that social work is more than a career. Social work is a calling to change the world.

*Reviewed by Peter A. Kindle, Ph.D., CPA, LMSW, assistant professor at the University of South Dakota. He can be contacted by e-mail at Peter.Kindle@usd.edu.*

---

*Raising Abel, by Carolyn Nash, CreateSpace, 2011, 332 pages, $15.99 paperback, $3.99 digital.*

Reading the back cover of *Raising Abel* by Carolyn Nash, one might expect the memoir to be the classic tale of how becoming a foster and then adoptive parent changed a woman's life. It doesn't take long before the reader discovers that this book is anything but typical. This is the story of a woman who proves that being someone's mother doesn't require giving birth to him. This is the story of just how much childhood trauma can alter someone's life. This is a story of how important mental health professionals can be for people in need. This is the story of low self-esteem, of high expectations, of unconditional love, and of torture that lives on far after the physical aspects end, of one mother's shortcomings and another's drive to be the perfect parent. In short, this is a chronicle that touches at least one aspect of most of us, giving us the gift of both another's very human experience and the parallels we may find between hers and our own.

Nash, describing her mother to her therapist, says, "I think my mom loved all of us the best she could, but she was so wrapped up in her own pain that that's all she could focus on. I don't think she even realized that she always came first and we came second. All my life, she has depended on me to make her happy. She truly *thinks* she wants the best for me, but at the same time, she wants me to make sure she's not lonely and that her problems and cares come first, mine a distant second" (p. 168).

Set over the course of the past eighteen years, Ms. Nash describes in incredible detail the rollercoaster ride that is the life of an abused child and a woman who became his mother. Initially, it seemed an odd choice for a review by *The New Social Worker* magazine, but the interactions with Nash's therapist pepper the content and provide a wonderful example of how to guide a client through her best and worst moments in ways that engage her, encourage her to do the work, and that uphold professional boundaries.

I hesitate to be more specific, because providing more details will potentially impede the experiences of living Carolyn Nash's life alongside her within these pages. The unexpected moments make it easy for the reader to become affected, to feel anger with the author, or to shed a tear in her joyous moments. Expect to set the book down several times because of the need for an emotional break and to find one's self further relating to the family who never had the option of pausing their story. There are many autobiographies and personal stories on the market, but none share the unedited truth the way *Raising Abel* does, leaving you at the end wanting to hug your children and Nash's.

*Reviewed by Kristen Marie (Kryss) Shane, MSW, LMSW.*

# Learning By Podcast With Jonathan Singer
## by Claudia J. Dewane, D.Ed., LCSW

In recent years, issues of complexity regarding the use of technology in the social work profession have been explored from many angles. There is no doubt that technological advances have had significant impact on social work practice.

Dr. Jonathan Singer is the founder of The Social Work Podcast, a unique learning vehicle. As described on *www. socialworkpodcast.com:* The Social Work Podcast provides information on all things social work, including direct practice (both clinical and community organizing), research, policy, education... and everything in between. The purpose of the podcast is to present useful information in a user-friendly format. Although the intended audience is social workers, the information will be useful to anyone in a helping profession (including psychology, nursing, psychiatry, counseling, and education)."

I interviewed Dr. Singer regarding the podcast and emerging technological issues in social work practice.

### 1. What is a podcast?

A podcast is an audio or video file that you can subscribe to and is "pushed" to your computer/media device when a new episode is available. While audio has been available on the Web since the mid-1990s, you had to visit the site regularly to see if there was a new episode. With podcasts, the episodes come to you.

### 2. What prompted you to develop the Social Work Podcast?

In 2007, I was teaching a practice theories course at the University of Pittsburgh's school of social work. I knew that the theories and ideas about integrating theory into practice would be really useful for students both in practice and for their licensure exams. I figured that the best way of archiving the material would be through audio recordings. Students wouldn't have listened to them during the semester, so there was no point in posting them to Blackboard. I talked about the more technical side of how I developed the podcast and the

Social Work Podcast Web site in a recent interview: *http://www.socialworkpodcast. com/2011/01/behind-scenes-at-social-work-podcast.html.*

### 3. Can you identify the most challenging and most rewarding aspects of the podcast initiative?

The most challenging aspect of the podcast is that it is a time-intensive effort, and I don't have nearly the time to put into it that I'd like to. The most rewarding aspect is connecting with experts in the field, listeners from all over the world who share their social work experiences, and feeling like I'm

*Jonathan Singer*

making a valuable contribution to the social work profession.

### 4. What role do podcasts play in social work education and practice?

There is no published research to establish the value of podcasts in social work education. The anonymous surveys I've conducted with my students suggest that they really like being able to listen to podcasts, for a couple of reasons: 1) They like the break from reading. Listening to episodes, particularly for students who struggle with reading comprehension, gives them a new way to learn important information. 2) Many podcasts are interviews with leading experts. These interviews tend to bring to life concepts that, on the page, seem to be academic or impractical.

I also have anecdotal evidence from social workers in the field. Social workers say that: 1) they listened to the podcast as a way of studying for the Bachelor's, Master's, and Clinical licensure exams,

and 2) the podcasts are portable. Social workers do a lot of home visits. The podcasts give them a way of learning something new, or re-acquainting them with ideas they might have learned but forgotten. The ultimate goal is to help social workers provide better services to clients.

### 5. Have you determined the extent of usage or success of the podcast in any way?

I base the "success" of the podcast on the e-mails I receive and the feedback I get from professors and students about the benefit of the podcast. The data I have tell me a lot about usage, but not much about success. I use Google Analytics and Webalizer as my main "web metrics" to get stats on the podcast. According to Google Analytics, between March 2007 and February 1, 2012, there were 500 million page views, from 200,000 unique visitors. In the past year (February 2011-February 2012) the Web site averaged 446 pageviews per day from 58,306 unique visitors. Visitors were from 166 countries/territories, stayed on the site just over 2 minutes, and 95% of visitors come from English speaking countries. I know that 2% of visitors used mobile devices like tablets or smartphones. The most popular episodes have been *Stages of Change, Theories for Clinical Social Work Practice*, and *The Culturagram*. Webalizer suggests that in the past year, I have had about 320 GB of downloads. The Social Work Podcast page on Facebook has more than 2,500 fans, and the Social Work Podcast Twitter feed has 1,600+ followers. What all this means is that since the podcast started in 2007, there has been a lot of interest in the episodes. For that, I'm grateful.

### 6. What are some other forms of technology that are available for use in social service delivery?

I wrote about a number of uses of technology in my chapter in *The Social Worker's Desk Reference*. Agencies can get confidential feedback from consumers and other stakeholders using Web-based surveys (for example, *sur-veymonkey.com* or *zoomerang. com*). Community organizers use online databases to keep track of members or send out e-mail blasts to mobilize people to contact legislators via e-mail, fax, and phone. Inexpensive calling plans and computer-to-computer services like Skype have made online therapy practical and affordable. For example, a Marine in Afghanistan is questioning his sexual orientation. He fears seeking services on the base (for many reasons), so he has sessions over the phone with a therapist in the USA.

Technology has also been used to help people to help themselves. There has been some very interesting research lately on the use of text messages as a way of reminding consumers to perform certain behavioral tasks, such as complete a checklist, take medication, write a journal entry, and so forth. Applications have also been developed for smartphones that allow you to do self-guided CBT and mindfulness exercises. These applications integrate rating scales, journaling, and other aspects of the treatment, and use the smartphone environment as a way of leading the user through the treatment. This approach to services is still in its infancy, but some research has suggested that for people with mild symptomology, self-guided therapy can be as effective as therapist-guided therapy.

### 7. What has been your experience with other forms of online learning?

I taught my first online course in the summer of 2011. I integrated synchronous learning with asynchronous learning. Students had to attend one one-hour online class per week and participate in various off-line projects. Official student feedback about the course was very positive. I've consulted with people about the use of podcasts and social media sites like Facebook and Twitter to create online learning communities. Faculty from the University at Buffalo's School of Social Work and I presented a faculty development institute at CSWE in 2010 on that topic.

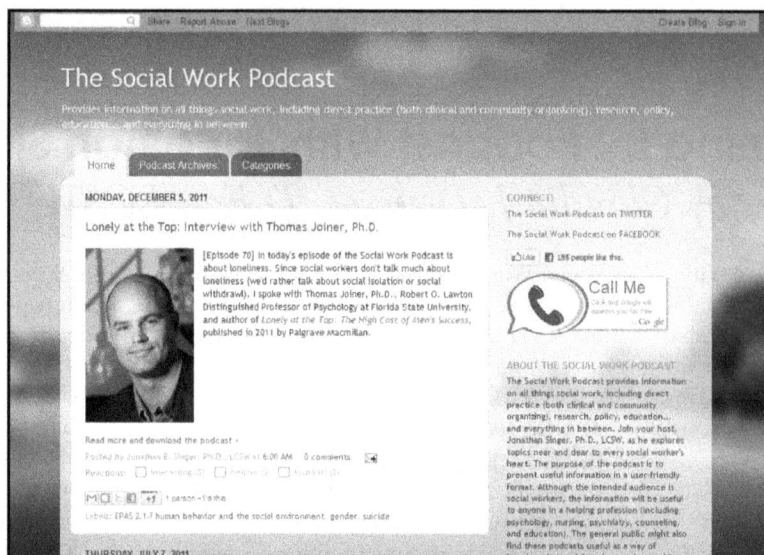

### 8. What do you think the most pressing technology issue is for social workers today?

Becoming familiar with it. If you're a social worker and you don't know about social networking sites, then you're missing a huge part of how people interact these days. If you're doing couples therapy, you need to know about how Facebook and other social media affect relationships, how people use cell phones and texting, and how people use these technologies to connect with others (in either faithful or unfaithful ways). If you work with kids, you need to know that even though Facebook has a policy that only people 13 and older can create accounts, many youth under age 13 are on Facebook.

Beyond social networking, social workers need to know about what information is available on the Web. A recent study from the Pew Foundation suggested that 85% of people turn to the Internet FIRST for medical advice. If social workers are not aware of what information is available, they won't be able to help clients differentiate good information from misinformation. Anyone who has ever had a client say, "My kid has ADHD because they took the quiz on the Novartis Web site," knows that overcoming misinformation can be as much work as providing good information in the first place.

### 9. The most recent NASW Code of Ethics addresses several areas that have never been addressed before in our profession. One of these areas is technology. What are some of the ethical and

legal implications of technology in social work practice?

Great question. I wrote a chapter on this topic for *The Social Workers' Desk Reference,* published in 2009, called "The Role and Regulations for Technology in Social Work Practice and E-therapy: Social Work 2.0." Perhaps the most important thing to know about that chapter is that some of the information is already out of date. The speed with which technology is changing suggests that the most basic implication is that social workers need to be mindful of how they use technology. Technological innovations used to occur once every ten or twenty years–now they occur monthly. For example, clinicians have been recording therapy sessions for decades. But the amount of time that has transpired between one technology and the next has shrunk from decades to years, e.g. reel-to-reel (20 years) > cassette (20 years) > VHS (10 years) > digital recorder (5 years) > laptop (three years) > webcam (2 years) > smart phone (1 year). Another example is the use of e-mail as a form of communication between client and clinician. When paper correspondence became electronic correspondence, ethical dilemmas arose over the risks to privacy and confidentiality. Although there are no longer concerns that checking e-mail on an agency's secure server with a unique login is an issue, the ability to check confidential e-mail from clients using a smart phone in public, or on a laptop over an unsecured Wi-Fi network at a coffee shop, presents new ethical dilemmas. Should clinicians "Google" their clients if they are on an unsecure connection? Should they Google their clients at all, regardless of whether the Internet connection is secure?

Social networking sites such as Facebook also present ethical issues for clinical social workers. For example, what should clinicians do if they realize that a friend on their social network is friends with their client? What ethical issues can be addressed by changing privacy settings, and what issues can only be resolved by the clinician deactivating his or her Facebook account? If a clinician is the only social worker in a school setting, and is aware of cyberbullying, should the clinician be required by administration to be Facebook friends with all students in the school in order to have access to information that might help intervention? Should social workers provide e-therapy to treat Internet addiction? These are just a few of the ethical dilemmas that today's social workers find themselves addressing.

**10. Speaking of cyberbullying, one of your most recent peer-reviewed publications appeared in the NASW journal *Children and Schools* regarding cyberbullying. Is there a "best practice" for working with families or kids experiencing cyberbullying?**

There is no "best practice" for cyberbullying. Some recommendations for parents include: 1) monitoring youths' Internet usage, 2) recognizing that cell phones are Internet machines with keypads, and 3) finding out if their child's school has a cyberbullying policy. If not, work with the administration to develop one. Some recommendations for youth include: 1) recognize that once you post a message or photo to the Internet via e-mail, social networking site like Facebook, or even a text message via cell phone, you have no control over what happens to that photo or text, 2) take control over who has access to your information by limiting your network in your privacy settings, and 3) use the same common sense online as you do offline regarding friendships or sharing information.

*Claudia J. Dewane, D.Ed., LCSW, is an associate professor in the College of Health Professions and Social Work, Temple University. She received a doctorate in adult education and health psychology from Penn State University and Master of Social Work from Columbia University. She is a Licensed Clinical Social Worker, maintains Board Certified Diplomate status in Clinical Social Work, and has a Certificate in Advanced Clinical Supervision. She is the founder of Clinical Support Associates, providing supervision, consultation, and training to professional social workers. She has presented numerous workshops on clinical, supervisory, and ethical issues in social work. She worked for the Department of Veterans Affairs for several years. Her clinical work has been in the areas of PTSD and military sexual trauma.*

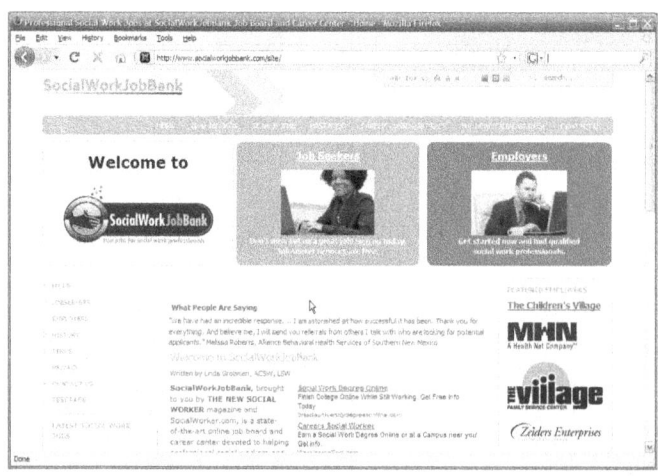

# CONTENTS

THE NEW SOCIAL WORKER®
Summer 2012
Volume 19, Number 3

## FEATURES

## DEPARTMENTS

# Publisher's Thoughts

Dear Reader,

This is an exciting time of year, as some social work students have just graduated and others are just starting on their journey toward a BSW or MSW degree. This year, for the second year in a row, we have put together a photo montage of some of the new social workers who are embarking on their new careers with their new degrees in hand. See page 23 for a sampling of these new professionals. I wish I had room to include ALL new social work graduates! You can find a slide show of these and other photos that were submitted at *http://www.flickr.com/photos/newsocialworker/sets/72157630388818324/*.

I mentioned in the last issue that I have been working on a couple of new book projects. One of these is coming very soon and is entitled *Riding the Mutual Aid Bus and Other Adventures in Group Work*. (See page 18.) This addition to the *Days in the Lives of Social Workers* series focuses on a variety of ways in which social workers work with groups. I am co-editing it with Jennifer Clements, Vice President of the International Association for Social Work With Groups. Keep your eyes open for more on this book.

In the meantime, in this issue, we have an article about an exercise one social worker has used in a group for foster parents. Are you working with groups? Maybe Joseph Berry's experience (page 16) will give you some ideas for working creatively with your own group.

If you haven't noticed, *The New Social Worker* is on Facebook, Twitter, Google+, and LinkedIn. We also have a Flickr photostream (see above mention of our slide show of new grads). Social media is everywhere, and social workers are a big part of it! In this issue, I profile @SWSCmedia, a new global network of social workers, founded by Claudia Megele. The group holds Twitter chats or "debates" twice a week and has had participants from 20 different countries. Read more about it on page 27.

Additional articles in this issue address FAQs about the NASW Code of Ethics, being a first-time field instructor, social work in Krygystan, social work in an HIV/AIDS clinic, an innovative "social work camp" for high school students in foster care, a social worker's mission, and more!

Do you have ideas or experiences you would like to share with our readers? Perhaps you would like to write an article or serve as an expert interviewee for a future issue! I am always looking for ideas on social work ethics, field placement, practice specialties, career development, technology, and other topics of interest to new social workers. Let me know if you have an idea!

Until next time–happy reading, and stay COOL this summer!

*Linda M. Grobman*

*The publisher/editor*

## Write for The New Social Worker

We are looking for articles from social work practitioners, students, and educators.

Some areas of particular interest are: social work ethics; student field placement; practice specialties; technology; "what every new social worker needs to know," and news of unusual, creative, or nontraditional social work.

Feature articles run 1,500-2,000 words in length. News articles are typically 100-150 words. Our style is conversational, practical, and educational. Write as if you are having a conversation with a student or colleague. What do you want him or her to know about the topic? What would you want to know? Use examples.

The best articles have a specific focus. If you are writing an ethics article, focus on a particular aspect of ethics. For example, analyze a specific portion of the NASW *Code of Ethics* (including examples), or talk about ethical issues unique to a particular practice setting. When possible, include one or two resources at the end of your article–books, additional reading materials, and/or Web sites.

We also want photos of social workers and social work students "in action" for our cover, and photos to accompany your news articles!

Send submissions to lindagrobman@socialworker.com.

# The New Social Worker
the social work careers magazine

**Summer 2012**
**Vol. 19, Number 3**

*Publisher/Editor*
Linda May Grobman, MSW, ACSW, LSW

*Contributing Writers*
Barbara Trainin Blank

THE NEW SOCIAL WORKER® (ISSN 1073-7871) is published four times a year by White Hat Communications, P.O. Box 5390, Harrisburg, PA 17110-0390. Phone: (717) 238-3787. Fax: (717) 238-2090. Send address corrections to: lindagrobman@socialworker.com

Advertising rates available on request.

Photo/art credits: Image from BigStockPhoto.com © Marek Uliasz (page 5), Svitlana Pavzyuk (page 17).

*The New Social Worker* is indexed/abstracted in *Social Work Abstracts*.

Send all editorial, advertising, subscription, and other correspondence to:

**THE NEW SOCIAL WORKER**

**White Hat Communications**
**P.O. Box 5390**
**Harrisburg, PA 17110-0390**
**(717) 238-3787 Phone**
**(717) 238-2090 Fax**

lindagrobman@socialworker.com

http://www.socialworker.com
http://www.facebook.com/newsocialworker
http://www.twitter.com/newsocialworker

**Print Edition:**
http://newsocialworker.magcloud.com

# Tayloe Compton

## by Barbara Trainin Blank

Tayloe Compton has a sense of wonderment that she has arrived at this point—earning a B.A. in social work in May from the University of North Carolina at Pembroke.

Along the way, she has overcome daunting challenges: her parents' separation when Compton was only two; long-term drug addiction; losing her first child–a son–because of that addiction; and nearly losing her second, a daughter. Most recently, she is also dealing with her father's health issues and dementia.

The difficulties also honed her "compassion for the underdog." She remembers in sixth or seventh grade sticking up for a boy who was being picked on. "But I also was guilty of picking on people; it was early signs of being an addict vs. being my true self," Compton explains. She is candid about the bumps along the road.

"I was raised by my father and his mother," she says. "I have no recollection of my mom, but subconsciously, I'm sure I do."

Originally, Compton had no plans to attend college. When she did, she didn't do well because of her addiction. She had assorted jobs afterward, including working at a photography business and waitressing for some 18 years, where drug and alcohol use were common.

Compton was married and divorced 20 years ago. Then, eight years ago, she became pregnant with a boyfriend. "I would have loved to be a mother and stop doing drugs," she says. "But I hated myself and was dissociated from my family, as well as a convicted felon because of the drugs. They took my son, Tyler, away in the hospital."

Compton was actually "relieved." She didn't know what to do with a child and wanted to provide him with "something better." Tyler, who turned eight in January, was taken in by a foster family, who later adopted him.

Compton became pregnant again, with another man. "I thought about abortion, but by the time I decided to do it, it was too late to abort, so I sought medical care. The doctors were kind." At five months' gestation, the fetus developed fluid and wasn't expected to live. But she did. "Both my children had to be on phenobarbital because of the drugs, but luckily had no [ill] effects," she says.

Her daughter, named Summer, also went into foster care. The family was interested in adopting her, but Compton had made up her mind. She was going to overcome her habit. After detoxing for two weeks, she underwent treatment, for the fourth time. This time was different. "I put a sign out in the backyard: 'No drugs or alcohol allowed.'" Although she lived 10 miles outside of town and had no car, Compton walked half a mile every day to call her sponsor. She got a job. At 38, she found her life turning around. "I'll always [technically] be a drug addict, but I feel free,"she adds.

When Summer was a year and three months old, she went to live with her mother. "It was a super-successful outcome–by the grace of God and timing. I got full custody. My child is a blessing in life every day. She is beautiful and happy," Tayloe says.

Compton had a neighbor who was chair of the board of Care Network, a food pantry/soup kitchen funded by several churches. She began to volunteer

*Tayloe Compton*

and eventually became a paid volunteer coordinator. "I loved the job," she says. "I had been homeless and on Food Stamps, so I understood the clients." Compton also realized she had leadership qualities.

That wouldn't have surprised Stephen Marson, professor of sociology at UNC-Pembroke. He met Compton two summers ago in a statistics course he was teaching. Despite her fear of using a computer, she was an impressively good student. Marson asked her to be his assistant for the *Journal of Social Work Values and Ethics*. "She did a bang-up job," says Marson. "She was more mature than average, with a level of earnestness. She kept feeling she wasn't doing enough." Compton also helped Marson with other writing and a research project. "If anyone was stuck with anything, she would get involved, offer to study together," he says. "When I told the students they needed to form study groups, she was the first one to do it."

It was her social worker who suggested that Compton go into the field. There have been obstacles. In February 2008, her stepmother–who at the time had been married to Compton's father

*Compton–continued on page 22*

# Ethics

## Frequently Asked Questions About the Code of Ethics of the National Association of Social Workers (NASW)

### by Mike Meacham, Ph.D., LCSW

The *NASW Code of Ethics* is a long document that provides guidelines for many complicated situations. As a new social worker or a social work student, you may have questions about the *Code*. I have provided some answers below. However, one must remember that clinical judgment allows us to determine our course of action with each individual case and circumstance. In the areas of ethics, morals, and values, there is often no one correct answer. (See the full *NASW Code of Ethics* at *http://www. socialworkers.org/pubs/code/default.asp.*)

### 1. What is the purpose of listing values as part of a code of ethics?

Sociologists define values as the most abstract level of beliefs in what is moral. Ethics are the particular statements about conduct for a profession. When decision-making about ethics becomes an issue, social workers may rely on the general beliefs of our conduct, as well as be guided by more specific guidelines within the *Code*.

### 2. Are there limits to how far a social worker is committed to a client?

Yes, Standard 1.01 mentions the legal obligations social workers have to society. Although social workers occasionally choose to ignore some illegal acts of clients during therapy, we have a commitment to the law, and we are responsible for the consequences of those decisions. Standard 3.09 states that social workers should abide by their commitment to employers, as well. Agency procedures and rules should be followed if they are not in conflict with the *Code,* which may at times limit our ability to help a client with a specific need.

### 3. Are there directions that we may use to decide if a client's self determination should be restricted?

Yes, Standard 1.02 states to do so if "in the social worker's professional judgment, a client's actions or potential actions pose a serious foreseeable and imminent risk to themselves or others." A general rule used by many social workers is "dangerous to self or others." Potential and imminent violence must be reported, according to the Tarasoff ruling. (See *http://tinyurl.com/newswtarasoff.*) Rules of behavior in the agency must be enforced. This leads to some different interpretations about self determination, depending on the environment. For example, a social worker may or may not report that a client is selling marijuana if he or she is working in an outpatient setting. But in prisons, drug sales are one of the leading causes of murder within the "walls" and should then be reported.

Standard 4.07 disallows endorsement from clients or soliciting clients informally, as this may create an undue influence.

### 4. What if I am not sure if a client is capable of understanding "informed consent"?

There are supports available. Psychological testing prior to our services may indicate IQ and ability to understand situations. The mental status exam will give evidence, as well. There is a "Kent Intelligence Exam" that is used to give the social worker some evidence that he or she tried to measure the level of client functioning. A team approach also helps.

Also, we need to obtain qualified interpreters for those who need them. (See Standard 1.03 b, 1.14.) It is important that the interpreter be aware of and preferably part of the specific culture of the client, because euphemisms differ among subcultures (e.g., specific meanings differ in Spanish at times, depending on the country of origin).

### 5. Is therapy over the telephone or by computer allowable?

Yes, but Standard 1.03e states that clients must be made aware of the limitations of distant forms of treatment.

### 6. Sometimes clients present with problems in areas about which I have little knowledge. What can I do in these cases?

Standard 1.04c states that social workers should "ensure the competence of their work and protect clients from harm." This standard in the *Code* originated from Hippocrates. We can refer clients to whom we are not capable of providing good treatment, and we have trainings, formal and informal education, research, consultation, and supervision to support us. At these times, a team approach is helpful. We may transfer a client, but Standard 3.08 tells us that we should minimize difficulties for the client in transfers by giving them adequate notice and explanation. Also, we should assure no duplication of services.

### 7. What infraction of the *Code* has resulted in the most negative actions against social workers?

In a 2000 study spanning ten years, author Kim Strom-Gottfried found that poor practice resulted in 160 violations, Sexual misbehavior resulted in 102 violations, and competence issues resulted in 86 violations.

### 8. How much should I know about diversity and culture to be competent?

In essence, competency means that a social worker is capable of working with clients as they relate to issues in their environment. Their social status, both achieved and ascribed, is a very important part of that environment. It is nearly impossible to be competent with every culture and subculture, but we can understand the theories and issues surrounding oppression, access, social justice, liberty, status liability, and other difficulties faced by all groups. We also can study the groups with which we practice to understand better their particular problems. A good start is to practice the value of "respect for human dignity," with which people from all cultures relate (see Standard 1.05). Standard 3.08 tells more about continuing education requirements, which at times address these issues. Standard 4.01 tells us more about competence.

## 9. What if my religious or other basic values conflict with the *Code of Ethics* in a particular instance?

Religion, politics, tradition, socialization, and other bases of our value system may have prohibitions or directions that are opposed to our interpretation of the *Code*. Our *Code* provides the written professional standards of conduct for social workers. Whereas we may choose to act on other beliefs as being more important than the *Code* (see Standard 1.06), we must understand clearly that once we act outside of the *Code,* we no longer are acting as social workers, but in another role. The client and agency should be made aware of such decisions. It may be important to note that people frequently use their value systems to support their

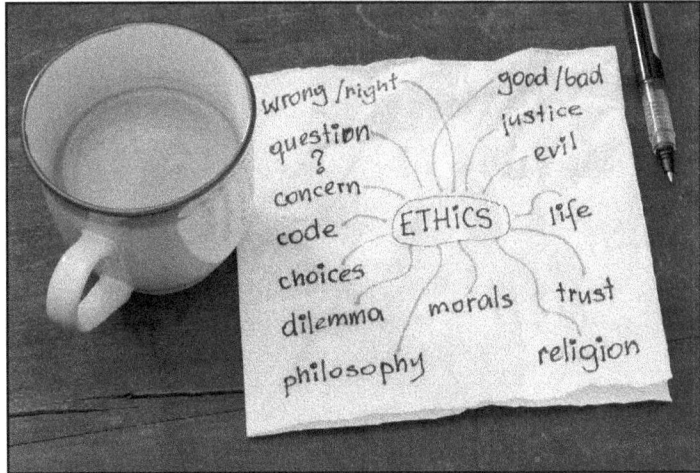

prejudices and dislikes, instead of using them to relate better with others and provide themselves more life satisfaction. Be aware of this before assuming that your values are the basis of your decision to act outside of the *Code*. Standard 4.08 more strictly narrows the boundaries between professional acts and extra-professional values.

## 10. I live and work in an area where I see my clients frequently at social settings, such as restaurants, church, while shopping, and so forth. Sometimes we serve on voluntary committees together. Am I in a dual relationship?

Not necessarily, but Standard 1.06 indicates you are close to being in one and, therefore, should be cautious. A dual relationship is one in which there is a conflict of interest. Seeing people in church, for example, need not be a conflict of interest if we go about our business there without undue interaction with the client. If there is a clear line, it is when a conflict of interest develops and social workers are in a position to take undue advantage of it.

## 11. When do I know if I am violating a client's privacy when asking about things related to his or her treatment?

Standard 1.07a implies that client/therapist interaction should be strictly related to the issues of treatment. During engagement and at other times, we may vary slightly to relate to the client better, but our goal is to help clients help themselves in treatment. As in any relationship, we will discover things about our clients that are interesting to us, but not necessarily related to treatment, and we should avoid exploring those issues. This is important when talking about any issue, no matter how mundane (such as mutual interest in gardening), but it has caused great damage in important areas. Sexual assault victims have been asked to describe the assault in detail, evidently only to fulfill the voyeuristic needs of some therapists, for example.

## 12. What if I am called to court to testify for a client. Should I release all information?

An attorney affiliated with your agency can give specific information on what you should release. As a general rule, you should release everything legally requested and no more. Standard 1.07c indicates that we should reveal only what is necessary in these circumstances.

## 13. I am concerned that my members in my group therapy sessions,

couples, and family therapy may break confidentiality. Will I be at fault for this?

Standard 1.07f states that in such cases, we must be careful to protect confidentiality by obtaining agreement among members to do so. We will be better protected to do so in writing. We also should inform clients that we cannot guarantee that others will conform to confidentiality agreements.

## 14. Am I required to allow a client to see his or her file?

Yes, unless you, as the social worker, can demonstrate that access to the file will cause harm. That is difficult to do. We can avoid much of the awkwardness in such situations by taking precautions not to state unnecessary negative information about the client and by sharing our concerns with him or her in therapy. This avoids surprises when the client asks to see the records.

We also must take care that all records are accurate and take special precautions to assure that records are kept safe from being seen by others (Standards 1.08, 3.04).

## 15. What should I do if a client appears to want more intimate contact with me?

Whereas touching within culturally appropriate boundaries is allowed (e.g., handshakes), we are to limit it to those boundaries. Sexual contact, harassment, and derogatory language are prohibited during treatment and afterwards. The code writers understood that under some circumstances, a social worker might happen to become involved (sometimes sexually) with an ex-client, and they made it the social worker's responsibility to show that the sexual relationship is not exploitive, which is near impossible. An example of this may be that sometimes attorneys or entire agencies hire social workers for particular tasks related to their clientele, or we are involved in community work. Since we are hired to do social work, they are our clients, but no therapeutic relationship existed, and romance may occur years later and be permissible. The best practice is to leave any sexual or similar intimacy out of your work, whether past or present. (See Standards 1.09, 1.10, 1.11, 1.12.)

**16. Are there causal factors that we may foresee to help us avoid becoming intimately involved with clients?**

There are many ways people become involved, ranging from social workers with poor character to people overwhelmed with romantic love. However, we can avoid many of these feelings with the realization that intimate feelings may be an important part of transference and countertransference issues instead of the "real thing." Some clients' poor self esteem permits them to demonstrate appreciation only in that manner. We can be helpful at such times instead of convincing or fantasizing ourselves into involvement.

**17. When should I begin to prepare clients for termination?**

As soon as possible. In situations in which the number of sessions is set, we can begin immediately. Interruption of services and termination may have a profound negative effect on clients when done poorly and tend to have at least a mild negative effect for a brief time even when done well. Clients need to prepare for the adjustment much in the manner they would prepare for any loss, and it is the social worker's responsibility to alert and help prepare them for this occurrence (see Standards 1.15, 1.16).

**18. I know social workers who gossip frequently about each other. Others do not believe in the work of particular professions recognized by the state and refuse to cooperate with them. Are these actions allowable behavior?**

No. Standards 2.01, 2.02, 2.03, 2.07, and 2.08 state that we should give an accurate and respectful view of other colleagues in social work and elsewhere and respect their privacy. We are to be careful to avoid conflicts of interest and exploitation. Disputes should be negotiated with the same standards in mind, and clients should never be involved (2.04).

**19. Are there steps to help a colleague who has developed an impairment that prohibits doing his or her job well?**

Yes, Standard 2.09 addresses this. If a social worker has knowledge or concern about an impaired colleague, the social worker should consult with that colleague and assist with taking remedial action. Then, if none is taken, the social worker should take action with NASW, licensing boards, and so forth. The same is true for incompetent colleagues under Standard 2.10.

**20. A social worker at my job purposely is acting unethically. What should I do?**

Many social workers either under-react or overreact to this difficult situation, but Standard 2.11 gives some pretty clear direction. The steps are: (a) discourage any such activity, (b) be knowledgeable about the *NASW Code,* (c) seek resolution by discussing the infraction with the colleague, and (d) when necessary, take the issue before the NASW or licensing board.

**21. I would like to volunteer to be a supervisor toward licensing for MSWs. Does the NASW have requirements I should meet?**

Yes, Standard 3.01 states that you must have the knowledge and skills to be able to give quality supervision. You must make clear boundaries, avoid dual relationships, and evaluate respectfully. Much the same is true for educators (see Standard 3.02), who also must ensure that clients with whom their students work understand that they are working with supervised students.

**22. Are social workers allowed the freedom to bill for services as they wish?**

No. Standards 1.13 and 3.05 inform us that we should have billing "fair, reasonable, and commensurate" with the services performed. We should not barter for services, accepting items other than money or its equivalent, unless there is a special situation in which the social worker believes the client or situation warrants it and can demonstrate that concern to the NASW. Charging private fees for agency practice is not allowed, and billing must accurately reflect the services rendered, to whom, and by whom.

**23. Once I become an administrator, am I still responsible to the *NASW Code?***

Yes. Administration is discussed under Standard 3.07, directing administrators to advocate for their clientele, be fair in resource allocation, assure staff supervision is adequate, and assure that the work environment encourages cooperation under the *NASW Code.*

**24. What if I have a chance for employment in an agency that acts against *NASW Code* guidelines?**

Standards 3.09 and 3.10 give direction on this question. Social workers should avoid employment in such agencies, although they should assure that their interpretation of the *Code* is not the issue, but that the agency clearly violates the code. They should make any agency where they work aware of their required need to comply with the Code and educate the agency on the Code. Social workers should follow the Code. We can engage in labor/management disputes as well, but still must act ethically.

**25. Part of the Code involves acting well as a professional. What does that mean?**

Standards 4.01, 4.02, 4.03, 4.04, 4.05, 4.06, 4.07, 4.08, and 4.09 direct social workers to act as professionals by (a) maintaining competence, (b) resisting discrimination, (c) not allowing private conduct to interfere with their responsibilities, (d) not being a part of deception, and (e) acknowledging impairments and taking steps to remediate them, including not practicing for a time, if required.

**26. How can I make social work a better profession?**

Your own example is a good start. Further instructions are found under Standard 5.01.

A social worker can improve the profession by furthering study, research, and discussion. Helping the community with our expertise is another way. We share our knowledge at conferences, workshops, and meetings, and we should prevent unauthorized persons from practicing social work.

**27. What does the Code include as standards of research?**

Especially after the systematic human suffering and death that occurred during World War II, there are several codes that the U.S. and the rest of the world accept as standards of research. They include: the Belmont Report, "The Common Rule," the United Nations Declaration on Human Rights, the United States Department of Health and Human Services Office of Research Integrity Rulings, and the World Medical Association Research Guidelines. Standard 5.02 demonstrates that the NASW abides by these rulings to protect human subjects of research and in reporting.

### 28. I am a student in an accredited social work program. Does the Code provide me any protections?

Yes, you are to be taught by competent professionals in their area of expertise. You are to be evaluated fairly and treated respectfully. You are to be protected from any harm or exploitation (see Standard 3.02) All sexual harassment and sexual contact statements in the Code apply to you, as well.

### 29. What if I am presenting on behalf of an organization and its policy is congruent with the Code, but I have doubts. Should I state my opinion or the agency's?

The important phrase is "on behalf of." If you are telling an audience about an organization as its representative, you are to "accurately represent the official and authorized positions of the organization" (see Standard 4.06b).

### 30. Do we have any more responsibilities?

Yes, social workers have responsibilities beyond their clients and their profession. We are to promote social justice, participate in the political process, assist within our area of expertise in public emergencies, and participate in other social action to promote a better society and environment for our clients and society as a whole.

## References

Strom-Gottfried, K. (2000). Ensuring ethical practice: An examination of NASW code violations, 1986-1997. *Social Work, 45* (3), 251-261.

*Mike Meacham, Ph.D., LCSW, is on the faculty at Valdosta State University, Department of Sociology, Anthropology, Criminal Justice and Marriage and Family Therapy.*

# Poetry

## Forget Us Not
### by Eitan Daniel, BSW

I get the call
First thing, suspected SIDS, the parent second
I gather myself best I can
It is my first few days at the job
So much still to learn, to do
It will all have to wait
There is no dilemma.

I race to emergency
Calming myself
Slowing down
Making it safely
Shaking my head at my choice of a shirt
It's bright orange.

A brief introduction
Last minute check-in
And I am in the room.

I see them both
Him
With his back to me
Rocking his baby
His silence
Does not conceal
The screams and anguish beneath.

She
Sitting upright
Absent minded holding a coffee cup
Staring into space
While stroking a gentle scalp
Lovingly
Achingly.

What can I possibly say?
I know what I want to say

And I do my best to do so tactfully
Yet it is too soon
The journey is up ahead
And we all know it.

I try and transmit care and compassion
But also strength and courage
Are they received?
I wonder.

The room is dark
Lit enough to face the reality.

It is not insulated from sound
I doubt it is truly a place to heal
But it may have to do
For now.

I look at the young baby
Pale and peaceful
Beyond this world's reach
I hear no angels singing
They ought to.

It is time for me to go
I leave and hope
They know I am not really far at all.

*Eitan Daniel is a social worker with more than 15 years counseling experience with a range of organizations such as Q Rail, Veteran and Veterans Families Counseling Service (VVCS) and North West Queensland Primary Health Care. He currently works as a Sids and Kids Grampians region grief counselor, completing a post grad in couple counseling, practicing Korean sword martial arts and is writing a nonfiction book.*

## What I Learned From My First Intern
### by Tina Landeen Panos, LCSW

I was so excited to get my first intern. My mind was busy ticking off the valuable bits of wisdom and knowledge I could impart to her. The years of schooling, the papers, the internships, the field experience, the naked clients (that's a story for another article)—I could share them all. I had been through so much, learned so much, and knew so much. This was going to be my chance to give back. I wasn't prepared for some of the lessons I would learn from her.

### #1: Question authority.

This sounds almost silly coming from me, as I tend to pride myself as being somewhat of a rebel, but after so many years in the field, it's safe to say that some of the "shiny" has worn off. Why we do some of the things we do doesn't always cross my mind. The paperwork, forms, and protocols seem to run into each other like a stream that tumbles from here to there. When presented with questions from my intern, I was forced to take notice of the processes I go through. I took some time to examine my work and either reaffirm its value or get rid of it.

Mindful practice has always been a goal of mine, and until I was really questioned about it, I thought I was doing it. I learned that continued questioning keeps the fidelity to one's practice.

### #2: Keep learning.

In finding some of the weaknesses in my intern's knowledge, I dutifully sought opportunities for trainings she could attend. Tagging along to these trainings that I always seemed too busy for previously gave some fresh light on practices I was currently using, as well as opening my eyes to new possibilities. Again, sometimes we are on such automatic pilot dealing with our day-to-day operations that we lose sight of the power of learning from each other. Isolating ourselves in our practice doesn't benefit us as clinicians or our clients. This leads me to my next lesson.

### #3: Appreciate your knowledge.

Have you ever had this moment? You're talking, and all of a sudden, you are outside of yourself listening and thinking, "Damn, I really sound like I know what I'm talking about." I really hope I'm not the only one that's ever thought that, but seriously, until I had my intern eagerly looking to me for answers, I hadn't realized just how much knowledge I had. Not to say that I know it all, but there is a lot that I do know. Another benefit—now I won't be so bitter

writing that student loan check. This brings me to my final lesson.

### #4: Perspective.

After all those classes, that interning, those lectures and clients, the way I see the world has really changed. How things look when you're an "expert" is vastly different from how they looked before all the experience. This is helpful to remember when your client isn't seeing things as they so obviously are to you... like when I'm imparting nuggets of wisdom to clients. Now I'll work harder to put it in a more palatable way for them.

"So, what's so hard about changing those negative thought patterns and distorted cognitions so that you can function with less maladaptive schemas?" Huh? Of course, this is a gross exaggeration for comedic effect. I would never talk like this to my clients. Besides, I work with teenagers, and they already know everything.

I've learned so much with my first intern. It's an experience I've enjoyed immensely and would recommend to other professionals interested in illuminating the minds of future social workers. This especially goes for other professionals who don't mind learning a thing or two themselves.

*Tina Landeen Panos is a licensed clinical social worker with a certification in child welfare. Currently, she is the clinical director at the Center for Brain Training in Jupiter, FL, a center providing neurofeedback therapy to clients.*

## Journal of Social Work Values and Ethics
*http://www.socialworker.com/jswve*

*The Journal of Social Work Values and Ethics* is an online, free, full-text peer-reviewed journal published by the publisher of *The New Social Worker*.

The *Journal,* edited by Stephen M. Marson, Ph.D., and Donna DeAngelis, MSW, and published twice a year, is available at *http://www.socialworker.com/jswve.* The *Journal* examines the ethical and values issues that impact and are interwoven with social work practice, research, and theory development.

See *http://www.socialworker.com/jswve/content/view/57/52/* for details. Register for free to receive the Table of Contents of each issue.

# Future Social Work Majors Learn, Work During UA Summer Camp

Fourteen high school juniors and seniors are spending five weeks learning about social work careers at the University of Alabama and working with social work agencies in the Tuscaloosa area this summer.

For the second consecutive year, UA is a host site for the National Social Work Enrichment Program's (NSEP) summer camp, a program designed to introduce high school students to social work as a potential college major and career.

The camp began June 4, when students moved into campus dormitories and began a "Careers in Social Work" course. Over the duration of the camp, students earn stipends by working with local United Way agencies, said Dr. Sebrena Jackson, NSEP founder.

"One of the key components is partnering with local agencies so the students can see the professional side of social work," said Jackson. "We're also trying to do a community service project. In the past, we've worked with Habitat for Humanity and gone to nursing homes to do bingo."

The students participating at UA are foster children who are enrolled in the Independent Living Program, a Department of Human Resources program aimed to guide youth toward success as adults. Additionally, DHS provides the majority of NSEP's funding.

Drs. Debra Nelson-Gardell and Javonda Williams, UA social work professors, attended the end-of-camp awards luncheon at Alabama A&M in 2010. They were impressed with the program and approached Jackson about hosting a camp at UA.

"Over the course of the year, we worked out all of the details, and we were able to host the camp last year for the first time," Williams said, "which was amazing, because the students were able to help with tornado recovery projects."

Williams, chair of the undergraduate social work program at UA, said the program is vital to future college students looking to major in social work, as most students aren't aware of the many career options for licensed social workers.

"I think this is the primary goal of the program," Williams said. "This valuable information is usually not compiled and clearly presented to students until they take an introduction to social work course at a university."

The students work with agencies from 9 a.m. to 2 p.m., Monday through Wednesday.

*UA undergraduate social work major Cambrin Daniel leads a class of high school students at the National Social Work Enrichment Program summer camp. Daniel is one of two UA students assisting Dr. Sebrena Jackson with the camp. UA is hosting the NSEP camp for the second year in a row.*

# Social Work on the Silk Road
## by Christine Tappan, MSW, CAGS

M y introduction to social work on the Silk Road started two years ago with a ceremonial toast of Bishkek Cognac and a slice of apple. Although not much of a drinker, as I partook of the cognac and fruit, a real and metaphorical warmth came over me as I imagined the vision to which we had all just committed: developing a more competent and confident generation of social workers in Kyrgyzstan. That toast set a plan in motion to train and educate social workers in the "land of the Tien Shan," to move beyond theory toward cutting-edge technical skills for assessing and working with children and families with desperate needs. These social workers would have more skills and knowledge than their predecessors for dealing with the increasing challenges facing Kyrgyz society, and the burn-out that ends so many careers after just a year or two in the field.

Social work is a profession built on hope–hope for change, hope for a better life for abused and neglected children,

the poor, the sick, the disabled, and the elderly. The sobering reality is that the values of freedom, justice, social responsibility, and human dignity drive a profession that often goes unrecognized and underappreciated, even pitied. Because of this, social workers worldwide face an uphill battle, striving to educate and retain a workforce that grapples with compassion fatigue while barely squeaking out a livable wage.

An entry-level social worker in Bishkek makes about $150 a month; in a village, half that salary is common. Even in the western world, the average pay for a social worker with a graduate degree is significantly less than others with a similar education. Most social workers will confess that making money is not what motivates them most. Helping to change the lives of others, to see children and families prosper–or just receiving a smile or words of thanks–is enough to keep them going. As Erkayim, a social work student at Bishkek Humanities University (BHU) said, "I want to be useful for society." His peer Nestyn added, "I just want to be able to help people with special needs solve their problems."

As the world economy grows increasingly complex, so do the needs of vulnerable children and families. The ever-expanding knowledge and technical skills a social worker must have to effectively support individuals in need is a global issue. However, in a budding democracy such as Kyrgyzstan, it is even more critical. And so I have come to know this country, many of its towns and villages, and a group of dreamers who believe as I do that a framework of child and family support is essential to every community in the world–and where this does not exist, it must be built.

Social work was founded as a profession in Kyrgyzstan in 1994. Many amazing individuals did "social work"

prior to this time, but once the profession was legally recognized, they began to formally build the path toward a structured and credible educational system. Several universities in Kyrgyzstan educate about 400 social workers per year. The limit to this endeavor is that much of the curriculum in the typical five-year undergraduate program is theoretical in nature, without a means to experience the work firsthand.

To achieve proficiency in critical technical skills–including assessment, investigation, interviewing, case planning, and community development–training and education must be both didactic and practical in nature.

Social work takes place in high-stress, complex environments, in homes, hospitals, or on the streets. Workers are often independently responsible for assessing and addressing multi-faceted safety, health, and well-being needs of children, their parents, and the communities where they live. The ultimate goal is to address issues such as drug and alcohol abuse, domestic violence, mental illness, and child abuse and neglect, all while enhancing family functioning, and improving child safety and family independence. Stamina and diplomacy are among the most important tools in the social worker's professional kit.

Because of training gaps, low pay, and emotional stress, social workers–particularly those who work with high-risk families in which abuse or neglect has occurred–face high burn-out rates and alarming professional turnover. Research shows that this dilemma hits close to home around the globe. The negative impact on families is felt in many heart-wrenching scenarios, such as more children being placed in foster care or orphanages.

Recognizing these issues, the Kyrgyz Association of Social Workers and department leadership and faculty at BHU, in partnership with governmental and non-governmental organizations in Kyrgyzstan, began discussions more than four years ago to develop a social work specialization focused on children and families. After researching international program alternatives, BHU determined that a consultative partnership with a child protection specialist in the United

States who had experience developing and working with competency-based training and educational programs for social workers would be the best option. That's where I came in.

I was brought into this project in 2009 by one of the original group of dreamers, Ruby Johnston from the NGO International Learning and Development Center (ILDC Kyrgyzstan). She, along with Vera Usenovna, President of the Association of Social Workers of Kyrgyz Republic and Orozaliev Erick Sadyckovich, Dean of Faculty of Social Work and Psychology at BHU, had been planning the project for some time. The barriers to the dream were many, including expert time for consultation on curriculum development, teaching approaches, course materials, and practicum design. Access to technology that would support the use of slides and video "models" for social work students to follow was nonexistent. Approval by governmental ministries to authorize the specialization was another hurdle. Through persistence and united vision, the dreamers cleared many of these barriers. The final step was finding what they came to call an "on the ground champion" to bring the project to fruition.

Ruby and I met in the United States while she was conducting training for my state child welfare agency. She knew my passion for teaching and my belief that teachers—and the way they teach—can inspire and build confidence in young, developing social workers, coaching them through the technical skills required to be effective. As one student from BHU shared with me, "The faculty at BHU inspires us. They tell us that we are the generation to change our society." But the faculty will tell you that despite their admirable efforts, they don't possess all of the knowledge and tools needed. Many have never been social workers in the field. They understand the theory behind the practice, but don't have teaching skills or resources necessary to help their students learn. For example,

there are few or no current social work textbooks to give students. So they teach mostly through lecture. When a textbook is available, it must be shared among 20, 30, or 40 students, or photocopies can be made for two soms per page, which adds up quickly. There's no access to technology. Faculty members consider themselves lucky if there's a chalkboard in the classroom.

And so I applied for the Fulbright Specialist Program as a Child Protection Specialist. BHU asked me to replicate a highly successful program model used throughout the United States and Canada to prepare social work professionals for employment in the child welfare field at the university level. The specific focus is a specialization for working with at-risk families and maltreated children. Upon graduation, students are prepared to immediately assume job responsibilities in child welfare organizations, and NGOs, without requiring extensive training and preparation.

The curriculum is an adaptation of the Core Curriculum for Child Welfare Caseworkers, developed and published by the Institute for Human Services (IHS), used throughout North America in both in-service training and university education settings. It has been translated into Russian and adopted by child welfare organizations in the Ukraine, Belarus, and Russia. The four-volume *Field Guide to Child Welfare,* circa 1998, is an internationally recognized practice resource. This social work bible-of-sorts authored by Judith S. Rycus and Ronald C. Hughes, Child Welfare League of America, serves as an essential companion to the core curriculum. The field guides have also been translated into Russian and are being shared in Russia, Ukraine, Belarus, and Lithuania with much success.

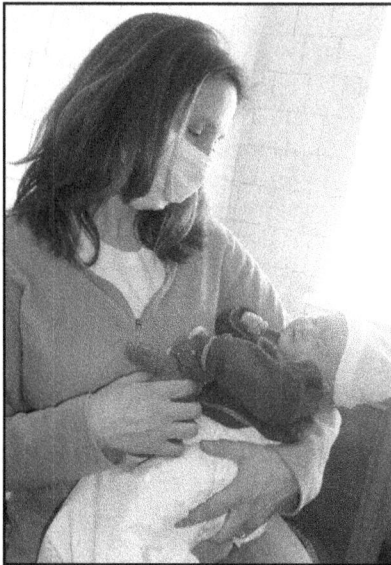

My role was to help the university learn how best to teach the teachers and, most importantly, to do this within Kyrgyzstan's educational and cultural contexts. I had a lot of learning to do myself. Maps and guidebooks were helpful in fixing my global bearings. But for me, the dream truly came alive when I came to this country to meet at length with faculty, students, NGO partners, and the Kyrgyz Association of Social Workers. Students and teachers helped me craft a program that would truly meet their learning needs and professional goals. Together, we determined that a one-year specialized course series with supervised work out in the real world best fit the needs of all.

Many students studying social work at BHU, pronounced in Russian "B'gu," have made life choices with serious consequences. One of the 20 third-year students selected for the new Children and Families specialization in social work says that her family was very concerned when she chose this profession, because there is a general perception that "social workers are servants."

"We have to prove how valuable our job is," says this young woman, who like her peers has entered the profession because of a central belief that family is the foundation and the purpose of life. "The

difficult social situations in the country bother me a lot. I want to take my part in changing it," says Nurgul.

These eloquent, sincere, fledgling do-gooders told me that they wanted to be a part of something that might help to change their country in a way that makes lives better for all families. Several expressed a desire to maintain the unique culture of Kyrgyzstan while encouraging open and honest societal dialogue about real problems in Kyrgyz society–alcoholism, poverty, domestic violence, and mental illness.

And they saw the specialization at BHU, "as a way to increase the prestige of the social work profession." These students, and students to come, are ready to check out of the "pity party" that plagues the social work profession and claim respect for the work they do.

When asked whether child abuse occurs in Kyrgyzstan, all the students I spoke with agree that it does and that few are open and willing to discuss why it occurs. It's a universal travesty deeply felt here.

One female social work student from Osh, in a sharing session, admitted that the custom of bride stealing keeps her from visiting her village.

"I am afraid if I go home, I will never come back."

This student and others who spoke to me on condition of anonymity said that this Kyrgyz tradition can be harmful to young girls and women, resulting in unwanted pregnancies and children who then are at high risk for abuse.

Child labor is another problem students expressed great concern about, even though they recognize that many parents must make their children work to bring enough money into the family for food and shelter.

"Parents don't feel good about this, though," one student shared. "They feel inadequate as a parent, have low self-esteem, and so they drink alcohol and sometimes beat or neglect their children."

In one planning conversation with students, I asked the miracle question: *If you woke up one year from now, and the children and families social work specialization was happening successfully, what would you be doing?*

Their responses made me all the more grateful to be a part of this project.

"I would be thinking about the family I have been working with for the year

and how they are doing. I'd be checking on their progress, seeing that they are doing better because of how I have built trust with them and showed them new ways to be a family." "I would feel comfortable and confident about the family I am working with and would feel I can work with them and help them because I have the best knowledge and skills. As a social worker I hope for this the most." "We [the students] wouldn't be strangers to the NGOs–we would be the type of specialists they want and need to help children and families."

These students believe social work could add value to Kyrgyz society, both in terms of reducing the costs of social problems and as working, educated professionals contributing economically.

I have been asked more times than I can count why I want to come to Kyrgyzstan to work with social work students and faculty. My response is always the same: I see hope in Kyrgyzstan. I see commitment, possibilities, and desire in the eyes of all the other dreamers who have been a part of this project. It's a practical magic.

As one student stated quite simply on the first day of class, "The difficult social situations in the country bother me a lot. I want to take my part in changing it–and this specialization can help me to do that." That's the spirit that has brought me to love Kyrgyzstan and the many social workers who will help to power the energy for change.

The project remains in need of funds to support teaching materials, such as textbooks, a laptop computer, and an LCD projector. Donations would be greatly appreciated and can be made through a U.S. and Canadian tax deductible nonprofit organization at the following address: *http://www.lambinternational. org/donations.htm*

*Christine Tappan, MSW, CAGS, is driven by the power of education and its ability to strengthen families and communities in every culture throughout the world. She earned her master's degree in social work at the University of Michigan and Certificate of Advanced Graduate Study in Special Education & Leadership at Plymouth State University in New Hampshire. Christine and her sister Cyndi Boschard Perkins, freelance writer, columnist, and editor, are in the process of collecting a series of stories about social workers and their experiences in Kyrgyzstan for their forthcoming book,* Social Work on the Silk Road.

# IS IT ETHICAL? 101 Scenarios In Everyday Social Work Practice
## A Discussion Workbook
### by Thomas Horn, MSW, RSW

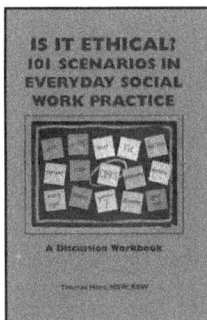

What would you do if you were asked to be your hairdresser's social worker? How about if you developed a crush on a client? Or if you unexpectedly received a $100 check in the mail from an agency to whom you had referred a client?

Social work is filled with these kinds of questions. They come up every day in professional life. Will your students be prepared to make the ethical decision?

Very few social workers go to work looking for ways to exploit, manipulate, or mislead the peopel with whom they work—clients, colleagues, managers, the government, or the general public. Yet, it is possible to cross into unethical behavior unintentionally, often as a result of poor decisions that are misguided. The line between ethical and unethical can become blurred.

This workbook provides students with 101 different everyday scenarios and challenges them to think about what the ethical and unethical choices might be in each situation. Through examining these scenarios on their own and in discussion with classmates and others, they will become more familiar with how to apply the ethical guidelines and standards that they will be required to follow as professional social workers.

Space is provided after each scenario for readers to write their own responses as they prepare to discuss the scenario with classmates, supervisors, and others. There is space for students to write their own scenarios, as well.

Resources are listed, including Code of Ethics Web addresses for nine different social work associations, as well as ethics journals.

*"...if you need a resource to begin a discussion of ethics in a classroom or agency in-service, this workbook qualifies for Social Work Ethics 101."* Paul Dovyak, ACSW, LISW-S, University of Rio Grande, Journal of Social Work Values and Ethics

**ABOUT THE AUTHOR**

Thomas Horn, MSW, RSW, is a Registered Social Worker (RSW) with both the Ontario College of Social Workers and Social Service Workers (OCSWSSW) in Ontario, Canada, and the General Social Care Council (GSCC) in England. Tom is also a graduate member of the British Psychological Society. He has worked in the social services field for more than 20 years in a variety of settings, including residential developmental care, residential and outpatient child and adolescent mental health, residential drug/alcohol treatment, and inpatient psychiatry. Currently, Tom works with an inpatient forensic mental health team at a large psychiatric hospital in Ontario. He routinely provides field supervision to social work students at the undergraduate and graduate levels.

2011 • ISBN: 978-1-929109-29-6 • 118 pages, 5½ by 8½ • $14.95 plus shipping

White Hat Communications, P.O. Box 5390, Harrisburg, PA 17110-0390  Phone: 717-238-3787  Fax: 717-238-2090  shop.whitehatcommunications.com

# Social Work in an HIV/AIDS Clinic

## by Joe Vanny Perez, LMSW

HIV (Human Immunodeficiency Virus) is a virus that destroys the immune system. Over time, most people with HIV become less able to fight off the germs that surround all of us every day, in our offices, on public transportation, on the street, and everywhere else. These germs usually do not make a person sick, but when the immune system gets weaker from HIV, these germs can cause infections and cancers that can kill a person. There are medications that fight HIV in the body and help the immune system stay stronger for a longer time. But there are no cures available for HIV.

As a social worker for New York Presbyterian Hospital's Center for Special Studies, I am part of a medical interdisciplinary team that specializes in providing medical care to patients with HIV/AIDS.

Working with patients with HIV/AIDS has allowed me to focus on a population that has often been neglected and stigmatized by our society. Social stigmas, homophobia, and lack of education have caused many People Living With HIV/AIDS (PLWHAs) to feel like outcasts in their own families and communities.

As an HIV/AIDS social worker, I help patients navigate the complicated levels of public assistance requirements and other hierarchal social services. I help them advocate for basic human necessities like food and shelter and help in finding community-based organizations (CBOs) that can offer support as they come to terms with having HIV/AIDS. I work with patients who are undocumented from other countries, helping them secure medical care and support to help them establish a steady foundation in a country (the U.S.) that may be new to them. I help lesbian, gay, bisexual, transgender, queer, and intersex (LGBTQI) patients tackle the double stigmatization of being treated as "different" and also living with HIV. Sometimes culture can have a negative impact on PLWHAs and their successes in managing the illness. Therefore, it is important that I incorporate cultural sensitivity into my daily work with patients tackling myths about HIV/AIDS by encouraging learning and advocacy.

I reinforce self-care and medication adherence alongside the medical team, which consists of a physician, nurse, psychiatrist, and social worker. I teach patients safer sex practices, encourage condom use, and provide a safe and nurturing environment that promotes healing and self-confidence. Ultimately, I help patients regain control of their lives through self-reflection and advocacy. Having the support of the multidisciplinary team can result in more successes, since each team member can help reinforce healthier lifestyles and encourage patient ownership of individual challenges utilizing the medical team as a foundation to build upon.

I provide short-term therapy for patients with concerns such as being recently diagnosed, disclosing their HIV status to loved ones, intimate partner violence, addictions (including substance and sexual), harm reduction, aging, and coping with grief and loss.

---

## A Hypothetical First Session

*(After introductions, I sit down with the client and begin an initial assessment, but cannot finish because the patient becomes upset)....*

SWer: *Please have a seat.*

Client: *(Not making eye contact) Thank you.*

SWer: *What brings you here today?*

Client: *I have not been feeling well these past few weeks. When I tested positive, I went into severe depression. Now, I feel like my body is breaking down. I have diarrhea, can't sleep well at night, nauseous.*

SWer: *How are you feeling right now?*

Client: *A little better. I thought you were just going to ask me to fill out a survey or something. This is different than what I am used to.*

SWer: *Well, we do care about our patients and make every effort to make them feel as comfortable as possible. Would you be ok with me asking you some personal questions?*

Client: *OK. Go ahead.*

SWer: *How were you infected? Was it through drugs or through sex/sexual contact?*

Client: *Sex*

SWer: *Sex with men or women? Or both?*

Client: *Men*

SWer: *When were you diagnosed with HIV?*

Client: *2006. November 2006. I remember that night. It was snowing hard outside. I kept looking out the window in his room thinking "how did I end up here in his bed?"*

SWer: *Did the person who infected you tell you about his HIV status beforehand?*

Client: *No. That is the unfair part. He should have told me and given me the chance to decide whether to use a condom or not! (Client becomes tearful). It has destroyed me!*

SWer: *What happened to you and him after you tested positive for HIV?*

Client: *He left me. He said I cheated on him because he was "clean." But he is the only person I have ever had sex with. He told me that he did not deserve to be put at risk. He said I was a "whore" and that I was going to die fast. Now, I am all alone.*

SWer: *I am so sorry to hear that. Is there anything you could have done at that time for yourself?*

Client: *I should have put a condom on him. He kept telling me "Trust me. Trust me baby. I'm clean." Now look at me. I'm sick. I am still in shock.*

SWer: *You have the right to feel that way and to be angry. It sounds like he was not honest with you from the beginning. But, I am glad you came to our clinic today. I am going to help you learn about our clinic and the services we can offer you. As a social worker, I can help you get in contact with support in the local community including referrals to support groups and individual therapy that can provide you a safe space to explore what living with this illness may mean to you. This can also give you an opportunity to meet people who may share similar experiences with you. Does this sound like something that may be helpful to you?*

Client: *Yeah. I am just scared. And lonely...*

SWer: *Please understand that the doctor and I are here to support you as best we can. At this clinic, we have a team-centered approach where we will always make every effort to schedule you to see both the doctor and social worker during the same visit. It will also allow us, as your providers, to communicate easily regarding your care and provide you with the best service possible. Feeling scared of the unknown and lonely are two sane responses to this traumatic life-altering journey you have been experiencing. Does this sound like something you may find useful at this time?*

Client: *Yes. You seem to care. I appreciate it.*

People of color continue to be at a disproportionate greater risk of being infected with HIV/AIDS. Lack of health insurance, inadequate medical attention, general poor health, and little or no access to proper education contribute directly to increased infection rates among these populations, representing a negatively increasing trend in new HIV infections. As social workers continue to develop cultural competency, complex psychosocial factors continue to evolve as HIV spreads across the globe.

Working with people of color, I have come to understand that social workers in my field are faced with not only working with the medical aspect of HIV/AIDS, but with other, just as powerful, forces that can create huge gaps in accessing medical and social services. Some of these forces include racism, discrimination, genocide, and ignorance.

Sometimes these forces can cause a patient to become ambivalent about his or her medical care, and this may result in poor adherence to medication regimens. A common problem I have seen with patients (not just people of color) is that they stop taking their medication because it may remind them of their illness, and somehow by taking the medication, they are admitting they are HIV-positive and/or have AIDS. To combat poor adherence, I help patients explore their fears about HIV, the impact of disclosing their HIV status with people in their immediate social circles, the influence of religion/folk/cultural beliefs, and ultimately encourage patients to establish support networks (either personal or through agencies), utilizing individual therapy and groups as a tool to network with other people who may share similar experiences.

Motivational interviewing can be a useful intervention with people struggling with medication adherence and safer sex practices. As I attempt to work with a patient who is ambivalent about behavior changes, I often think, "Is the patient able to understand core concepts I am trying to teach? Is he or she able to reflect upon the positive and negative attributes of the choices being made? How can I reframe the message I am attempting to convey in a way that the patient can relate to? What are the patient's strengths and weaknesses? Does the patient advocate for other people? If so, how? How has the patient managed ambivalence in the past?"

HIV/AIDS is an exciting field that is constantly changing as medicine evolves. It will challenge social workers to understand complex psychosocial factors, societal stigmatization, and human injustice, and encourage advocacy on mezzo and macro levels, including advocacy on multi-tiered levels as government funding for HIV/AIDS programs is reduced. It will also encourage social workers to help patients navigate bureaucratic systems while recognizing individuality, self-respect, and self-worth.

For further information, please visit:
*http://www.thebody.com*
*http://www.thebodypro.com*
*http://aids.gov*
*http://avert.org*
*http://www.aidsinfo.nih.gov*
*http://www.poz.com*

*Joe Vanny Pérez, LMSW, has worked as a social worker at the Center for Special Studies/NY-Presbyterian Hospital for five years, focusing on HIV/AIDS. He holds a master's degree in social work from New York University and a B.A. in sociology and art history from Hunter College-City University of New York. In 1990-1991, Mr. Pérez served in Operation Desert Storm as part of a United States Army unit embedded in Iraq and Saudi Arabia.*

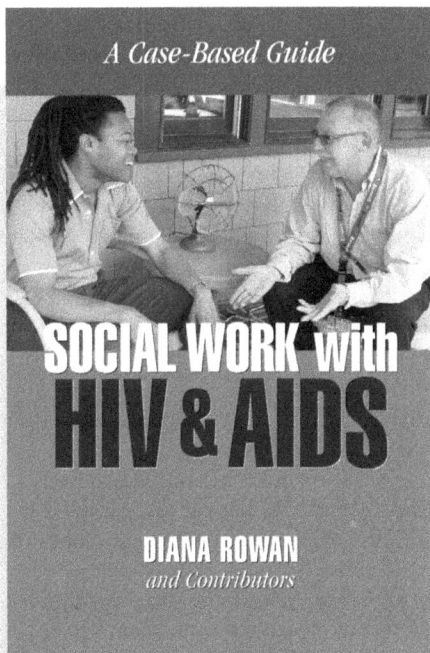

# A Foster Child Removal Experience:
# A Narrative Concerning Entry Into the Foster Care System

*by Joseph P. Berry, BSW*

I work as a behavior specialist in Kansas City, Missouri. Spofford Home is a residential treatment center for children with emotional and behavioral disturbances. My duties include being accountable for daily structure and reinforcement of treatment plans. In addition to my experiences at Spofford Home, I have also volunteered at Crittenton Children's Center, another residential treatment center in the Kansas City area. While at Crittenton, I interacted with male adolescent and pre-adolescent units and assisted with therapy sessions in chemical dependency groups. The combination of my experiences in these organizations, combined with my increasing knowledge of the child welfare system through my practicum placement at the Johnson County Children's Division in Warrensburg, MO, provided frequent opportunities to share what I had learned thus far in my career.

During my practicum, we had to lead group sessions, and I wanted to lead groups on something that was

## Foster Child Removal Experience

Close your eyes and imagine.... It is 2 a.m., and you have been asleep for quite a while now. Startled, you wake up at the sound of a knock on the front door of your house. You see the hall light turn on and see the shadow of your mom and dad's footsteps walk past your bedroom door. The stairs creak in the familiar way they often do on the fifth and seventh stairs, as you hear your parents walking down them.

You sit up in bed as you hear the front door being unlocked and the doorknob turn. Then you begin to hear voices talking softly. You can clearly make out the voices of your parents, but you are unable to identify the other two voices. The only word you can make out is the word "remove," which is then followed by a bunch of other words you don't quite understand.

All of a sudden, you start hearing your dad talking louder and saying something about not having the right and having no proof. You can hear your mom crying between your father's raised voice. Suddenly, you hear footsteps coming up the stairs and can hear people walking outside your bedroom door. You hear the familiar creak of the floor and you know that there is someone outside your bedroom door. You pull the covers up to your chin, hoping that whatever is going on will just stop and this is all just a dream. You hear your dad outside your door talking to the other people, this time saying, "They need their mom and dad. You have no right to do this."

You hear one of the other voices saying a lot of words you don't understand, and then you pull the covers tightly around you as you see the doorknob slowly start to turn. You see your mom walk into the room. You can tell she has been crying. She asks you to get out of bed and get dressed. You slowly get out of bed and look at her for a second before walking to your dresser to put on your clothes. As you finish putting on your shirt, your mom asks you to take all your clothes out of your dresser. You watch as she picks up your half-open backpack on the floor and starts to put your clothes in it. You walk over to her and hand her the clothes in your hand and watch as she puts more of your clothes in the backpack.

You don't know what to think. Are we moving? Maybe this is a surprise vacation. *Yeah, that must be it,* you think to yourself. Your mom helps you grab the rest of your clothes and tells you to follow her downstairs. As you walk downstairs, you see your dad talking with two other grown-ups. One grown-up looks like a policeman, and the other has lots of papers. The person with all the papers walks up to you holding a black trash bag and says you can put the rest of your clothes in the bag so you don't have to hold them. You hesitantly look up at your mom, and she doesn't say anything, only nodding slowly in a way that tells you it is okay to put your clothes in the trash bag.

The paper lady doesn't seem very scary, but why did she ask you to put your clothes in a trash bag? She bends down to pick you up, and you are still so tired that you wrap your arms around her neck. You turn your head to look at your mom and see that she is crying. As the paper lady begins to walk toward your front door, you see your dad talking to the policeman. The policeman says one last thing to your dad and starts walking toward the door behind you and the paper lady.

It is kind of cool outside, and it's even cooler because you wish you could be back under the covers in your warm bed. The policeman opens the car door for the lady with the papers, and you are placed in the back seat of her car and buckled in. The lady with the papers says something you can't hear to the policeman and then gets in the driver's seat of the car. She turns around and looks at you.

All you can manage to ask her is, "Where are we going?" The lady with the papers says there have been some problems and that you will have to live in a safer place for a while until the problems can get worked out. You are confused and have so many questions going through your head, but the only one that you can make out to ask her is, "Why?" She tells you that right now your home is not the safest place for you, and for you to be safe, you have to go live somewhere else for a while. The car is silent after she says this, and it seems almost as if time is standing still. The lady with the papers turns around and turns the key to start the car. The paper lady turns around as she backs out of your driveway, and you watch your house all the way until she turns at the end of the street.

As you slowly open your eyes, please allow yourself to feel free to make any comments on emotions or feelings you may have experienced at any point during the exercise.

to accurately capture the emotions and imagery present within a removal experience in addition to helping promote a mindset conducive to the topics I would be discussing within the training session.

*Joseph P. Berry, BSW, is a graduate of the Department of Social Work at the University of Central Missouri. He is currently employed at Spofford Home, an adolescent residential treatment facility, as a behavior specialist, where he works with children who have behavioral and emotional disturbances. Joseph has also been employed and volunteered at a number of facilities, including Crittenton Children's Center, Johnson County Children's Division, Trinity Nursing and Rehabilitation Center, and Clare Bridge of Leawood. His current interests include child welfare, issues relating to secure/insecure attachment in adolescents, and childhood behavior disorders.*

familiar to me. Based on my interactions with many children in the residential facilities, I chose to lead Foster Parent Support Group Training for Children's Division and Division of Family Services in the Johnson County area. My training discussed common topics related to foster parenting, such as: foster parents' interactions and ability to understand and empathize with foster children previously living in environments addicted to chaos, common behaviors of foster children and ways of reinforcing positive alternatives, foster parents' potential risk for vicarious trauma (witness to hearing about someone's trauma and abuse can cause personal trauma over time through accumulation), appropriate ways of reacting to a child's behaviors and maintaining healthy boundaries, burnout prevention, and the effects of compassion fatigue.

The Foster Parent Support Group Trainings were primarily attended by foster parents and the Children's Service Worker for the division where I was presenting. During several of my training sessions, I was privileged to welcome foster children who were accompanying their foster parents. This allowed for conversations that truly allowed for insight into the mindset of a foster child in the child welfare system.

Prior to beginning discussion about my main training topics, I wanted to grasp the audience's attention with a first-person narrative I wrote from the view of a child being removed from his or her parents' custody. The narrative was primarily intended to evoke emotional responses exhibiting empathy for the trauma a foster child faces when removed from parental custody.

After completion of the narrative, I observed nonverbal behaviors of the group members and prompted discussion among the audience members by inquiring about the emotions aroused by the "Foster Child Removal Experience." During some training sessions, the exercise brought some foster parents to tears as they responded, saying, "I've never thought about how traumatizing it would actually be to be removed from my parents and home." Other reactions from foster parents included: "This really helps me to see how I really don't know what my child has gone through when she tells me, 'You'll never understand and nobody ever does!'" Many of the foster parents also reported that the narrative made them feel more empathetic toward their foster children and helped them to realize where some common behavioral issues may originate.

Foster children in attendance stated the narrative described "exactly how I felt when it happened," and accurately depicted "how scared I was and all the questions that were going through my head." The responses of the foster parents, combined with the reactions of foster children present during the narrative experience, truly helped to confirm the success of my intent for the exercise, which was

# Riding the Mutual Aid Bus and Other Adventures in Group Work

## A Days in the Lives of Social Workers Collection

Linda May Grobman, MSW, ACSW, LSW,
and Jennifer Clements, Ph.D., LCSW, Co-Editors

The fourth volume in the *Days in the Lives of Social Workers* series focuses on social workers' experiences with groups. This collection of first-person narratives brings to life the many ways in which social workers use group work with clients of all ages, in all settings, and across a variety of populations. Readers will clearly see the power of mutual aid and group process in these stories. Developed in collaboration with the International Association for Social Work With Groups, the book includes the full text of the Standards for the Practice of Social Work With Groups.

*"This book presents a lovely compilation of group work vignettes—slices of practice life—that reflect a range of populations, issues, and settings in which group work takes place....The informal approach to presentation makes the case examples very user-friendly."*

Dominique Moyse Steinberg, DSW, Adjunct Faculty, Smith College SSW, CEO, CustomElderCare®

## Table of Contents

See http://www.daysinthelivesofsocialworkers. com for more information.

## ABOUT THE EDITORS

*Linda May Grobman, MSW, ACSW, LSW,* is the publisher/editor of *The New Social Worker* magazine. She edited the books *Days in the Lives of Social Workers* and *More Days in the Lives of Social Workers,* and co-edited *Days in the Lives of Gerontological Social Workers.* Linda received her MSW from the University of Georgia and has practiced in mental health and medical settings. She is a former chapter staff member of the National Association of Social Workers.

*Jennifer Clements, PhD, LCSW,* is currently an Associate Professor of Social Work at Shippensburg University of Pennsylvania. She is Vice President of the International Association for Social Work with Groups and a passionate group worker. She has worked in child welfare practice for 15 years, leading numerous groups with children and adolescents.

ISBN: 978-1-929109-33-3 • 2013 • 5.5 x 8.5 • $22.95 plus shipping

# Your Community Needs You

## Make a Difference at Home

Earn a Master of Social Work
Online from the Top-Ranked
USC School of Social Work

**USC** School
of Social Work

http://msw.usc.edu/NewSocialWorkerMag

# A Social Worker's Mission

## by *Jessica Bradstreet, LCSW*

I am a social worker. I'm often burnt-out, stressed out, and have to-do lists everywhere I turn around. My computer desktop might just earn me an Axis 1 diagnosis of Obsessive Compulsive Disorder, as I have files within files within files, all appropriately named and organized according to job duty the file falls under, category within that job duty, subcategories, and on and on. My Outlook inbox, another madhouse, with "flagged" e-mails to follow up on (I know I must drive people crazy with the number of times I check up on and re-check up on things–this is my public apology to those people), and e-mail archive files with saved important information, also organized into different folders by category and relevance.

I have worked hard to get where I am. Yet, as a social worker, I know that one must continue fighting, because it does not matter most days how hard you work. There is still more work to be done. When I leave my job at the end of the day, someone else does not pick up the shift. When I am done for the day, the job is not shut off like a computer. I work with people...they don't stop at 5 p.m. as I am driving home in traffic.

No, no matter what time I drive home, whether it's an early day because I have completed all of my to-dos for that day, or whether it's been a very long day, people keep living, keep needing, and the fight still rages on. On an early day, some argue that I am still not so lucky, because on that early day, I may still be responding to e-mails or calls until after 10 p.m. (the calls are usually me staffing and consulting with the employees that I supervise, don't want you thinking I'm talking to clients that late!). Was it really an early day? I'm not sure. I am over-worked and under-paid.

Frankly, I work my butt off. But I don't always see it that way. One of the things I can say is that I do not punch in on a time clock. I manage my own time (for the most part), and I am my own boss (pretty much, although I work for a private agency). There are a few positives!

However, there is always work to be done, things not getting done, and my own professional reputation is still blooming. So, I charge on. To the next day, the next crisis, the next need. I

do not have near enough support or resources to do my job. But still, I fight my way to get as much as I can get done, done. I have not given up.

Occasionally, I am recognized or appreciated. Sometimes (not often enough), something good happens for one of the foster children in my program. Something I've fought for, the fighting pays off. A child who needed to see a dentist gets to see a dentist. An adoption happens. A child "gets better" with the hard work and help of a good team.

I guess that is what keeps me going. At the end of the day, I know that without some of my hard work, my team's good skills, my annoying e-mails, and my kick-butt organizational skills, something that needs to happen might not happen. And there is always more work to be done. More good work. By a good social worker.

The reason I do it–foster children. Children taken away from their families

> The reason I do it—foster children. Children taken away from their families because of abuse and neglect. They all have a story, a need, and many layers of personality and being.

because of abuse and neglect. They all have a story, a need, and many layers of personality and being. They are all taken, and they are put into a system that sometimes does more damage for them than the damage done to them on their home-front. You see, one thing that I truly believe in–although I am speaking as a professional, not a mother–is that children need stable, healthy families who teach them right from wrong and nurture and love them in a safe home.

Many children in our country, next door, at our neighborhood schools, are not getting this need met. Shame on those parents. Or shame on their parents for allowing the ignorance to carry over into another generation. Or shame on our country for not providing more education, prevention, and resources to stop this cycle. Whoever is to blame, rightfully so, they are taken away. And foster care begins.

Many good things can come from this removal, sometimes even permanent

healing for a child or a new permanent home. However, my point is that any and every child needs this second chance at the life that he or she deserves after the first one, which is out of my realm of control, is done to them.

As a young child, I knew that I wanted to help people. I was raised by a bleeding heart mother (not a social worker) to rescue stray animals, feed the homeless man every Sunday on the way home from church, and feel sorry for the children who did not have.

Growing up, I–like every other child–dreamt of what I wanted to be "when I grew up." I once wanted to be a veterinarian, then decided I could not ever stand to put an animal to sleep, so I decided to go along with something in the "hospital helping" arena. So, after high school, I went to community college with a plan for a two-year degree. I had not found anything I was truly passionate about, but I honestly did not know there was such a passion at that time.

In my beginning college courses, I became curious about what else was out there. I began a preoccupation with what made serial killers turn into serial killers. At that time, I decided that what I really wanted to be was an F.B.I. agent, a forensic psychologist, chasing down and exploring the minds of serial killers. After this "awakening," I knew that I wanted more college than a two-year degree. I was ready to spread my wings into a four-year college.

Once there, I learned that this "dream job" of mine was not a field with many openings, and the mere thought of wearing a police uniform seemed revolting. I changed my major to psychology, only to learn that that was not my calling, either. Too many theories–not raw "helping."

I visited the social work department on a whim, a recommendation from my sister-in-law, who raved about the many opportunities of a social worker. I changed my major that day.

I began volunteering, deciding to try my hand at child welfare. I have never once looked back since finding this "passion." I began on my path as a volunteer Guardian ad Litem. In this volunteer position, as a college student with no degree, I was assigned my own cases. It was raw, all right. I felt like I was doing something that mattered. I became important in someone's life who needed the compassion I had to offer. I felt as if I was working front stage with an important cause. I have felt like an important asset to the field ever since.

I continued on to receive my master's degree in social work. I began working right away, obtaining a job as a caseworker. Here, I began to learn the gut and grit of a social worker. The training I received in no way taught me how to do my job, I was thrown to the wolves, with a degree, a heart, and rent to pay. I trudged through. I made my way, learned the ropes, returned phone calls on my way to and from work, researched people's needs, found referral sources, typed like a speed demon, and ran multi-tasking circles around my office and around the city of Jacksonville, FL.

Soon, a position opened up where I could be a master's level therapist for troubled foster kids. I thought I had hit the jackpot. I put in my one month's notice, worked late to properly and professionally transfer my cases, and off I went to my next venture. I was now armed with some real experience and had a few tricks up my sleeve about the oh-so-confusing and overwhelming child welfare and dependency system world.

I kept soaring. I did not stop. Within one year of being a therapist within a small, therapeutic foster care agency, I was promoted to Program Supervisor. I was two years out of graduate school, 26 years old, and I was sharp as a whip, creating organization within the entire program's systems of managing paperwork, intake, services, and so forth, while also managing a caseload.

I am now the ripe age of 28 years old. I have received my license within the state of Florida, I am a Licensed Clinical Social Worker. I am fortunate to be able to be flexible with my time (single, no children). I am also blessed with a calling, and I am a bright, fighting advocate with a heart made for foster children. I like to think that the agency that I work for appreciates me, or will appreciate me, but I can only hope and believe that if they're letting me manage my own program without breathing down my neck too much, I must be doing okay in their eyes.

Sometimes, and quite often, my relationships, social life, and sleep are affected by my job. I have learned to enjoy quiet, peaceful nights in and often trade them for going out. I do still, however, make sure that I am able to take some time to unwind and enjoy myself. Most times, somewhere in my head, or at any time, a work task lingers, an idea pops into my head for how I can better advocate, or my phone rings with an emergency.

Sometimes, as a social worker, it's a question you've never heard. Something you do not know the answer to. You are learning every day and no day is the same. Find the answer, figure out what to do. You're a social worker. This is your job.

I enjoy voicing my "social work" or "child welfare" opinions, but always try to remain objective, open, and professional. I am still a young social worker, and there is much to be learned. But I believe that the foster care system deserves more funding, more resources, and better advocates. I do not know if this will ever be accomplished.

I tell myself I do not wish to ever burn out of this field. I want to be a foster care ranger. I want to be remembered. I want to make a difference. However, in the dark times, I sometimes wonder, "How much more can I take?" The foster care system needs more and better advocates, maybe smaller caseloads, more training. I often see things slipping through the cracks and things not being handled appropriately or in a timely manner. There are people working with these children who do not understand their need for urgency, their trauma. Maybe some of these people are burnt out. Yet, still, these are children's lives and needs.

Some foster families are not held to the standards that they should be. Proper parenting of our abandoned children is sometimes not the focus. I've seen times when the risk of a lawsuit trumps the best interest of a child. Sometimes, it's like, God forbid we get in trouble for taking a risk for the possibility of betterment on a child's behalf.

Foster care adoptions are not always given the attention that they need. The children (when old enough) are not involved, the entire team is not always included in selecting a family, adoptive families sometimes are not given enough information, or the prospective parents lack the knowledge of the sometimes complex personalities of our little ones who have been subjected to abuse and a troubled system. Biological families are given too much time and not enough good resources to get themselves together and do right by their children once they are given back. I firmly believe that each move for a child is a separate loss. Children are often denied the truth, and our nation's youth are further shown that the world cannot be trusted.

I believe, as a social worker, that it is my duty to advocate by any means possible on behalf of a child's best interests. I handle things not outlined in my job description, offer above-and-beyond support, and try to adhere to my mission of ensuring that all of a child's needs are met somewhere along the way of them crossing my path. I honor the importance of continuing training in my field and am often enrolling in the next (free or low-cost) training course, reading about a "hot" topic, or somehow expanding my network and knowledge base.

This, my friends, is the life of a social worker. A social worker, whom if I do say so myself, is dang good. And who is also a fighter, a lover, an advocate, sick of seeing children suffering, and stressed out.

I encourage you, fellow people of our nation, to care. Care about children, foster children, and how these lives can so suddenly be changed, and how these changes affect them in the long and short run. These are your neighbors, your children's school/play mates, the next generation.

I encourage you, advocates, policy makers, to hear this out. Find my passion and fight for it.

I encourage parents to become educated. Parenting, attachment, bonding, behavior management, the importance of nurturing, all of these important topics of prevention.

I encourage those with a burning flame for this cause, to do something big. And do something good.

I encourage you, those wishing to go into the field or those in the field, to find balance. Do not lose your mind, but certainly, do not let a child's needs wait.

Is this possible? I am not so sure myself. But I seek to find this balance, as I am thankful and, forever, a social worker.

*Jessica Bradstreet, LCSW, received a bachelor's and master's degree from the Florida State University College of Social Work. She has worked in the child welfare system in Jacksonville, FL, since 2007, as a caseworker for foster children, a child therapist for therapeutic foster care children, and now as a program supervisor of a therapeutic foster care program. Jessica became licensed in 2011.*

# Phi Alpha Honor Society for Social Work

The deadline for the Phi Alpha individual scholarship was May 30.

The scholarship opportunity was a huge success, and three winners will be announced on September 1. The national office received more than 200 applications. Phi Alpha is committed to serving our members with opportunities to help achieve individual and chapter recognition in the field of social work. Please visit Phi Alpha at *http://www.PhiAlpha.org* and on Facebook.

Enjoy your summer,
Tammy Hamilton
Executive Secretary

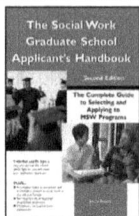

*Compton–continued from page 3*

for 25 years–was killed in a riding accident. "I had not yet restored my relationship with my family," she says, "but I made plans to move to Southern Pines, NC, to be with my father, who now lives with me and my daughter."

She started studying in a community college's substance abuse program, where a professor reiterated her suitability for social work. "Eventually, I want to be fully licensed," Compton says. "Social work offers so many areas of choice. I'm interested in people overall–how they got to where they are, their strengths and murky areas."

She had intended to continue with an MSW degree in the fall, but right now says her 86-year-old father is her "job." She's also general service representative of her 12-step recovery program and hopes to get a part-time job. "I'm open to anything, one day at a time," she says. Still, in five years, Compton would like to be a licensed clinical social worker and also complete a program in substance abuse. Compton is considering a career as a military social worker–Fort Bragg is only 35 minutes from her home, and she is interested in PTSD–or maybe work in a prison or in-patient residential treatment center.

In her spare time, Compton loves to ride horses, which she calls her "winter hobby." Her summer one is gardening. She has no significant other now, but that's okay.

What's harder to find okay is that she and her son's adoptive parents have minimal communication–even though she has a good relationship with Summer's former foster parents. "If it's meant to be, some day I'll see him," Compton says.

Her calm and courage in the face of adversity are, Marson says, "inspirational."

*Barbara Trainin Blank is a freelance writer based in Harrisburg, PA.*

FOLLOW ME ON TWITTER

**The New Social Worker is on Twitter! Follow us at:**
*http://www.twitter.com/newsocialworker*

# Congratulations 2012 Social Work Graduates!

See slide show with more photos at http://www.flickr.com/photos/newsocialworker/sets/72157630388818324/

Noele Brabon, MSW, University at Albany

California State University, Northridge, 2012 MSW Graduates

Andrea Reed, MSW, Ohio University

Brittany O'Neill, BSW, George Mason University

Phylicia Massey, MSW, Florida State University, December 2011

Eva D. Goodman, B.A. in Social Work, Christopher Newport University

Crystal Brown, BSW, Northwestern State University

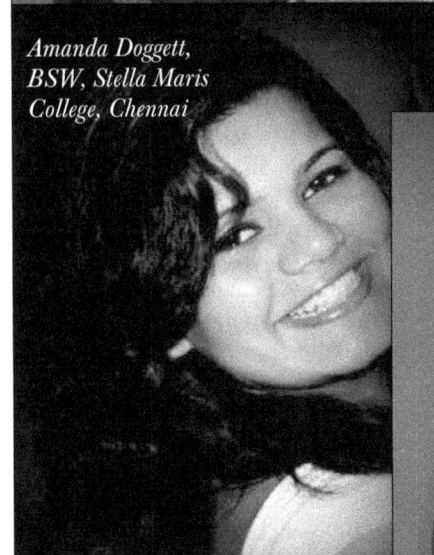

Amanda Doggett, BSW, Stella Maris College, Chennai

Michael L. Brown, MSW, Radford University

Carl Deertz Jr. (MSW), Preston Nguyen Tang (BSW), and Tess Banko (MSW), San Diego State University

# Reviews

*Narrative Approaches in Social Work Practice: A Life Span, Culturally Centered, Strengths Perspective*, by Edith M. Freeman, Charles C Thomas Publisher, Springfield, IL, 2011, 244 pages, $54.95 hardcover, $34.95 paperback.

This text begins with the challenge to outline narrative approaches from four theoretical perspectives: life span development, social construction, spirituality, and culture. The author prudently divides the text into two sections. The first part lays the foundation of the narrative approach, offering a chapter for each of the five principles: timing and context of narrative; the shared experience and transformation, naming, and unpacking: the assessment-intervention; meaning-making; and social-political-cultural intervention. Within each chapter, there are clear descriptions of the principle's elements and significance, as well as the corresponding practice skills. Furthermore, the author offers greater clarity to the reader through poignant case examples, figures and tables to summarize key points, and consistent cross-referencing to the other principles and their corresponding practice skills.

In the second portion, the author seeks to equip readers with advanced practice skills to be used across the life span. Beginning with children, the author offers prevention, early intervention, and treatment strategies through the use of play, interpretive, and improvisational narrative approaches. Other chapters include: youth and narrative transitions to explore choice and consequence, "re-authoring" narratives concerning gender and adult development, older adults and life narrative for well-being and peer support, resolution-based metaphor for couples and families in conflict, and common marginalized and exception narratives for multisystemic advocacy and change. The author sustains consistent and substantive content throughout the text, in spite of the comprehensive breadth in approach. That said, the theoretical and practical narratives of spirituality are not integrated into the text to the extent of the other perspectives.

This text merits utility in the clinician's and clinical supervisor's toolkit, as well as the educator's syllabus. Beyond providing lucid explanations of how and why individuals tell and retell narratives, narrative typology, and practice skills, the author describes the nuances of therapeutic interactions with clients that a seasoned clinician seeks to impart during supervision. For the classroom, the author strategically fashions chapters to be read sequentially or individually for topical study. This text stands as a cutting-edge resource for social workers as they advocate for the profession's legitimacy in an environment increasingly driven by evidence-based practice and outcome evaluations.

*Reviewed by Joshua Hammer, MSW, MA, Program and Research Assistant, Institute for Urban Initiatives.*

---

*Lesbian and Gay Couples: Lives, Issues, and Practice*, by Ski Hunter, Lyceum Books, Chicago, IL, 2012, 208 pages, $29.95.

Author Ski Hunter has a background in psychology, an MSW, and a Ph.D. in social work, and readers benefit from it all. Within the pages of this thin paperback is a wealth of knowledge that provides both a general overview and a number of specific issues related to lesbian and gay couples. The extremely detailed table of contents makes this a perfect resource for someone looking for one specific piece of information. The book as a whole allows for an overall increase in knowledge in an area of the social work field to which many students and practitioners aren't often introduced.

Although the book purports to be intended for social work students, practitioners, and couples, it is likely that the audience best served is the student population. Be prepared, though—this book is clearly written by someone with a mind for research, and the vignettes—though helpful—are short and to the point, with the vast majority of the book filled with facts rather than discussions, and there are no practice models recommended. As Hunter acknowledges, however, it is best used as supplemental reading rather than as a primary source of information. For someone seeking an up-to-date collection of research related to sexual orientation and to the specific issues that arise when sexual minorities pair and work to build a life together, this is a great resource.

*Reviewed by Kristen Marie (Kryss) Shane, MSW, LMSW*

---

*Social Work in Rural Communities (5th edition), by Leon Ginsberg (Ed.), Council on Social Work Education, Alexandria, VA, 2011, 422 pages, $28.95 paperback.*

Ginsberg, recipient of the 2011 Council on Social Work Education Significant Lifetime Achievement in Social Work award, describes this collection of 20 new chapters as a compendium on rural social work practice. As such, it maintains a 40-year history of CSWE attention to social work practice in rural communities. However, rather than comprehensive, this collection is idiosyncratic without an over-arching theme. Although many of the chapters may be individually useful in a variety of courses in the social work curriculum, I believe this volume will be more useful as a reference tool or supplemental readings, rather than a textbook, for social work faculty teaching students in rural areas.

The first nine chapters addressing the basics of rural social work practice contain an excellent introductory chapter, a useful discussion of dual relationships in rural practice (chapter 6), meaningful consideration of student competencies for rural practice (chapter 7), and a thorough discussion of recruitment and retention issues in rural practice (chapter 8). The other chapters are either too specific geographically or limited to a focus on information technology to warrant inclusion in the basics section, in my view, although the attempt to look at rurality from a strengths-based perspective (chapter 2) and to include an international focus on rural community development (chapter 3) will be of interest to a limited readership. Social work historians may find the treatment of Appalachian settlement houses essential (chapter 9).

The second section of the book contains six chapters addressing specific rural populations. It is in this section that the book most closely approaches a compendium with strong summaries of rural social work practice with youth; children following natural disasters; reentry; Native Americans; the Amish; and lesbian, gay, bisexual, transgendered, and questioning people. The reader will find that each of these chapters contains updated information on the needs of the special population, obstacles to effective practice in rural areas, and practical suggestions for social workers engaged in these practice arenas. Although grouped with the third section in the book, chapter sixteen seems more appropriately placed in the second section, because it focuses on the influx of immigrants into rural America and the challenges this increased diversity brings.

The final section of the book includes four chapters (without chapter 16) that address interpersonal abuse in rural communities, rural healthcare disparities, rural mental health practices, and rural oncology. The last two chapters may be particularly useful in a practice class, because of the case examples provided.

Demographic shifts in rural America are inadequately covered in this compendium. Rural America is aging more rapidly than urban and suburban America. The resulting impact on rural public education systems and school consolidations threaten the sustainability of many rural communities. Regional consolidation into hub communities provides the semblance of urban amenities, but does so at the expense of resource depletion in the countryside. Under-resourced public education systems may not be up to the task of preparing graduates to effectively compete in the broader economy, thereby exacerbating rural poverty and its correlates. A comprehensive treatment of social work in rural communities should include a chapter on aging, poverty, and substance abuse.

Despite these limitations, I believe that every social work educator who is preparing students for rural practice should have a copy of this book available to them. Supplemental readings from this book are appropriate for courses addressing families, ethics, policy, mental health issues, and diversity issues. It is often difficult to locate succinct summary chapters to support class discussions, and many of the chapters in this volume do so admirably.

*Reviewed by Peter A. Kindle, Ph.D., CPA, LMSW, assistant professor at the University of South Dakota.*

---

*The Use of Self: The Essence of Professional Education, by Ray Fox, Chicago, Lyceum Books, 2011, 192 pages, $34.95.*

Advances in research are expediting the evolution of social work education and practice. Whereas the previous training of professionals relied heavily on transmission of practice wisdom, new technologies are catalyzing greater sophistication in many aspects of service provision, from approaches to assessment and diagnosis to the implementation and delivery of interventions. As both producers and consumers of research, social workers posit a range of responses to these changes. Analyses of these de-

velopments mostly identify the changes that social workers in direct practice are enacting; few treatments give consideration to the simultaneous transformations being leveraged in social work education.

As a seasoned practitioner and teacher, Dr. Ray Fox offers a meaningful contribution to these discussions. *The Use of Self* asserts that the profession's attention to the integration of science with practice-based training has neglected the artistry of social work. This prioritizing of the creative forms the foundation of his book, which can be experienced as a reimagining of educational models and as a roadmap for establishing different relationships in the classroom.

Successful social work training, Fox asserts, is predicated on reflection and relationship. Educators convey to students much more than substantive content; self-awareness in the classroom allows for the in vivo demonstration of how it is to be with clients. "Teaching and practice are isomorphs.... There is a strong congruence between what happens in the classroom and what happens in the practitioner's office," he asserts (p. 6). Indeed, Fox's descriptions of education—and the language with which he communicates these ideas—read more like a clinical manual than a treatise on teaching. For Fox, lessons learned through teacher-student relationships are readily portable to student-client interactions. Through co-creating a variety of relational dynamics in the classroom—such as initiating and sustaining an alliance, mirroring, and empathic resonance—students are able to experience and reproduce professional bonds that are safe, goal-oriented, flexible, and client-centered. At once philosophical and practical, Fox provides tangible examples of how to foster relational and reflective processes in the classroom. Lesson plans integrating art, music, journaling, photography and other alternative approaches are detailed.

Although novel, the validity of some of the author's assumptions warrants questioning. That the profession is sufficiently and successfully introducing findings from science into curricula is debatable. In fact, some argue that the disconnect between training, service delivery, and new knowledge remains the field's greatest liability. Further, suggesting that these more creative approaches to "being" with students are introduced into all sequences of social work education fails to acknowledge the assets and limitations of the profession's academy. For example, the social work professoriate continues to experience a shortage of faculty with experience in direct practice; the scarce practitioners-turned-educators seem to be

the target audience of this book. Further, the learnability of this approach is limited. Perspectives on self and relationship described in the text are mostly cultivated from years of clinical supervision and reflection, but are not easily acquired in workshops or other venues aimed at instituting new teaching skills. Additionally, the privileging of science over the use of self may actually be preferable in some domains of education—like research and policy—in which more traditional approaches to information-sharing may be most conducive to the attainment of this kind of knowledge.

*The Use of Self* can serve as a guide for new teachers eager to facilitate classroom experiences employing their practice-informed expertise. Veteran social work educators can benefit from this resource, as well. The unique approaches proposed by Fox—and the suggestions he provides for integrating artistry with science—can differently infuse variety, intuition, and creativity into teaching and learning processes.

*Reviewed by Jeff T. Steen, LCSW, doctoral student in social work at New York University, New York, NY.*

---

*Transgender 101: A Simple Guide to a Complex Issue, by Nicholas M. Teich, Foreword by Jameson Green, Columbia University Press, New York, 2012, 160 pages, $20.00.*

*The Lives of Transgender People, by Genny Beemyn & Susan Rankin, Columbia University Press, New York, 2011, 248 pages, $27.50.*

With President Obama, the NAACP, and Colin Powell's recent statements in support of same-sex marriage, America has its eye on the LGBT population, and clearly, we have been making great strides in the understanding and acceptance of lesbian, gay, and bisexual relationships. However the transgender population remains a mystery to many. These two books are great quantitative options to demystify this group and to debunk rumors and myths, doing so by educating the reader in a way that is more broad than the common storytelling method.

In *Transgender 101: A Simple Guide to a Complex Issue*, author Nicholas M. Teich is quite open about approaching this topic from a logical and scientific standpoint. For a social worker who is more focused on the medical model, for example, this may be a book more geared for you, with a focus on terminology and data. Within the pages, Teich discusses gender binary, which pronoun to use when, what the transitioning process is, different implications for trans people of different ages, legal difficulties, and discrimination considerations. In addition, Teich's social work background shines while discussing the impact of the current and future inclusion of transgender diagnoses within the DSM. Although the book could have spent more time acknowledging the genderqueer and gender variant/gender non-conforming populations, for a person who is looking for a more generalized overview of the transgender population in a way that is fact-minded, this book is a great option for comprehensive and approachable learning.

Conversely, *The Lives of Transgender People* is essentially a research study of approximately 3,500 transgender people, mixed with information obtained from more than 400 of the subjects. Although the quotes at the beginning of each chapter and the photographs of participants help to make the read a bit more personalized, there is a much drier feel in the sections that involve tables and statistics. This is a very different way to approach learning about the transgender experience from the more common personal storytelling, and, although the reader will not likely walk away feeling an emotional connection, the large number of the study's participants certainly acknowledges commonalities in the transgender experience throughout the spectrum of identifications.

Overall, both books are helpful options to aid in the better understanding of transgenderism. Having up-to-date options such as these to become better educated social workers (and/or to share with clients) further allows us to maintain the *Code of Ethics* requirement that we advocate for those in need while also allowing us each to learn in the way that is most effective for each individual reader.

*Reviewed by Kristen Marie (Kryss) Shane, LSW, LMSW.*

---

*Social Work Practice and the Law. by Lyn K. Slater and Kara R. Finck, New York, Springer, 2012, 421 pages, $70.00.*

*Social Work Practice and the Law* presents the idea that knowledge of the legal system can be a powerful tool for effective social work practice. Written by a social worker and an attorney, rather than focusing on the often-adversarial relationship between social workers and the legal system, the authors invite social workers to become involved in the legal process to advocate for and protect client best interests.

The book begins with an overview of ethics and social workers' roles in legal settings. Then it is organized around the different types of legal proceedings, including civil, criminal, and administrative. The authors first lead the reader through the process of the proceedings and identify the roles and responsibilities of the various players. The book then focuses on how social work and the law intersect, and how and where legally informed social workers can intervene. The social worker's role in alternative legal venues, such as drug courts, mediation, and conferencing, is also discussed.

The book illustrates each of these types of legal proceedings using one case example—the case of Michelle Jones. Following one case through each of the various legal systems creates some cohesion throughout the book and illustrates how one client can be involved in multiple implicit and explicit legal issues. However, the authors would have been better served providing a variety of case examples. This would have allowed for a more comprehensive look at how the legal system affects clients with different types of backgrounds and needs.

Of particular interest is the book's focus on client experiences of the legal system and the racial disparities that exist on every level. Understanding these disparities and how social workers can either help clients identify and advocate for their legal rights or advocate for system change is crucial to the social worker's effectiveness in the legal setting.

Providing an exhaustive text on every law affecting social work practice in every state would be cumbersome and confusing, and *Social Work Practice and the Law* does not attempt to do so. This book is designed to be a starting place for social workers as they begin to navigate within the legal system. In light of this, perhaps most useful is the text's frequent reference to Web sites and organizations that the social worker can use to access more specific state-level legal information.

*Social Work Practice and the Law* is a good starting place for those who want to understand the court system, as well as for those who are interested in developing collaborative relationships between social workers and attorneys. This text can best be supplemented with information on state law, but it still has a valuable place on any social worker's reference shelf.

*Reviewed by Laura Gale, LCSW, adjunct lecturer for the University of Southern California School of Social Work Virtual Academic Center.*

## Be a Book Reviewer

If you are a social work practitioner, educator, or student who loves to read, let us know your areas of interest and send us a short sample of your writing. We will then consider you when we are assigning books for review in *The New Social Worker* and on our Web site. Send writing sample, interest list, credentials, and contact information to: *lindagrobman@socialworker.com*

# @SWSCmedia—Bringing Social Workers Together Globally

## by Linda May Grobman, ACSW, LSW

With the rapidly changing technology all around us, it seems that new online social work communities and resources are springing up all the time.

One such community and a leading resource in this area is @SWSCmedia. According to its Web site at http://swscmedia.wordpress.com/, "@SWSCmedia is a knowledge community of practice that brings social work and social care practitioners, organisations, academics, researchers, students, policy makers, users of service and other allied professionals, stakeholders or enthusiasts, and interested parties together, to discuss issues, innovations, opportunities, dilemmas, and challenges, as well as relevant developments in relation to social work and/or social care."

The UK-based group has about 4,000 followers and has attracted as many as 100 participants interacting simultaneously in some of its Twitter "debates."

Claudia Megele (@ClaudiaMegele), a Senior Lecturer and Module Leader for MSc Step up to Social Work Programme at the University of Hertfordshire who also holds psychotherapy clinics both privately and at NHS, recognized the power of Twitter to connect people professionally and to enhance learning. She explains, "As a researcher, I was interested in social psychology and psychoanalytic sociology of Twitter, and as an academic, I could see its enormous potential for social learning, knowledge dissemination, and community building. We have used Twitter in creative ways, ranging from debates/chats to case study discussions, speeches, focus groups, mock interviews, and panel discussions." Megele's vision was to create an open access community for all, and the network has indeed become a global knowledge and learning community. In addition to being the founder of @SWSCmedia, Megele also started the @MHChat and @U4Change networks.

In October 2011, Megele announced the first @SWSCmedia debate, and the network has grown substantially ever since. @SWSCmedia debates are held Tuesdays (8:00 p.m. UK), often with a guest speaker. A second weekly debate is held every Sunday (6:00 p.m. UK) focusing on case studies, focus groups, student issues, and other activities. The debates have attracted people primarily from the UK and the U.S. and have overall participation from more than 20 countries.

"We started by offering Learning through Sharing, and it has been very well received. We are very proud of the quality of our work and delighted to serve our global community. In fact, our debates will be incorporated in social work curricula at selected universities," says Megele. "It is an eclectic space and will be even more so as we move to the next level and continue to engage everyone from university professors and researchers to students and practitioners to users and providers of services. It's a fantastic platform for social learning and knowledge and information sharing."

*So, what exactly is a Twitter debate?* you might ask. In simple terms, it is a fast-paced, live, real-time online chat that takes place on Twitter. Through the use of a hashtag (#SWSCmedia, in this case), participants can see what others are saying on the current debate topic.

@SWSCmedia, which stands for Social Work/Social Care & Media, operates primarily through the use of a blog (http://swscmedia.wordpress.com/), Twitter (@SWSCmedia), and LinkedIn group (http://www.linkedin.com/groups?gid=4010412). A brief review of the @SWSCmedia site/blog reveals that recent topics of discussion have included adoption reform, cyberbullying, workplace stress, ethics, professional conduct, social media, and many more.

Megele explains, "One of our main objectives is to bridge the gap between theories; research; and practice of social work, social care, and allied professions. Social media are changing and challenging both the medium and content of communication...and continue to transform our sociality as well as our thinking, being, and ways of relating to one another. In this context, we are leveraging social media to enhance the professional identity and the praxis of social work and social care."

Megele concludes, "Social media will continue to transform every aspect of our lives, ranging from research and education to systems and services. We at @SWSCmedia aim to seize this opportunity to enhance social work and social care education, research, and praxis."

The blog's "About" page provides detailed instructions on how to participate in the group's Twitter debates.

Follow @SWSCmedia on Twitter to stay informed of upcoming debate times and topics.

*Linda May Grobman, ACSW, LSW, is the publisher and editor of THE NEW SOCIAL WORKER magazine.*

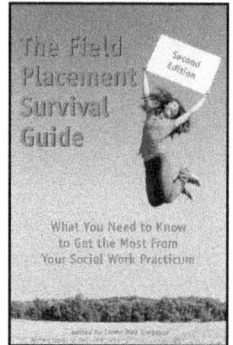

## Network With *The New Social Worker!*

As of July 2, 2012, we have reached 14,820 fans (or "likers") of our page on Facebook at *http://www.facebook.com/newsocialworker.*

Besides providing information about *The New Social Worker* magazine, the page has features of a typical Facebook timeline. We list upcoming events and send updates to our "likers" when there is something interesting happening!

Are you on Facebook? Do you love *The New Social Worker?* Show us how much you care! Be one of our Facebook "likers" and help us reach 20,000 (and beyond)!

We also have a Facebook page for our SocialWorkJobBank.com site! Go to *http://www.facebook.com/socialworkjobbank* to "like" this page. New job postings at *http://www.socialworkjobbank.*

*com* are now automatically posted to the Facebook page, as well.

Finally, stay up-to-date on our latest books at *http://www.facebook.com/whitehatcommunications.*

In addition, we'd like to know how *you* are using Facebook. Have you found it a useful tool for networking with social work colleagues, searching for a job, or fundraising for your agency? Write to lindagrobman@socialworker.com and let us know.

Facebook address: *http://www.facebook.com/newsocialworker*
***Also check out our other pages:***
http://www.facebook.com/socialworkjobbank
http://www.facebook.com/newsocialworkerbookclub
http://www.facebook.com/whitehatcommunications

AND...look for The New Social Worker's group on LinkedIn.com:
**http://www.linkedin.com/groups?gid=3041069**

Twitter: **http://www.twitter.com/newsocialworker**

Google+: **https://plus.google.com/u/0/101612885418842828982**

# CONTENTS

THE NEW SOCIAL WORKER®
Fall 2012
Volume 19, Number 4

## FEATURES

**American Red Cross**

## DEPARTMENTS

# Publisher's Thoughts

Dear Reader,

I hope you had a great summer and are now in the full swing of the fall season.

This year is a presidential election year, and I have already heard of many social workers and students (like the ones on our front cover from La Salle University) who have become involved in such activities as voter registration, advocacy regarding the voter ID laws, campaigning for candidates, and the like. As social workers, we have ethical responsibilities to clients, colleagues, practice settings, and **the broader society.** I encourage you to review the *NASW Code of Ethics,* and then think about which candidates' positions are in line with our ethical responsibilities to society. Be an advocate by being involved! Don't forget to cast your vote this November.

*Linda Grobman (right) with friends of The New Social Worker—Susan Mankita, Karen Zgoda (seated), and Kryss Shane, at the NASW conference.*

Over the summer, 1,000 social workers gathered in Washington, DC, for the "Restoring Hope" conference of the National Association of Social Workers. I was pleased to participate as a presenter and an exhibitor. Read my blog post about it at *http://blog.socialworker.com/2012/07/the-power-of-face-to-face-conference.html.*

I mentioned previously that I was working with my co-editor, Jennifer Clements, on a new book, *Riding the Mutual Aid Bus and Other Adventures in Group Work.* (See back cover.) I am pleased to tell you that this book is available NOW. Also, in the coming issues, we will be featuring a series of articles about group work.

Starting in the next issue, Allan Barsky, the new chair of NASW's National Ethics Committee, will be a regular ethics contributor to *THE NEW SOCIAL WORKER.* In this issue, we are featuring an excerpt from Barsky's book, *Clinicians in Court.*

In August 2012, Hurricane Isaac headed toward the U.S., leaving fatalities in Louisiana, Florida, and Mississippi. Many feared a repeat of Hurricane Katrina. The American Red Cross was ready with its new digital disaster volunteer program, spreading support and virtual hugs throughout cyberspace. Read about this new program, as well as the new Disaster Distress Helpline, on pages 30 and 31.

If you are planning to apply to graduate school in social work, don't miss Robin Wingo's article on page 18. Also, head over to our **new** Social Work Graduate School Site at *http://www.socialworkgradschool.com!*

Additional articles in this issue address burnout and self-care, homeless education, workplace safety for social workers, time machines in hospice social work, student research participation, and more!

Until next time—happy reading, and enjoy the changing colors of the leaves!

*Linda M. Grobman*

# Write for The New Social Worker

We are looking for articles from social work practitioners, students, and educators. Some areas of particular interest are: social work ethics; student field placement; practice specialties; technology; "what every new social worker needs to know," and news of unusual, creative, or nontraditional social work.

Feature articles run 1,500-2,000 words in length. News articles are typically 100-150 words. Our style is conversational, practical, and educational. Write as if you are having a conversation with a student or colleague. What do you want him or her to know about the topic? What would you want to know? Use examples.

The best articles have a specific focus. If you are writing an ethics article, focus on a particular aspect of ethics. For example, analyze a specific portion of the NASW *Code of Ethics* (including examples), or talk about ethical issues unique to a particular practice setting. When possible, include one or two resources at the end of your article—books, additional reading materials, and/or Web sites.

We also want photos of social workers and social work students "in action" for our cover, and photos to accompany your news articles!

Send submissions to lindagrobman@socialworker.com.

# The New Social Worker®
*the social work careers magazine*

## Fall 2012
## Vol. 19, Number 4

*Publisher/Editor*
Linda May Grobman, MSW, ACSW, LSW

*Contributing Writers*
Barbara Trainin Blank

THE NEW SOCIAL WORKER® (ISSN 1073-7871) is published four times a year by White Hat Communications, P.O. Box 5390, Harrisburg, PA 17110-0390. Phone: (717) 238-3787. Fax: (717) 238-2090. Send address corrections to: lindagrobman@socialworker.com

Advertising rates available on request.

Photo/art credits: Image from BigStockPhoto.com © Ari Sanjaya (page 4), Phatic-Photography (page 6), Ramona Smiers (page 10), Cheng En Lim (page 14), and Wolfgang Filser (page 18).

*The New Social Worker* is indexed/abstracted in *Social Work Abstracts.*

## Editorial Advisory Board
Rachel Greene Baldino, MSW, LCSW
Vivian Bergel, Ph.D., ACSW, LSW
Fred Buttell, Ph.D., LCSW
Joseph Davenport, Ph.D.
Judith Davenport, Ph.D., LCSW
Sam Hickman, MSW, ACSW, LCSW
Jan Ligon, Ph.D., LCSW, ACSW
Joanne Cruz Tenery, MSSW

Send all editorial, advertising, subscription, and other correspondence to:

**THE NEW SOCIAL WORKER**

**White Hat Communications**
**P.O. Box 5390**
**Harrisburg, PA 17110-0390**
**(717) 238-3787 Phone**
**(717) 238-2090 Fax**

lindagrobman@socialworker.com

http://www.socialworker.com
http://www.facebook.com/newsocialworker
http://www.twitter.com/newsocialworker

**Print Edition:**
http://newsocialworker.magcloud.com

# Christine Webb

*by Barbara Trainin Blank*

Christine Lauren Webb has what she calls a "social work disposition." An intense desire to help others has led her to volunteer in a Haitian village through Kings Cross Missionaries and to lend a listening ear wherever she is.

This inclination also explains, at least in part, Webb's openness in discussing the challenges in her own life. She'd like other people, especially young people, to learn from them.

Webb is young herself—only 23—with one year to go in the BSW program at the University of Indiana at Bloomington. It is a milestone she might not have reached if not for the realization that she had serious drug and alcohol problems.

She denied those problems for a while because she was otherwise fairly functional—although, as she acknowledged later, many of her relationships were troubled.

Webb had begun to use drug and alcohol after her parents' divorce when she just graduated high school. (Both of them later remarried.) She might have continued on that path had not one particular college course changed her life.

It was a course about substance abuse—to which she often came stoned or hung over. "It didn't register that I was where I needed to be,"

Webb says. "The class taught us how to identify an addict and how you could be emotionally dependent on a drug without being physically dependent—that dependence could be different from abuse."

Judy L. Malschick, adjunct professor at the School of Social Work, who had developed the course and teaches it, had no idea at the time that her student suffered from addiction. "She revealed that after the class was over in an e-mail, in a kind of appreciation, along with a message that the class had saved her life," Malschick says.

What Webb did acknowledge during the class was that other members of her family had addiction problems. "I admired the collegial way in which Christine worked on group projects," the professor adds. "Her ability to share about these issues encouraged other students to speak about theirs."

The later revelations not only enabled Webb to face her addictions, but to reach her potential. "It's since she came out with her own problems that she has really demonstrated a leadership role," Malschick says. "She has done a lot of volunteer work. I connected her with the executive director of Amethyst House, where I do contract work. She has spoken to groups there to inspire others, and to my class—as part of a panel. It's incredibly important to get speakers the students can connect with, and she's close to their age. She has an amazing style."

A transitional living facility with in- and outpatient services, Amethyst House has many clients who are in college. "That's the age when many people first experience abuse and possible addiction," Webb says.

She also volunteers at Martha's House, where she began doing intake work when the homeless shelter was short staffed. "It was my first experience with active listening and finding dignity and worth in everyone," she says.

Webb had to struggle to find that dignity and sense of self-worth in herself. For a time, she was able to give up drugs

*Christine Webb*

and alcohol—but then she relapsed. "Maybe it's because I had proven myself," she says. "But two months later, I almost choked to death on my own vomit, and that was a wake-up call. I found a 12-step program that worked for me. I was really ready."

Webb has spent nearly her entire life in Indiana, growing up in Lafayette. One sister goes to IU, as well, and another to its "rival school," Purdue. But she seems like a citizen of the world.

Webb is active in Fair Talk at IU, a grass-roots organization that raises awareness about HJR6, a suggested amendment to the State Constitution that marriage must be between a man and woman. "There's already a law banning gay marriage in the state," she comments, "so to add this is insulting."

Webb also worked with Stone Belt, a nonprofit that provides group homes and day services to people with developmental disabilities. There she learned an important lesson. "The clients who were encouraged to express themselves soared, but when they're completely taken care of or seen as a burden in their homes, they didn't do well. A lot of it is environment."

*Webb—continued on page 22*

# Ethics

# Clinicians in Court: Thwarting Disclosure
## by Allan Barsky, JD, MSW, Ph.D.

*Editor's Note: This article is an excerpt from Allan Barsky's book,* Clinicians in Court, *which addresses issues facing social workers when they are called on to testify. This excerpt addresses the issue of disclosing records in court. Look for more from Dr. Barsky in upcoming issues of THE NEW SOCIAL WORKER.*

Treating clinicians often wish they could prevent disclosure of records. Some reasons are ethically justifiable, others not. Clinicians treating victims of sexual assault, for example, may be concerned that their clients will be subjected to intense scrutiny before and during the trial of the alleged perpetrator. Historically, defense attorneys could subpoena complainants' records from clinicians, crisis services, and transition houses in order to discredit the complainant by saying that she is emotionally unstable, tends to fabricate stories, or is motivated to lie because she is trying to hide having had sex with someone else. For the most part, current evidentiary rules prohibit use of evidence of the victim's past sexual behavior or alleged sexual predisposition, although there are some exceptions (see Federal Rules of Evidence, 2010, Rule 412, at *http://www.law.cornell.edu/rules/fre/rule_412*). Also, most states have laws granting privilege to advocates, crisis counselors, and transition house staff working with victims of domestic violence, according to the American Bar Association.

Still, there are many other areas of practice where clinical records could be subpoenaed and the client could be embarrassed. Consider, for instance, a client who has received vocational counseling. The counselor's records may include information about the client's problems, including poor performance in school or prior work settings, irresponsible behavior leading to dismissal, or ethically questionable behavior. If a clinician wants to protect his client from disclosure of this type of information in a public legal process, there are several options, described below. Unfortunately, each option has major drawbacks. Before adopting any of these options, consult with your attorney, professional association, or other expert on law and professional ethics.

## Minimal Records

To protect their clients, some clinicians resort to maintaining minimal records (e.g., limiting details to the name of the client, the problem presented, and the dates seen). They deliberately exclude any information that could harm the credibility of the complainant or embarrass her. Unfortunately, some of this information may be clinically important, legally relevant, and ethically necessary. Suicidal or homicidal thoughts, alcohol or drug use, and high levels of stress are just a few examples. Although minimal records may thwart disclosure in legal processes, they may not meet the standards required for competent clinical practice. Further, the clinician may still be called to testify about client information not included in case records. If you want to keep minimal records, ensure that these records are consistent with agency policy, laws regulating your agency, and your professional code of ethics.

## Double Records

Some clinicians keep two sets of records—an official set and a personal set. The official set excludes potentially damaging information. The personal set includes all information, assessments, and speculations that the clinician uses for her own purposes. Although some clinicians believe that a subpoena applies only to the official records, all records are subject to subpoena. Some clinicians hide the fact that they have a set of unofficial records. However, if found out, failure to disclose all records can result in obstruction of justice or contempt of court charges against the clinician. The question raised by some clinicians is, "How will anyone know?" The real question is, "What does your sense of ethics and risk taking tell you?" Few agencies or professional associations would officially condone hiding a second set of records. There is no ethical foundation for keeping two sets of records. Ethically as well as statutorily, one set of records is what is appropriate.

## Coded Information

Some clinicians use secret coding to make parts of their records indecipherable to people unfamiliar with the coding. Some codes are so subtle that the reader does not even know that coding is being used (e.g., a double asterisk may denote past suicide attempts; "FLK" for funny looking kid). During a hearing, you may be asked to explain your codes or shorthand. Some codes may not be directly significant to the case but may indicate bias, lack of respect, or lack of professionalism. If it appears that you have deliberately tried to mislead the reader, your credibility as a witness may

---

[1]TTFO is sometimes used as slang for "told to f**k oneself." If asked what the initials mean, the practitioner might say "to take fluids only." Patients have sued agencies based on derogatory notations in their records.

be called into question.[1] Further, if someone else in your agency needs to refer to
your records, will she understand what
you have written? As indicated earlier,
if you know in advance that your case
may be involved in a legal proceeding,
you may have an ethical obligation to
maintain clear notes without the use of
code or shorthand. This will ensure that
others reviewing your work–in court or
otherwise–can understand the meaning
of your records. If you want to use ac-
ronyms or abbreviations in records, the
professional approach is to include a key
that accurately explains the meanings of
these terms.

## Doctoring or Disposing of Documents

If there is no impending legal process, clinicians are free to amend their
records. In many agencies, supervisors or
agency attorneys periodically review case
records and suggest changes to avoid future problems (e.g., to remove judgmen-
tal language, bias, or speculation). Clinicians are also free to dispose of records,
within the policies of the agency and the
standards of the profession. Michael's
mediation association, for example, suggests that mediators maintain records for
at least six months after mediation has
been terminated. However, if a clinician
is aware of an impending legal process
or has been subpoenaed, doctoring or
destroying documents can result in such
charges as contempt of court or obstruction of justice, malpractice suits, and
professional disciplinary actions. Once
again, the question may arise, "How
will anyone know?" Before shredding
your files, you might want to explore
the frequency with which fraudulently
motivated shredding has been unearthed
and exposed.

Even if you have no records, you
may still be called as a witness. You may
have limited value as a witness, particularly if you have no current recollection
of the events in question. However,
keeping records might actually help
your client, since premature disposal of
records can hurt your credibility as a witness. Finally, a clinician without records
may be more vulnerable to malpractice
suits (e.g., where a client later alleges that
the clinician induced a false memory of
abuse) or complaints before a licensing
board for failure to comply with ethical
standards of record keeping.

## Lying

When clinicians are involved in
legal processes, they are expected to tell
the truth. Depending on their priority of
values, some clinicians may be tempted
to intentionally lie to protect clients or
themselves. Frieda believes her records
will embarrass Paula, so Frieda considers telling Alice that she has already
destroyed them. Sam does not want to
be called as a witness, so he wonders
whether to tell the court he has no current recollection of any of his notes (a
convenient memory lapse). These types
of tactics can thwart disclosure. However, you risk charges of perjury and
professional misconduct, as well as a negative perception for both you and your
profession. Professional organizations,
agencies, and judges will rarely condone
lying, even if the witness honestly believe
she has good intentions.[2]

Given the forgoing dilemmas, how
does a clinician balance these risks and
conflicting interests? If a significant part
of your mandate is to collect evidence,
this takes precedence in the way that
you gather and store information. If
your primary role is that of a helping
professional, then your records should be
designed primarily to meet your needs
as a treating clinician. Bear in mind the
potential legal pitfalls. In many fields of
practice there are few conflicts between
the clinical and legal requirements for
proper record keeping. In areas where
conflicts arise, there may be no ideal
solution.

*Dr. Allan Barsky is Professor of Social Work
at Florida Atlantic University School of
Social Work and Chair of the National Ethics
Committee of the National Association of
Social Workers (NASW). He is the author of
Ethics and Values in Social Work (Oxford
University Press), Conflict Resolution for
the Helping Professions (Brooks/Cole), and
Clinicians in Court (Guilford Press). The
views expressed in this article do not necessar-
ily reflect the views of any organizations with
which Dr. Barsky is affiliated.*

*This article is reprinted from Clinicians in
Court, 2E, by Allan E. Barsky. Reprinted
with permission of The Guilford Press, New
York © 2012 The Guilford Press.*

[2]The types of rare examples include necessity (e.g., lying in order to prevent a person from being killed when
there is no other alternative) or to escape pernicious
treatment by a rogue state (e.g., Jews and other perse-
cuted people who lied to escape Nazi Germany).

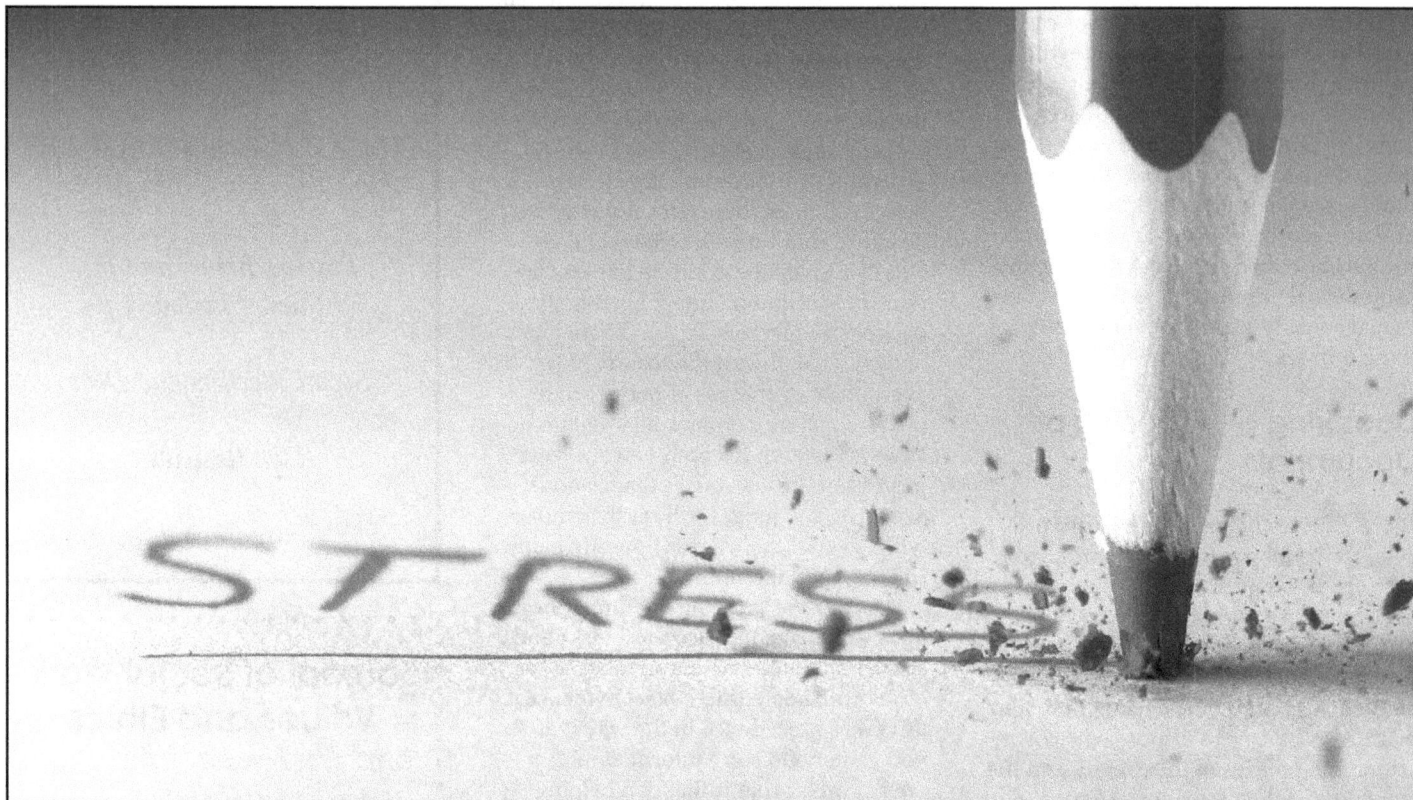

## What I Wish I Had Known: Burnout and Self-Care in Our Social Work Profession
### by SaraKay Smullens, MSW, LCSW, CGP, CFLE, BCD

*Editor's Note: Although burnout, compassion fatigue, and vicarious trauma can occur at any level of practice, it is especially relevant to learn about them in preparation for one's first experience in the field—otherwise known as field placement!*

The training to become a social worker is arduous, demanding, and complex. My concentration was clinical social work, which during my graduate education was known as casework. I well remember studying my basic curriculum; taking more electives than were required; receiving excellent supervision of my clinical work with individuals, couples, families, and groups; and before it was required, taking many continuing education classes.

Suffice it to say, I learned a great deal—but what it seemed that no one shared with me during these years, or seemed to discuss among themselves as either teachers or therapists, was the sheer exhaustion experienced in clinical

work as we do our very best to meet the needs of others day after day, year after year. When one of my deeply trusted supervisors died, and I met his wife for the first time, she told me that sometimes he would return home too exhausted to even speak, and that a frequent statement she heard from a man who obviously treasured his clinical work, teaching, and writing was: "They feel better, but I surely do not." How well I understood this feeling, I thought. How well so many in our field must understand this feeling. And yet many of us lack the attendant knowledge that can assess and direct this feeling, which is called "burnout" in the literature—or knowledge of the necessary practices to heal and soothe ourselves, which are collectively known as "self-care." What I have learned over the years is the necessity of addressing this complicated exhaustion before the feeling of depletion leads to dysfunction and beyond. With this in mind, I share the precise information that I wish I had known about "burn-

out" and "self care" in the early years of my work, with references for your further study.

### The Problem of Burnout

"Burnout" as a term was first applied by Freudenberger (1975) to describe what happens when a practitioner becomes increasingly "inoperative." According to Freudenberger, this progressive state of inoperability can take many different forms, from simple rigidity, in which "the person becomes 'closed' to any input," to an increased resignation, irritability, and quickness to anger. As burnout worsens, however, its effects turn more serious. An individual may become paranoid or self-medicate with legal or illegal substances. Eventually, a social worker afflicted with burnout may leave a promising career that he or she has worked very hard to attain or be removed from a position by a forced resignation or firing.

In the intervening 37 years, burnout has been the focus of several studies, each of which has affirmed the phenomenon (van der Vennet, 2002). We may instinctively realize that therapeutic work is "grueling and demanding" with "moderate depression, mild anxiety, emotional exhaustion, and disrupted relationships" as some of its frequent, yet common, effects (Norcross, 2000). We may even have gotten used to some of the factors promoting burnout such as "inadequate supervision and mentorship, glamorized expectations...and acute performance anxiety" (Skovholt, Grier, & Hanson, 2001). Yet, as social workers, we may still not pay full attention to the reality of burnout until suddenly everything seems overwhelming. At such times, we may lack the knowledge of what is transpiring or the critical faculties to assess our experience objectively that would enable us to take proper measures to restore balance to our lives.

To explore and understand the phenomenon of burnout before it is too late, researchers have found it useful to introduce several components of the term or attendant syndromes, specifically compassion fatigue, vicarious trauma, and secondary traumatic stress. Although there is a great deal of overlap among these terms, each of them poses a particular risk and originates from a different place in the practitioner's experience or psychology.

## Compassion Fatigue

Compassion fatigue is perhaps the most general term of the three and describes "the overall experience of emotional and physical fatigue that social service professionals experience due to chronic use of empathy when treating patients who are suffering in some way" (Newell & MacNeil, 2010). There is evidence that compassion fatigue increases when a social worker sees that a client is not "getting better" (Corcoran, 1987). Yet, a large part of compassion fatigue is built directly into the fabric of the kind of work we do. Although we may strive for a relationship with our clients that is collaborative, our goal is not a relationship that is reciprocal. In many important ways, reciprocity is unethical, even illegal. Although recognizing this fact can lead to an important setting of boundaries, including financial boundaries (charging clients, collecting co-pays), or deciding how missed appointments are handled, compassion fatigue may reflect a deeper

"inability to say no," one of the hazards that "can exacerbate the difficult nature of the work" (Skovholt, Grier, & Hanson, 2001).

In our work, although we are surrounded by people all day long, there is not a balanced give and take. Concentration is on clients, not ourselves. In the truest sense, we are alone—we are the givers, and our fulfillment comes from seeing the growth, hope, and new direction in those with whom we are privileged to work. The fulfillment of our professional commitment demands that we ever do our best and give as much as possible in the ethical ways that are the underpinnings of the social work profession. With this awareness, common sense predicts that burnout is a potential threat waiting for us in the wings. However, as we all know, common sense and clear thinking can be eroded when our own unfinished emotional business propels us. Although there are many therapists who describe fulfilling childhoods that are secure and stable, research indicates that the majority who come into our field have known profound pain and loss during their formative years (Elliott & Guy, 1993). Most have experienced one or a combination of five patterns of emotional abuse, which has led to the relentless need to give to others what we wish we had received, coupled by an inability to care for oneself and set limits in order to counteract exhaustion (Smullens, 2010). Social workers, therefore, are especially prone to compassion fatigue, not only because of the nature of our work, but often because our own natures have inspired us to enter this precise field.

## Vicarious Trauma and Secondary Traumatic Stress

Vicarious trauma (also known by the closely related term "secondary traumatic stress") results from a social worker's direct exposure to victims of trauma. Unlike compassion fatigue, vicarious trauma may have a more immediate onset (Newell & MacNeil, 2010), as such exposure triggers the immediate re-experiencing of painful occasions from the practitioner's personal history. As mentioned above, social workers are far more likely to have painful personal histories than those working in other professions or vocations. Elliott & Guy (1993) found, for example, that women working in the mental health professions were more frequently traumatized as children by physical abuse, alcoholism,

emotional and sexual abuse, and familial conflict than were women working in other fields. Additionally, women therapists appear to come from more chaotic families of origin, with significantly lesser experiences of familial cohesion, moral emphasis, and achievement orientation.

Although I have separated vicarious trauma from compassion fatigue for ease of categorization, it is quite likely that they influence each other—that is, vicarious trauma provokes and promotes compassion fatigue, while the origins of compassion fatigue—an inability to establish proper boundaries—can be found in the social worker's trauma history. Unfinished emotional business can involve all aspects of our personal and professional lives. Do we have issues with members of our family of origin that are unresolved and drain present relationships, keeping us from seeing clearly? Do we long to do the impossible for a deceased or suffering parent? Do we long to establish closeness with a family member who has continuously made it clear that this is not a mutual desire? Are there present issues regarding a partner, or sexual preference? Are we struggling to find the intimacy we crave, yet still eludes us? The list, in myriad forms, can go on and on. It is essential to remember that when our clients bring these very same issues to us that we have not faced, burnout and the depression that accompanies it can and will set in, leading to emotional exhaustion, depersonalization, and a decreased sense of personal accomplishments.

Through the agencies of compassion fatigue and vicarious trauma, burnout systematically decreases our ability to relate to our clients, which strikes at the heart of our self-identification as a healer or positive force in society. This in turn results in increased disaffection for our work, disconnection, and isolation. This isolation may in fact already be present; Koeske and Koeske (1989) found that in addition to demanding work loads, one of the causes for burnout was low social support, particularly low coworker support.

Fortunately, as Poulin & Walter (1993) noted in their one-year study of nearly a thousand social workers, just as burnout is associated with personal and professional factors, adjustment to those factors prevents future or further burnout from occurring. Further, it can reverse burnout that has occurred. In other words, there is a cure for burnout—not a permanent cure, or a cure-all, but a process that can be engaged to restore balance in our personal and professional lives. That cure is self-care.

## Self-Care as the Antidote to Burnout

Lately, there has been increased attention on the concept of self-care–the balancing activities in which social workers can engage to preserve personal longevity and happiness, their relationships, and their careers. These activities of self-care span a wide range and can include: receiving support from mentors or a peer group, the importance of relaxation (including vacations), personal endeavors that are non-professional activities, and the need to balance wellness with one's professional life.

By engaging in self-care, we can assert our right to be well and reintroduce our own needs into the equation. Hearing this call may be a difficult first step, as social workers might feel guilt about needing to take care of ourselves–especially since, as was pointed out previously, mental health workers are more likely to "come from chaotic families of origin" where they adopted codependent/parenting roles.

In a study comparing psychotherapists and physicists, psychotherapists were significantly more likely to perceive themselves as assuming a care-taking role than were physicists (Fussell & Bonney, 1990). The same study showed that psychotherapists also experienced significantly more parent-child role inversion (parentification) than did the physicists. This does not mean that the caregiver choice of career is a negative thing; it can be a healthy and healing choice, once we recognize the need to engage in self-care. When we do embrace self-care, we find many different strategies at our disposal that span the entire gamut of human experience. There are self-care solutions in the emotional, physical, social, intellectual, sexual, and spiritual dimensions of life that underscore our humanity.

There have been several attempts to categorize self-care strategies, notably: Mahoney (1997) and Norcross (2000). Norcross outlines 10 self-care strategies, including seemingly obvious–yet incredibly valuable–pieces of advice, such as recognizing the hazards of psychological practice and beginning with self-awareness and self-liberation. Three of Nor-

cross's strategies are of special note, and I will now discuss these in greater detail.

### 1. Employ stimulus control and counterconditioning when possible.

This strategy is actually two common sense, personal organization strategies in one, which I refer to as "necessary selective gifts to oneself" in a setting where you will spend more daytime hours than you spend at home. The first, "creating a professional greenhouse at work" (Skovholt, Grier, & Hanson, 2001), involves decisions such as the resolve to eat lunch at one's desk as little as possible, the importance of social exchange as well as a comfortable chair, providing calming music as background for writing and thinking, and taking plants to your office. (A personal aside about plants: I well know that forgetting to water them is a sure wake-up call that you are not giving yourself what you need.)

> By engaging in self-care, we can assert our right to be well and reintroduce our own needs into the equation.

The second part of this strategy is the "counterconditioning" that physical activities, healing modalities, and the diversion of reading and films, to cite some examples, can provide. Is there a gym you can visit first thing in the morning or after hours? Would it center you to visit a place for worship during your lunch break or on your way home? Would you like to hear a book-on-tape at certain hours? In one study of self-care strategies, Mahoney (1997) reported pleasure reading, physical exercise, hobbies/artistic pursuits, and recreational vacations as the most commonly reported self-care activities, followed by practicing meditation and prayer, doing volunteer work, and keeping a personal diary.

### 2. Seek personal therapy.

Nearly 90% of mental health workers seek personal therapy before, during, and after their professional training (Mahoney, 1997). In addition, more than 90% of those who do seek personal therapy derive satisfaction and growth from their experiences therein, creating more fulfilling lives (Norcross, 2000). Toward this end, when we need consultation, we must seek it; and if such consultation directs us

to deeper psychological work, we must not deny this necessity

### 3. Diversify, diversify, diversify.

Whereas clinical responsibilities can totally deplete us, we can also use our hard won skills in various ways that replenish us. Many find balance, camaraderie, and stimulation through ongoing discussion groups with colleagues. Others find it by shifting client focus. For instance, those of us concentrating primarily in group therapy can also turn to individual, conjoint, and family therapy for a small part of our practice. I have found it invigorating to combine marital work and group therapy in an unusual way. For marital clients with complex problems, I place the couple in separate groups, trying to find one in each group who will remind each of his or her partner.

Another important sustaining resource is to use hard won skills in areas other than clinical practice. A few years ago, for example, I became a clinical consultant to a local Philadelphia theater company, meeting with directors and cast members to discuss the lives of actual clients (disguising all recognizable aspects of lives, of course) that parallel lives and events in the plays. My most memorable experience was consulting work done on the very controversial play *Blackbird,* by David Harrower. *Blackbird* is a play about sexual abuse, as well as the pain and loneliness that can lead to this horrific act. One of the most poignant moments in my professional life occurred during a TalkBack for this play, when an audience member confided that she had been abused, and her assailant had never owned this abuse or apologized. But she explained that events in this play felt as if an apology had been made to her, and would help her to heal.

My life and work have taught me that the strongest lesson in avoiding burnout through self-care is to accept that we are human, and in that we are each limited and–yes–flawed. Despite best intentions and very hard work, we will each experience failure, and our losses and the losses of those dear to us will bring the most unbearable pain imaginable.

Yet, with all of the pain and loss of life, we can, if we will it, grow and learn and move forward in our life journey. If we hold on to this, we can understand how important self-care is. It will give us the strength to claim the joys of living and endure what we must. And it will help us to assure that our clients are able, whenever possible, to do the same.

## References

Corcoran, K. J. (1987). The association of burnout and social work practitioners' impressions of their clients. *Journal of Social Service Research, 10* (1), 57-66.

Elliott, D. M., & Guy, J. D. (1993). Mental health professionals versus non-mental-health professionals: Childhood trauma and adult functioning. *Professional Psychology: Research and Practice, 24* (1), 83-90.

Freudenberger, H. J. (1975). The staff burn-out syndrome in alternative institutions. *Psychotherapy: Theory, Research and Practice, 12* (1), 73-82.

Fussell, F. W., & Bonney, W. C. (1990). A comparative study of childhood experiences of psychotherapists and physicists: Implications for clinical practice. *Psychotherapy, 27* (4), 505-512.

Koeske, G. F., & Koeske, R. D. (1989). Workload and burnout: Can social support and perceived accomplishment help? *Social Work, 34* (3), 243-248.

Mahoney, M. J. (1997). Psychotherapists' personal problems and self-care patterns. *Professional Psychology: Research and Practice, 28* (1), 14-16.

Newell, J. M., & MacNeil, G. (2010). Professional burnout, secondary traumatic stress, and compassion fatigue: A review of theoretical terms, risk factors, and preventive methods for clinicians. *Best Practices in Mental Health: An International Journal, 6* (2), 57-68.

Norcross, J. C. (2000). Psychotherapist self-care: Practitioner-tested, research-informed strategies. *Professional Psychology: Research and Practice, 31* (6), 710-713.

Poulin, J. & Walter, C. (1993). Social worker burnout: A longitudinal study. *Social Work Research & Abstracts, 29* (4), 5-11.

Skovholt, T. M., Grier, T. L., & Hanson, M. R. (2001). Career counseling for longevity: Self-care and burnout prevention strategies for counselor resilience. *Journal of Career Development, 27* (3), 167-176.

Smullens, S. (2010). The codification and treatment of emotional abuse in structured group therapy. *International Journal of Group Psychotherapy 60* (1), 111-130.

van der Vennet, R. (2002). A study of mental health workers in an art therapy group to reduce secondary trauma and burnout. *Dissertation Abstracts International, 63* (9-B), 4389. (UMI No. 3065615).

*SaraKay Smullens, MSW, LCSW, CGP, CFLE, BCD, whose private and pro bono clinical social work practice is in Philadelphia, is a certified group psychotherapist and family life educator. She is a recipient of a Lifetime Achievement Award from the Pennsylvania chapter of NASW, which recognized her longstanding community organization, advocacy, and activism, as well as the codification of patterns of emotional abuse and the development of the model to address it. SaraKay is the best-selling author of* Whoever Said Life Is Fair: A Guide to Growing Through Life's Injustices *and* Setting YourSelf Free: Breaking the Cycle of Emotional Abuse in Family, Friendships, Work, and Love.

# Homeless Education: Providing Stable Education for Children and Youth in Transition

## By Sonya O. Hunte, MSW

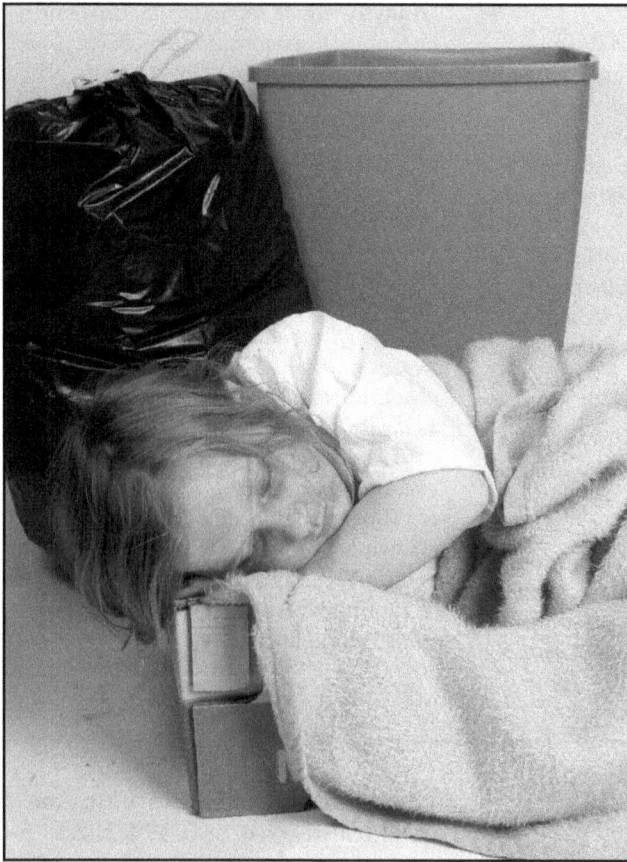

*A*mericans were astonished as they viewed the *60 Minutes* special, *Hard Times Generation: Families Living in Cars*. The special focused on the issue of family homelessness in central Florida. Particularly highlighted were children and youth facing homelessness in the Seminole County school district. There was hope in the story—the resilience of families and the efforts of Homeless Education Liaison, Beth Davalos.

*Meet homeless child, John Scofield, Jr., who is six years of age. John and Yvette Scofield had been having marital discord for some time. One Friday evening, the argument escalated, and John hit Yvette—a bruised eye, cheek, and lip resulted. Scared for her life and that of John Jr., Yvette fled the home. Mrs. Scofield left her home scared and without any income or access to monetary resources. Yvette's friend volunteered at a domestic violence shelter, Renewed Hope, about two years earlier in a neighboring county. After living in her car for two nights, Yvette checked into that very shelter on Sunday morning. Fearing returning to her old neighborhood*

*and John Jr.'s school, Yvette asked her case manager about other school options for John Jr. After all, Yvette wanted John Jr. to have a consistent education, despite their now transitional state. The shelter case manager recalled information from a McKinney-Vento training given by the local school district's Homeless Education Liaison at the shelter site. The case manager shared with Yvette that John Jr. could attend the school zoned for the shelter. John Jr. was registered and attended classes at his new school that Monday morning with guidance from the school social worker and registrar.*

Homeless education is a movement mostly known to school-based and child welfare social workers. Guided by the McKinney-Vento Homeless Assistance Act, this form of education seeks to provide parameters for eliminating barriers to school enrollment, attendance, and academic success for children and youth facing homelessness. Named after Representatives Stewart B. McKinney of Connecticut and Bruce F. Vento of Minnesota, the McKinney-Vento Act's purpose is to close the achievement gap of students in transition with accountability, flexibility, and choice, so no child is left behind. This law, reauthorized as Title X, Part C, of the No Child Left Behind Act in January 2002, defines homelessness and provides school-based services targeting the needs of those who are in transition.

Since 2007, Americans have been feeling the effects of the housing crisis. Daily media messages on the debt ceiling, increasing unemployment rates, job availability, and the housing market's implications confirm what we already know—there is an economic downturn. These factors matter and greatly influence the issue of homelessness in America. In particular, family homeless-

ness brings additional factors like educating children into play.

According to the National Center on Family Homelessness, America's Youngest Outcasts 2010, there are 1.6 million children facing homelessness each year. The U.S. Department of Education reports that in the school year 2009, 954,914 children and youth were considered homeless. The McKinney-Vento Act is an intersection of the child welfare, education, housing, health care, and other social welfare systems.

The Act explicitly defines those who lack fixed, regular, and adequate nighttime shelter as homeless. The Act further discusses the types of nighttime residences that would qualify a student as being homeless. Those residences are hotels and motels, shelters and transitional facilities, unsheltered and living spaces not fit for human habitation, families who are doubled up with another family because of economic hardship, and children awaiting foster care. Each state has the ability to create statewide policy and legislation in an effort to provide an explicit definition on awaiting foster care. Children who are in foster care cannot be considered McKinney-Vento eligible; however, there are supports for this population directed by the Fostering Connections Act. Also covered under this Act are unaccompanied youth, students who are not in the physical custody of a parent or guardian.

*Meet Nichole Porowsky, age 20, who has been couch surfing for the past three months. She had been thrown out by her parents after disclosing that she was four months pregnant. Nichole found herself living under a bridge after running out of friends who allowed her to stay at their place. Nichole walked into StandUp For Kids, an organization that provides resources for youth who mainly live on the street. After meeting Kendra, a volunteer with StandUp For Kids, Nichole decided to enroll in school as a part of her independence plan.*

*Nichole had not been to school in the previous three months, although she was four classes shy of receiving her high school diploma. Kendra contacted the Kings County Public School System's Homeless Education Liaison for assistance. Within hours, Nichole* was enrolled in school and given school supplies and a bus pass. The liaison also made a referral for Nichole to meet with a doula and social worker at the Second Chance Homes as a supportive housing option. The homeless liaison was able to contact the Second Chance Homes, because she established a formal community partnership after a review of data indicated that unaccompanied youth who were either parents or expecting a child dropped out of school for a lack of parenting supports. The Memorandum of Understanding between Second Chance Homes and the school district outlined that eligible students would receive a doula, available housing, life skills training, and free child care for the duration of their time in school. Nichole was also introduced to her school social worker for additional school and community based supports.

Each school district is charged and mandated by law to identify a staff member called the Homeless Education Liaison. The liaison's role is to identify and provide supports for students facing transition. Supports take on many forms, including technical assistance to parents and school administration, data coordination, grant writing and monitoring, and program development. This person, typically a social worker, has the opportunity to provide supports to ensure that each homeless student is able to remain in school and thrive. The work is not done in isolation, but in partnership with internal and external stakeholders. The stakeholders include but are not limited to parents, school nutrition, housing agencies, shelters, and the local Continuum of Care. Liaisons are provided technical assistance by state Departments of Education, homeless education consultants, and the National Association for the Education of Homeless Children and Youth.

Stable educational environments provide children with social and supportive relationships with peers, educators, and the community that surrounds the school. Steady education is mostly maintained by providing transportation, social services, and educational enrichment opportunities for homeless students. Often, when families are forced to move frequently, children may attend a few different schools within a school year. Homeless students are typically provided with transportation supports to remain in their school of origin. The school of origin is the school that the child attended when permanently housed or the last school of attendance. There are times when attending a new school may be a better fit for

a student. For example, when a family is fleeing a domestic violence perpetrator, it may be in the student's best interest to attend a new school where he or she is least likely to be located by the harmful party.

In summary, if you know a family that meets the above definition of homelessness, utilize their school district's Homeless Education Liaison as a resource. The McKinney-Vento law makes provisions and supports students who are in transition by providing transportation, educational, and social service supports to result in a stable and successful education. The ultimate goals of the McKinney-Vento Homeless Assistance Act are to have students be promoted in grade, meet and exceed standardized test requirements, graduate from high school, become gainfully employed, and be active citizens.

For additional resources on McKinney-Vento, visit:

McKinney-Vento full text and Policy Guidance: *http://center.serve.org/nche/*

National Association for the Education of Homeless Children and Youth (NAE-HCY): *http://www.naechy.org*

National Law Center on Homelessness and Poverty (NLCHP): *http://www.nlchp.org*

## References

Bassuk, E. L., Murphy, C., Thompson Coupe, N., Kenney, R. R., & Beach, C. A. (2011, December). State Report Card of Child Homelessness: America's Youngest Outcasts 2010. The National Center on Family Homelessness. Retrieved April 20, 2012, from *http://www.homelesschildrenamerica.org/media/NCFH_AmericaOutcast2010_web.pdf.*

Pelley, S. (2011, November 27). Hard times generation: Families living in cars. 60 Minutes. Retrieved April 20, 2012, from *http://www.cbsnews.com/8301-18560_162-57330802/hard-times-generation-families-living-in-cars/?tag=currentVideoInfo;videoMetaInfo.*

Webb, J. (2011, January 26). Assistant Deputy Secretary to participate in homeless count in Durham, North Carolina. U.S. Department of Education. Retrieved April 20, 2012, from *http://www.ed.gov/news/media-advisories/assistant-deputy-secretary-participate-homeless-count-durham-north-carolina.*

*Sonya O. Hunte, MSW, is a Homeless Education Liaison with the Atlanta Public Schools. Her social work career has spanned over a decade in direct service and program management within child welfare, juvenile justice, and education settings. She is a speaker, author, social service consultant, and entrepreneur, serving as the CEO of Hunte Community Development Consulting LLC.*

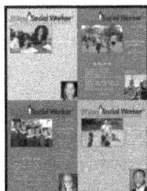

# Workplace Safety for Social Workers: A Student's Analysis and Opinion

*by Shannon Alther, MSW*

Workplace safety is a significant concern for many social workers. According to a study by the Center for Health Workforce Studies and the National Association of Social Workers (NASW) in 2004, 10,000 licensed social workers were surveyed on workplace safety, and 44% of the respondents felt that they were "faced with personal safety issues in their primary employment practice" (http://workforce.socialworkers.org/whatsnew/safety.pdf). Another national study of NASW members in 2005 indicates even more disturbing results for social workers (http://www.naswma.org/displaycommon.cfm?an=1&subarticlenbr=51). Of 1,029 NASW members surveyed, "62% had been subjected to psychological aggression within the previous year, with 85.5% experiencing this at some point in their careers; and 14.7% had experienced physical assault perpetrated by clients in the previous year, with 30.2% having experienced it at some point in their career" (http://www.naswma.org/displaycommon.cfm? an=1&subarticlenbr=51).

Other studies have shown rates indicating that 50-88% of social workers have experienced violence in the workplace (Spencer & Munch, 2003). These rates are alarmingly high, especially throughout the course of a social worker's career (http://www.naswma.org/displaycommon.cfm?an=1&subarticlenbr=51).

## Discussion

As a master's level, second-year social work student researching this issue, I kept coming back to several questions. If workplace safety is such a concern, why hasn't my field agency taken time to train us on safety matters more thoroughly? Why hasn't this issue been addressed at school in our curriculum? Why haven't we learned skills to keep clients and ourselves safe? Why don't we have stronger penalties for crimes committed against social workers? And why isn't there more literature and research addressing workplace violence for social workers?

My thoughts on these questions initially led me back to the core values of social work.

We are trained as social workers to look for our clients' strengths, to advocate for them and to offer hope, but we are not trained to assess the client's potential to harm us and to advocate for our own safety needs. Is it that we overlook ourselves to better serve our clients? One possible answer to this question, according to Weaver, is that social workers are in denial about the potential for violence, because it allows them to do their jobs without being fearful (Blank, 2005).

My research on this topic shows that there are a variety of factors that contribute to social workers not advocating for their safety, particularly within

> If we truly want to take care of our clients, we must change our thinking to also include taking care of ourselves.

the agency setting. As Spencer and Munch (2003) discuss, there are several studies that show that social workers underreport incidents of client violence. There are many factors that may lead to underreporting, including agency attitudes about safety, agency reporting requirements, and social worker beliefs about the nature of the job (Spencer & Munch, 2003). Many agencies do not give workplace safety a high enough priority by developing a safety plan, or by training staff on risk assessment skills, verbal de-escalation techniques, and non-violent self-defense (see http://www.naswma.org/displaycommon.cfm?an=1&subarticlenbr=51).

My own experiences and research indicate that social workers receive little training on workplace safety and crisis management, compared to other professions. For example, when I was working in a rural elementary school last year for my field placement, we participated in regularly scheduled lock down drills to practice what to do in the event of an intruder entering the school or a violent encounter. In contrast, my current mental health agency placement does not

have a "violence plan," nor do we practice what to do in a violent encounter. The most training I have received at my agency is instruction to find a supervisor in the event that a client escalates or becomes aggressive. There has been virtually no communication on basic safety practices, such as de-escalation skills, non-violent forms of self-defense, risk reduction, or a safety plan of action, and to my knowledge we do not have a safety manual, even though we have a safety committee (Saturno, 2012; http://www.socialworkers.org/profession/centennial/violence.htm). In my field placement, I have had more instruction on what to do during a fire than I have had on what to do when a client escalates or becomes aggressive.

Another profession that receives a significant amount of training on mental health crisis situations is law enforcement. In some jurisdictions, police officers receive 40 hours of training in de-escalation skills and managing crisis situations, through the Crisis Intervention Team (CIT) training curriculum (Oliva, Morgan & Compton, 2010). CIT focuses on effective communication, which includes de-escalation skills such as active listening, using open and closed ended questions, using mirroring and summarizing statements, and role playing. In addition, the police officers are observed and reviewed during role plays by an expert panel, to improve their skills. Even though police officers may encounter more mental health crisis situations than social workers, the disparity in training is significant.

Social work schools could use training techniques in their practice courses to enhance their teaching, by utilizing the skills already learned of active listening, using questioning, mirroring and summarizing statements, and applying them to crisis situations and role playing. De-escalation skills would be useful to help students learn how to defuse anger with clients before the situation potentially becomes violent.

Even though social worker safety is not really addressed in schools, a study by Criss (2009) indicates that of 595 social work students surveyed, "41.7%

directly experienced client violence during their practicum. The highest rate of the violence reported by students was verbal abuse (37.5%) while the lowest rate of reported violence was physical assault (3.5%)." In another study by Agbai-olunkwa (2002), data indicate that 42.9% of MSW students felt that "they were inadequately prepared by classroom experience to handle threats to their personal safety in field placement." Social work schools leave the responsibility of teaching workplace safety up to placement agencies (Spencer & Munch, 2003). However, not all agencies have good safety policies and worker training in place.

The emphasis on workplace safety is lacking within our agencies and in our professional organizations. According to the NASW *Code of Ethics,* there is no ethical standard for social workers to implement workplace safety; however, social workers are ethically bound to "advocate for changes in policy and legislation to improve social conditions in order to meet basic human needs and promote social justice" (http://www.naswdc.org/pubs/code/code.asp). So we, as social workers, are bound to advocate for our clients and the community, but we ultimately ignore our own basic needs for safety and social justice.

According to the NASW, advocating for workplace safety for social workers falls under this standard for Social and Political Action (http://www.socialworktoday.com/archive/exc_032511.shtml). Essentially, by not advocating for ourselves, we are not being ethical. Even though workplace safety has not taken a prominent role in our professional organizations and many of our work settings, more attention has been given to this issue within the last 12 years (since 2000). According to a library search of peer-reviewed articles using the search terms "workplace safety" and "social workers," from 1950 to 2012, there was one relevant article published in 2007. Even though articles in the peer reviewed literature are virtually nonexistent, there have been several informal articles written about this subject since 2003 (see references). This shift in focus has occurred as a result of several social worker deaths across the country that were due to client violence from 2004-2008 (http://www.naswma.org/displaycommon.cfm?an=1&subarticlenbr=51).

Currently, there is legislation at the state and national levels that has been proposed or enacted to address safety issues after the deaths of these social workers–the Teri Zenner Social Work Safety Act (national), The Social Worker Safety Bill (West Virginia), The Boni Frederick Bill (Kentucky), and An Act to Promote the Public Health Through Workplace Safety for Social Workers. This legislation addresses issues on several fronts, from increasing penalties for physical crimes committed against social workers to increasing funding to provide safety measures, and requiring workplaces to provide safety plans and conduct risk assessments. The Terri Zenner Social Work Safety Act is still waiting for passage, and currently only three states have guidelines for promoting workplace safety for social workers, notably California, New Jersey, and Washington (http://www.naswma.org/displaycommon.cfm?an=1&subarticlenbr=51).

## Conclusion

Violence against social workers is a significant problem and can lead to a social worker being ineffective in practice (Spencer & Munch, 2003). If we truly want to take care of our clients, we must change our thinking to also include taking care of ourselves. Even though the chances of an assault becoming a fatality are low, we must address the emotional and physical consequences to ourselves, particularly with regard to verbal abuse and physical aggression (Sioco, 2010). It is up to us as social workers to advocate for ourselves and to educate ourselves on de-escalation skills, risk assessment, safety planning, non-violent forms of self-defense, and to promote workplace safety within our agencies and advocate for protective legislation.

Our schools need to teach us how to protect ourselves and our clients, so we can continue to help individuals and communities and practice within our knowledge base. We need to give ourselves the same care and attention that we give our clients, and our agencies, schools, communities–and professional organizations need to support us in our endeavors.

## References

Agbai-Olunkwa, M. (2002). Female MSW students' perceptions of personal safety in field placement. *Masters Abstracts International, 40* (2), 353-442.

Blank, B. T. (2005). Safety first: Paying heed to and preventing professional risks. *The New Social Worker.* http://www.socialworker.com/home/Feature_Articles/General/Safety_First%3A_Paying_Heed_to_and_Preventing_Professional_Risks/.

Criss, P. M. (2009). Prevalence of client violence against social work students and its effects on fear of future violence, occupational commitment, and career withdrawal intentions. *Dissertation.* ISBN: 978-1-1096-2129-7.

National Association of Social Workers. *About NASW: Code of ethics.* http://www.naswdc.org/pubs/code/code.asp.

National Association of Social Workers. Center for workforce studies. http://workforce.socialworkers.org/whatsnew/safety.pdf.

National Association of Social Workers Massachusetts. *Creating a climate of safety.* http://www.naswma.org/displaycommon.cfm?an=1&subarticlenbr=51.

National Association of Social Workers Massachusetts. *Committee for the study and prevention of violence against social workers: Safety guidelines.* http://www.socialworkers.org/profession/centennial/violence.htm.

Oliva, J., Morgan, R., & Compton, M. (2010). A practical overview of de-escalation skills in law enforcement: Helping individuals in crisis while reducing police liability and injury. *Journal of Police Crisis Negotiations, 10,* 15-29.

Saturno, S. (2012). *Violent crime and social worker safety.* http://www.socialworktoday.com/archive/exc_032511.shtml.

Sioco, M. (2010). Safety on the job: How managers can help workers. *Children's Voice (March/April),* 20-23.

Spencer, P., & Munch, S. (2003). Client violence toward social workers: The role of management in community mental health programs. *Social Work, 48* (4), 532-542.

*Shannon Alther graduated with her MSW in May 2012. She wrote this article as part of her coursework. She has an interest in clinical social work and school social work. She lives with her children and husband in Connecticut. She can be reached at shannon.alther@charter.net.*

# Evidence of Time Machines
## by Rich Kenney, MSSW

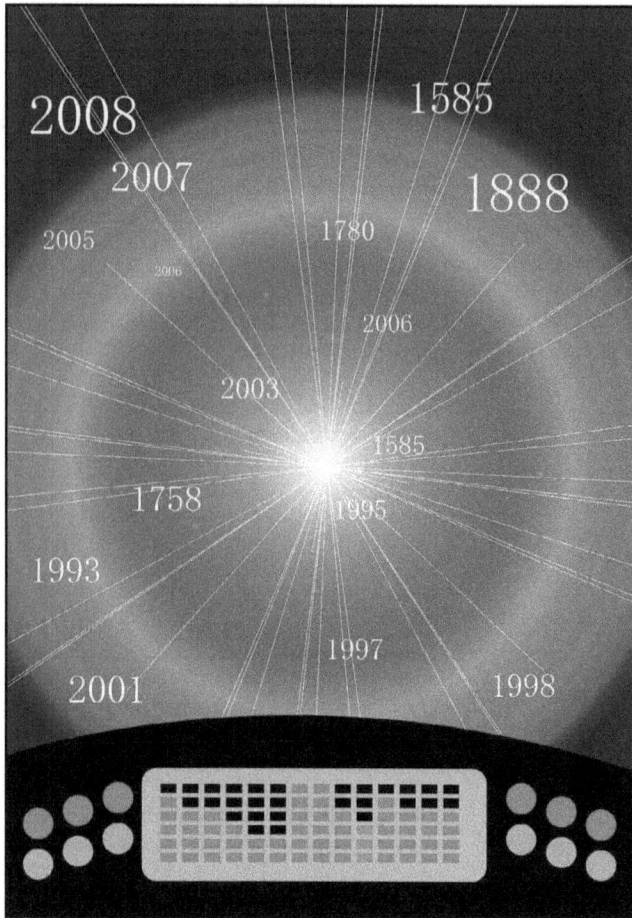

2008  1585
2007  1888
2005  1780
2006
2006
2003
1585
1758  1995
1993
1997
2001  1998

*We all have our time machines, don't we?*
*Those that take us back are memories.... And*
*those that carry us forward, are dreams.*
*Uber-Morlock from the movie,*
*The Time Machine*

Who needs wormholes or cosmic strings when you have a slide trombone and a bag of cotton? Postulates of special relativity and concepts of the Alcubierre drive are beyond my comprehension. They fall within the realm of physics and, like wormholes and cosmic strings, are related to theories pertaining to time travel. I am not a physicist; I am a social worker. What I do know, however, is that time travel is not just for scientists. Hospice social workers can dabble in time machines, too. At least, I do.

For the past few years, I have been working with hospice patients in Oklahoma. Hospice is an option for people when their life-limiting illnesses no longer respond to cure-oriented treatments. In addition to assisting patients and their families with end-of-life issues and care, I help them to return to the past.

While physicists look for ways to apply the possibilities of quantum mechanics and symmetric polygon arrangements, I explore the realities of the powers of old paintbrushes and Klingon warrior swords. These are some of the time travel tools I use in life review, the process of looking back to the past with the goal of bringing new meaning and perspective into the present. It provides hospice patients with opportunities to recount and re-evaluate their life stories.

## A Bag of Cotton

"There's an animal in Gloretha's house and it's not hers."

That was the part of the nurse's telephone message I kept thinking about while driving to Muskogee from Tulsa to see Gloretha, a petite, ninety-one-year-old woman with emphysema. In reading her chart earlier that day, I learned that she lived alone in a "cluttered and unclean abode." Another report noted that, despite her breathing difficulties, she was "feisty and frank."

When I sat on Gloretha's worn couch after giving her my business card, dust quickly filled the room.

"I don't want no prayers or bedpans," she said. "I want to live my last days. I want to smoke Pall Malls at the casino."

"Casino?" I asked.

"Slots at the Hard Rock every Friday," she said. "Cab takes me."

Pots and pans rattled down the hallway.

"That cat again," she said, sensing my surprise. "He come up from the hole under my sink. Follow me."

Gloretha led me into her kitchen, then leaned against the counter. "Go ahead," she said, pointing to the cabinet.

I gripped the handle and cautiously opened it. Without warning, something grabbed me. Shaken, I turned around.

There was Gloretha, her frail hand clutching my elbow. Her innocent laughter filled the tiny, ramshackle house. It was wondrous... childlike. Then, her long cough, cutting the moment short and reminding us of the present.

Over the next few weeks, I found services to help clean and repair Gloretha's residence. We even found a home for Potsandpans, her kitchen-crashing tomcat. One day, I noticed a bag of cotton hanging from the wall in her living room. Inside were several cotton balls.

"Just a child when I picked it," she told me. "Reminds me when I was young, when times was hard. Cotton brings me back."

Gloretha asked me to hand her the eighty-year-old bag so she could hold the cotton balls. She described the struggles of picking cotton in the fields of Webbers Falls in the late 1920s to earn money for her family.

"Bought my sister a winter coat for six dollars with cotton money," she boasted. "Fought them green worms and grasshoppers all day."

She cupped the balls in her palms. "These remind me to live."

A time machine. Evidence.

## The Sword

Cockroaches fell from the ceiling like scattered raindrops. When one landed on or near Roland, he picked it up and crushed it between his thumb and forefinger.

"Sorry about the bugs," he said, struggling to reposition himself in bed - all four hundred pounds. "One got stuck in my ear last year. Needed surgery to remove it. Flick them my way if they get on you."

I glanced up at the ceiling to see a dozen roaches. Another one crawled along the blade of a sword hanging on the wall beside me.

"That's quite a weapon," I said.

"It's a bat'leth, the one used by Klingon warriors. Remember Star Trek?"

"I do," I said, watching his mood brighten.

"Used to bring that to Trekkie conventions. I was the doorman. Best days of my life."

I took down the crescent-shaped sword and carefully handed it to him.

"Man, I haven't held this in years."

For the next half hour, Roland forgot about the cockroaches and the squalor of his makeshift bedroom separated by a moldy shower curtain from the rest of the rooming house. He forgot about the heart condition, obesity, and severe depression that ruled his life. He was no longer sixty-four and sickly.

"With this, I was somebody," he said. "No one made fun of me."

In the weeks that followed, Roland was somebody—a time travel warrior.

## The Slide Trombone

Edgar was cooking breakfast the first day I visited his apartment. The enticing smell of bacon and pancakes wafted through his slightly opened door. When he didn't answer, I pushed it and called his name.

A wisp of a man stepped out from the kitchen. "You must be the social worker. C'mon in."

I stepped inside the sparsely-furnished living room. An unmade sofa bed faced a stereo system. A jazz album jacket leaned against one of the speakers. There was a music stand and a fold-up, auditorium chair. One framed, black-and-white photograph of a man playing a slide trombone hung on the wall.

"Have a seat in here," he said, waving me into the kitchen and moving aside sheet music from the dinette table.

"Smells good," I said, savoring the scents of the small feast on the stove.

"Oh, I probably won't eat any of this."

As I sat down, I noticed an over-flowing trash bucket containing several days' worth of previous breakfasts.

"I cook this because it reminds me of my Molly," he explained. "Makes me feel like she's right here with me."

Edgar was eighty and dying of pancreatic cancer. His wife had passed away a few weeks earlier.

"Only thing I have left is that sheet music."

I studied a page of penciled notes. "Did you write this?"

"That's what I do," he said. "Better, though, when I have my trombone."

"Where is it?"

"Hock shop," he said. "That's where it goes when I'm running low on cash."

For the next hour, Edgar told me about how he "played with all the jazz heavyweights," like Arnett Cobb and Jimmy McCracklin.

"Played on the Dick Clark Show in the fifties," he said. "Where I met Molly."

The sparkle in Edgar's eyes said it all. I had to find a pawn shop... to see about a time machine.

*A former hospice social worker in Tulsa, Rich Kenney, MSSW, is now director of the Social Work Program and an assistant professor at Chadron State College in Chadron, Nebraska. He is a graduate of the University of Texas with a master's degree in social work, and received a creative writing fellowship in poetry from the Arizona Commission on the Arts.*

*When not writing, Rich enjoys playing chess and shooting birds (with a camera). He's also dabbled in rainbow-spotting from the deserts of Arizona and the meadows of Oklahoma all the way to the sandy beaches of Cape Cod. He and his wife, Linda, live in Chadron, Nebraska.*

# Being Who We Are, Every Day, Everywhere

*by Novia S. Reid, LCSW*

If you can remember the day you announced to your family and friends that you were pursuing a career in social work, how was the news received? Was there excitement, joy, and sincerity believing you were about to embark on a career that would change lives? Or was there concern, doubt, confusion, or wonder? Did you hear: "There is no money in social work." "Why not choose something else?" "Social work? You want to be a social worker?" "Is there nothing else you want to do?"

*Novia and her students at the famous Suncheon Bay for an outing.*

From the moment I entered Miami Dade College in Miami, FL, I declared social work as my major and never once did I change it. When many asked why I chose it, I was not completely sure at the time. The only answer I can remember giving was, "I want to." It was likely not the most convincing answer, but it was the only one I knew. Now, when people ask why I became a social worker, I confidently and genuinely say, "Social work chose me." It is a calling with endless possibilities.

I was aware that social workers were underpaid and undervalued, but what I knew about how much of an impact they had on the lives of others, how they cared for children and families and tried to make the world a better place for those who lived in it—that is what struck the cords of my heart. I wished to become a part of those who had paved the way and helped so many people. In this field, care, compassion, healing, and hope seemed to have no limits. Regardless of the many diverse positions we hold, such as a child protective investiga-

tor, school social worker, therapist, or residential coordinator, our reasons for choosing this career are often the same. Each presents a unique chance to impart changes in the lives of those who need us most.

There are blessings in these occupations, but office politics, unpleasant supervisors, and too much work for one person to handle can often cause these blessings to feel like burdens. Soon it becomes easy to lose the desire that once led you to pursue this great career. Although our desires and hearts can be shattered by the many obstacles we face, there is still a world that needs us to be who we were called to be—"helpers at heart." Not many experience the joy we do, which comes from being who we are at heart. I want to encourage us all that although our profession is not perfect, it is unlike any other. It truly represents a great mission. You could have chosen another profession, but there was something about being a social worker that resounded in your heart.

Always remember that there is remarkability in us! Separate from the various positions we attain, the very essence of who we are is our compassion—our desire to help others and be an inspiring agent of change.

We do not need a title to be who we are. How do I know? I experienced this while being a missionary teacher in South Korea. One day, a student asked me, "What is your profession?" I said, "I am a social worker." She said, "That's why you're so friendly and kind." I paused, and then it dawned on me that here, my title was that of a missionary teacher, not a social worker. Yet, I was recognized by my actions.

Yes, titles are important, because society requires them to recognize our duties, to draw upon the distinctions between ours and other professions, and many other reasons. But one thing titles do not do is define us. Our words and actions do. Being who we are, every day, comes naturally. It is the very reason why we are recognized without declaring our titles. Of all the blessings that come from what we do, that's the greatest!

Take time to remind yourself that when days become hard, cases appear hopeless, and your efforts go unnoticed,

it's people like my student who recognize and appreciate the naturalness of who we are that make it all worthwhile. Consider it an honor to be who you are, primarily because more often than not, people can tell who you are by your character.

We have a gift, and it is a gift that gets noticed by others even when we ourselves are unaware of what gift is being received through us. It is not difficult to be who we are, because the very reasons we chose to become social workers are the very things that my student saw in me when she decided to ask, "Are you a social worker?" When we view being a social worker through the eyes of many we meet, they will say it comes naturally through us, and indeed it does. This is why we are who we are every day, everywhere. There is nothing more beautiful and awe-inspiring than being who you are every day, everywhere. Therefore, take esteem in it!

*Novia S Reid, LCSW, resides in Miami, FL, with her family. She is a licensed clinical social worker with a passion for marital and couples therapy. She has served as a missionary teacher in Suncheon, South Korea.*

# Your Social Work Graduate School Application: 14 Tips To Help You Get an Acceptance Letter

*by Robin R. Wingo, MSW, LISW*

Applying for graduate school is a big step! Whether you are just graduating with your bachelor's in social work or you have been out for a few years, preparing that application takes time, energy, and careful consideration. Your grades are only one indicator of readiness for graduate study. It is highly likely that you will be asked to write a professional statement or essay along with completing a standardized application form. Although some admissions committees conduct personal admissions interviews, your first representation will be in writing, and your readiness will be evaluated on how you present yourself, your experiences, and your professional aspirations.

Every graduate school's application process is different. Some are fully online and others use hardcopy, but they are all looking for the same thing—students who can clearly and thoughtfully make

a case for how they are the best fit for acceptance into that particular graduate program.

As that applicant, you want to be successful, but making the most of the application process is a relatively unexamined process. Each program will provide forms and directions as part of the application, but little direction is provided regarding what works to meet the expectations. The following are some key thoughts for putting your best application forward.

## 1. Don't just download applications!

Each graduate program is looking for students who match its educational mission and goals. Go to the Web site of each program that interests you, and review! Decide whether you are a good fit for that particular program. Applying only to programs that are located close by may not be a successful strategy if you can't make a good case for fit. Take opportunities in the application to write about why you are a good fit.

## 2. Read the application carefully, and follow directions!

That sounds like a no-brainer, but often in the haste to complete an application, key information will be missed or ignored. Use a highlighter to target items that use the words "must," "demonstrate," "provide examples," or "identify." Read the instructions for the professional statement or essay carefully and make note of the expectations!

## 3. Attend a pre-admissions meeting or ask to meet with a faculty member to talk about the program and your fit.

Go prepared! Read the Web site and the application and prepare questions. Make sure you introduce yourself.

## 4. Give yourself ample time to think, write, revise, edit, get feedback from an impartial reviewer, revise, edit, and submit!

Make sure your spelling, syntax, grammar, and punctuation are correct. Make sure your word choices clearly and accurately depict your thinking and that your ideas are presented in a professional manner. As you no, its easy two half misteaks even win wee are being vary careful too due it rite! (sic)

## 5. If you aren't confident about your writing skills, during the application process, you might consider taking a writing class or working with an editor to improve your writing skills.

Graduate students can tell you they do a LOT of writing, and it is a skill you will use in every class.

## 6. If you are applying in your senior year or are a new graduate, keep in mind that the coursework, volunteer experiences, and field practica you completed have increased your knowledge and skills.

Don't underestimate their value! Focus on your strengths and what you have to contribute, rather than on whatever deficits you may think you have. Rather than, "I hope to learn...," think about saying, "I have learned and applied...," or, "The skills I developed have led me to...." Graduate programs are looking for learners who will contribute to the learning environment. Give them examples of what you have to offer!

## 7. If you have been out practicing at the bachelor's level, use your educational and work experience to highlight what you have accomplished, where you are headed professionally, and what you will contribute.

Draw specific examples from your work (without breaching confidentiality) to demonstrate skills, leadership, creativity, ethical practice, and professionalism. Sharing your successes is not bragging!

## 8. Some programs request that a résumé be submitted along with your application.

Make sure it is up-to-date and formatted in a clear manner. Current students can use the college/university career development center for consultation in creating a résumé. Typically, alumna can use the college/university career center, if convenient, for up to a year. Online sites also exist for templates and suggested formats. Consider dropping off employment or activities that occurred in high school or earlier.

## 9. Be honest in your application, your résumé, and your professional statement/essay.

Accurately portray your work experience, skills, and knowledge. If asked to identify challenges or deficits, instead of simply stating, "I overschedule" (for example), frame your response with what you are doing to remediate that—"As overscheduling is a challenge, I am careful to schedule time for completing paperwork and meetings using a day planner."

## 10. Write your professional statement or essay for a specific program.

Generic letters read that way! Some ideas, phrasing, or perspectives may fit with many programs, but tailor your writing to the mission and admissions criteria of each program. And keep the names straight—nothing is more off-putting than to have one's institution referred to by a competitor's name!

## 11. Do you have specialized experience related to a specific part of the program mission?

Do you have professional expertise that would be augmented by study in an area of the curriculum or with a particular faculty member? Do you have experiences that would enhance the student body? Make sure that it is included in your professional statement or essay.

## 12. References are always required!

Applications will likely have reference forms or specific points they want covered by a reference. Be clear about what kind of reference you need. There is a difference between someone who watched you grow up and thinks you are fabulous no matter what you do (personal reference) and a professional reference who can speak to the specific qualities that graduate programs are looking for, such as leadership, ethical behavior, and academic readiness. Supervisors (past or present), instructors (past or present), or colleagues who have had sufficient time to know you and your work are all po-

tential references. Talk to the people you ask to be a professional reference and make sure they are willing to address the specific questions the program is asking. Provide them with your résumé as an information source, and remind them of examples of your work. A letter that specifically addresses your application, the criteria, and your readiness for graduate study can make a difference. After you are accepted, thank them for their help.

## 13. Avoid anything that can make your application and or professional statement or essay difficult to read.

Colorful paper, exotic fonts, and illustrations are not appropriate for this type of writing. A white or linen colored paper, with an easy-to-read font of a reasonable size (Times New Roman, 12 point, for example), printed clearly and cleanly, are good choices.

## 14. Carefully review what should be mailed or done online, and by whom.

Some programs only accept references online, whereas others require them to be mailed in with the application. An 8½ x 11 envelope for mailing is a better choice than folding multiple pages into a legal size envelope.

Realistically, the graduate school application process is competitive, and you may not get in the first time you apply. Don't give up! Sometimes graduate programs will offer you feedback—ask! Attend another information session, if available. Talk with a mentor about how to improve your chances. Talk with the admissions person about classes you can take at a graduate level to demonstrate your readiness and improve your GPA. Work and get additional experience. Developing a relationship with a social work program in your area can help you know if it is a good fit. If you have a BSW/BSSW, consider becoming a field instructor for an undergraduate student. Don't give up! Rework the application and reapply! Many successful social workers did not get into graduate school with their first application!

*Robin R. Wingo, MSW, LISW, joined the Department of Social Work at Minnesota State University, Mankato faculty in 2001. She received her MSW from the University of Missouri-Columbia. She annually reviews applications for admissions to the MSW program.*

# Letters to the Editor

Dear *The New Social Worker Online* Team,

I have been such an immense intermittent benefactor of your collective efforts in regularly bringing out the e-editions of *THE NEW SOCIAL WORKER* ONLINE, that today I have sat down to write this e-mail.

Ms. Linda Grobman, please accept my heartfelt appreciation and thanks. I am roughly 9,000 miles away from you, but I feel so much a part of the concerns of U.S. professional social workers. In each issue, you offer so much to ponder, reflect, and compare. I am a modest learner and teacher of social work at the Faculty of Social Work, The M.S. University in Baroda, Gujarat, India. I feel, although the nature and details of the social problems faced there and here are different, the disciplinary concerns are quite same. But I always felt that the social work education is best imparted in the U.S. We too have tried to indigenize it to suit our ecological requirements, but there is heavy academic sourcing from the U.S. in terms of the books, journals, individual scholars, and so on.

Wishing you, the team, and *THE NEW SOCIAL WORKER ONLINE* all the very best. You are really doing a good work.

Sincerely,
Professor Chhaya Patel

Ms. Grobman,

Thank you so much for offering this valuable resource. I have been accepted into a pre-social work program at Auburn University-Montgomery in Alabama where I live. This newsletter has been so good for me. It allows me to read real-life social work stories, seeing all the good, bad, ugly sides of this field...ALL REAL, very, very HELPFUL to me in deciding whether or NOT to actually pursue this field! (Still undecided.)

God Bless,
Aris Vaughan

# Research

# 10 Benefits of Student Participation in Undergraduate Social Work Research

by Lucas J. Gogliotti, BASW, Justin J. Pung, BASW, and Suzanne L. Cross, Ph.D., ACSW, LMSW

Undergraduate research can be incredibly beneficial to social work students. Students may feel too busy to take on the burden of another obligation, but a research project is worth the added responsibility. Lucas Gogliotti and Justin Pung, two social work seniors at Michigan State University, have had the experience of working on a research team with Dr. Suzanne Cross, an associate professor at MSU, and Dr. Angelique Day, who was working at the time as a community agency employee.

This quantitative and qualitative research study, entitled, *Best Practices for the Recruitment and Retention of American Indian Social Work Students,* was conducted from 2008-2011. The two students joined the research team in the fall semester of 2010. Each student received the Provost University Research Initiative (PURI) Award, which provided funding for them while they participated in the research. Justin focused his literature review on the recruitment and Lucas on the retention of American Indian students in social work programs. In addition, both students conducted individual interviews and learned research methods, data analysis, and manuscript development. They participated in poster presentations at the NASW-Michigan Chapter conference, the school of social work research festival, and (for Justin) the Council on Social Work Education Annual Program Meeting (CSWE-APM).

The students' experience was invaluable, and they want to encourage other students to extend themselves to yield the benefits of undergraduate research. Therefore, Lucas and Justin have developed a list of ten benefits of social work undergraduate research.

## 1. Relationships With Faculty

Developing relationships with social work faculty provides a great experience to spend time with established professionals. Involvement in a research project allows a student one-on-one time and/or small group interactions with a faculty member. During this relationship, students learn in-depth the actual processes of research, an experience they are likely not to have had in a research course. This relationship also allows the faculty member the opportunity to observe the student's research skill sets more directly than in a classroom setting. Conducting research can be confusing and difficult to grasp at times. However, with the help and support of my faculty advisor, I (Lucas) was able to gain a firm understanding of the process. I got course credit for my research project, but I didn't have to share the attention of the professor with 20 other students.

## 2. Organizational Skills

In professional settings, it is necessary to manage numerous responsibilities while still staying composed. Adding a research project to classes and extracurricular activities is a good chance for a student to practice this essential skill. Granted, the life of a college student is anything but calm and free of stress, especially during senior year. Yet, it is vital students get involved in research projects if they can, as early as the sophomore or junior year. Personally, I (Justin) have already seen the impact that participating in research has had on my time management skills. During the fall semester of my senior year, I enrolled in 15 credits, spent 16 hours a week or more at my field placement, had a part-time job, and was the treasurer/secretary for a student social work organization. I was not stressed out over any of this, because putting extra time into research during my junior year prepared me to handle multiple commitments.

## 3. Learn the Research Process

Social workers are aware that research, policy, and practice are forever linked. Therefore, it is advantageous to become familiar with research methods before entering the field. The complexities of research can be intimidating at first, but students are not without help in a project. We were fortunate to learn research methodology from a professional social worker, who worked for a community agency and is now a professor at Wayne State University. At first, I (Justin) had a difficult time understanding the statistical concepts we worked with, such as Pearson's Chi Square. As the project continued, however, I gained a better understanding of them, and my senior year statistics class felt mostly like review after having this first exposure. Thanks to this experience, we both feel confident conducting more research at the graduate and professional levels.

## 4. Learn Interview Skills

Conducting interviews for a research project is the perfect way to practice interviewing skills. Many undergraduate students have had little or no experience conducting formal interviews prior to their field placements in the senior year. Even new social workers may be nervous when conducting one-on-one interviews as recent hires in a professional setting. As student research assistants, we had a great opportunity to hone skills as interviewers and to develop our own personal interview styles. We were able to conduct phone interviews with American Indian social work students. These interviews were low pressure and highly structured. They gave us a chance to learn about ourselves as interviewers, and we felt prepared to conduct interviews in our field placements because of this experience.

## 5. Cultural Competence

Social work students learn very quickly that they serve a wide range of clients. It is important, therefore, to step out of one's comfort zone early and take on a research project with a focus on a diverse population. Although both of us can trace a portion of our heritage to American Indians, we were not intimately familiar with the realities that they currently face. Researching the recruitment and retention of American Indian/Alaskan Native college students has motivated us to develop a deeper connection with this population and our heritage within it. Through this research project, I (Justin) found that I enjoy working with and learning about diverse populations. It was a worthwhile experience. I feel all aspiring social workers should not pass up such an invaluable opportunity to increase their cultural competence.

## 6. Letters of Reference

Most MSW programs require applicants for admission to have three letters of recommendation. Professors are a great source to draw upon for reference letters. Nevertheless, most students have had limited, if any, out of classroom conversation with their faculty. Thus, it is difficult to receive a faculty reference that will share the student's knowledge, commitment, and lessons learned during the research process. Involvement in research projects provides a great opportunity for the students to spend the time with faculty to build a "letter of recommendation worthy relationship." I (Lucas) was able to receive two letters of recommendation from my research advisors. These letters were thorough and complete, because I had the time to build a relationship with the referees and they were able to highlight my positive qualities as a researcher.

## 7. Potential To Get Published

Few undergraduates are co-authors of a published journal article. We are on the verge of claiming that title, as the manuscript produced from the research is close to submission to a peer-reviewed journal. If undergraduates become published co-authors, they have the knowledge that they have accomplished something many students do not even attempt until they are in graduate school. It should be noted that not all research projects will result in publication, but the opportunity is there. We feel fortunate that we could be published co-authors so early in our careers. I (Lucas) hope to become a professor one day, so having a journal article on my résumé as an undergraduate is a huge asset. Students interested in this potential benefit should approach professors and ask if they need research assistants for any of their projects.

## 8. Conferences

The idea of attending a professional social work conference may not appeal to some undergraduate students, but it is a great opportunity. Undergraduate researchers may be given the opportunity to co-present their research at professional conferences. This gives the student a chance to stand up in front of professional social workers and faculty to explain research findings. It's also a good chance to get rid of some of the public speaking "nerves" that students have, because audiences at conferences are usually welcoming to college students. We were given the opportunity to present at three different professional conferences. The experience in presenting will help us immensely in graduate school and as professionals when audiences will have higher expectations.

## 9. Résumé

Students need to engage in activities that will convince graduate schools and employers that it would be a mistake on their part not to choose them. A student's chances will improve if he or she can proudly put "Research" beside a bullet point. When graduate schools come across an applicant who committed to research, they most likely see someone that is prepared to take on the rigors of graduate-level coursework. Employers will probably note that students took the initiative to apply their academic skills to a real world issue, and expect that they can transition well into the workplace. As I (Justin) spoke to representatives from graduate schools, I found them to be impressed that I had conducted research and presented it a number of times at conferences. Once they knew what I had accomplished, it felt more like they were trying to convince me to come to their program, not me trying to convince them why I should be accepted. There are few rock solid means to prevent a résumé from being passed over, so students should strongly consider involvement in research.

## 10. Potential To Earn Money

As most undergraduate social work students know, a majority of the jobs that a student can get outside of flipping burgers are volunteer positions. Even though volunteering is a learning experi-ence and makes you feel warm and fuzzy inside, it doesn't pay for tuition, bills, and textbooks. Undergraduate research can be a great way to earn money doing something that actually relates to social work. Not all research jobs pay money, but when they do, it is a great addition to the previously mentioned benefits. Your earnings may equal that of a part-time job, allow for more independent time management, and come with developing critical thinking, development of research knowledge, skills, and experience. We were able to receive a grant that paid us $1,000 a semester. We would have participated in a research project voluntarily, but the income really helped us. For an undergraduate social work student looking for a job, a paid research position is one of the best available.

*Lucas J. Gogliotti, BASW, was a senior at Michigan State University in the School of Social Work at the time this article was written. He is now a student in the MSW program at the University of Michigan. Lucas served as the BSW student representative on the NASW-MI Board of Directors.*

*Justin J. Pung, BASW, was a senior at Michigan State University in the School of Social Work at the time of this writing. He is now pursuing an MSW degree at Loyola University Chicago. He was Secretary/Treasurer for MSU's Phi Alpha Chapter.*

*Suzanne L. Cross, Ph.D., ACSW, LMSW, is an associate professor at Michigan State University School of Social Work. She enjoys working with students on research projects to increase and broaden their learning experiences. Her research interests include historical trauma, grand families, student recruitment and retention, and collaboration with tribal nations. Dr. Cross was selected for the 2012 Mit Joyner Gerontology Award for her work with American Indian elders.*

## STUDENT SOCIAL WORK ORGANIZATIONS

Please send us a short **news** article about your group's activities. Also, send us **photos** of your club in action–we may even feature you on our front cover!

It's easy to share your club's activities with our readers. Send your news/photos to:

Linda Grobman, ACSW, LSW, Editor/Publisher
THE NEW SOCIAL WORKER
P.O. Box 5390, Harrisburg, PA 17110-0390
or to *lindagrobman@socialworker.com*

## Greetings From the Phi Alpha Honor Society for Social Work National Office

Phi Alpha has awarded the following chapters the "Chapter Service Award" for 2012 with a $500 check, beautiful plaque, and travel expenses to CSWE-APM in Washington, DC:

- Boise State University–Dr. Misty Wall, Advisor and Shirlene Elledge, President
- Florida International University–Dr. Mary Helen Hayden, Advisor and Nicola Bryan, Betsy Godoy-Rosado, Presidents
- Texas A&M University–Dr. Claudia Rappaport, Advisor and Rebecca Saunders, Jennifer Brietzke, Presidents
- University of Arkansas–Michael Collie, LCSW, Advisor and Tina Smith, President

Congratulations to all the winners, and thank you to all chapters that applied for the Chapter Service Award and to the advisors that served as judges in various regions.

The Phi Alpha Poster Board Presentation will be hosted at CSWE-APM in Washington, DC, in November. Please visit *http://www.phialpha.org* or e-mail *phialphainfo@etsu.edu* for more information.

Kind Regards,
Tammy Hamilton, Executive Secretary

*Webb–continued from page 3*

An outdoor environment is where Webb would like to be if she had her druthers–hiking, meditating, camping, and enjoying wildlife. She also likes cooking and the company of her boyfriend, a fellow social work student.

"It's really cool to date someone with a similar personality type," she says. "If I feel upset I can't help someone, or get too emotionally involved, he can rein me back in."

Webb's choice of social work was based partly on her inveterate desire to help, and partly on a social worker she met during a hospitalization for emotional issues. "He provided me with resources and helped me make the transition to outside the hospital," she recalls.

But while she's definitive about wanting to be a social worker, Webb is uncertain about her specific plans. Ultimately, she'd like to get an MSW, but would like to "explore" for a while before coming to further decisions. She expects she'll go wherever she feels "called and needed," but also suspects her "dream job" will be working with those in recovery.

Webb's required senior year practicum, however, will involve working with people with HIV/AIDS and on prevention.

She may seem hugely altruistic, but Webb insists that reaching out to other people–especially those with addiction issues–is in a way "self-serving. "In order to recover and stay sober, I have to help others," she says.

There is another motivation. "The reason I am willing to have a conversation and expose a very dark part of my life I'm not proud of is that I really want to work on breaking the stigma of drug and alcohol addiction, so people can recover from it. So I'm willing to air my dirty laundry."

*Barbara Trainin Blank is a freelance writer based in Harrisburg, PA.*

# Social Work Students in Action!

William Woods University senior BSW students and Dr. Elizabeth Wilson during a visit to the Missouri State Capitol as part of the Missouri Association of Social Welfare's (MASW) annual advocacy day.

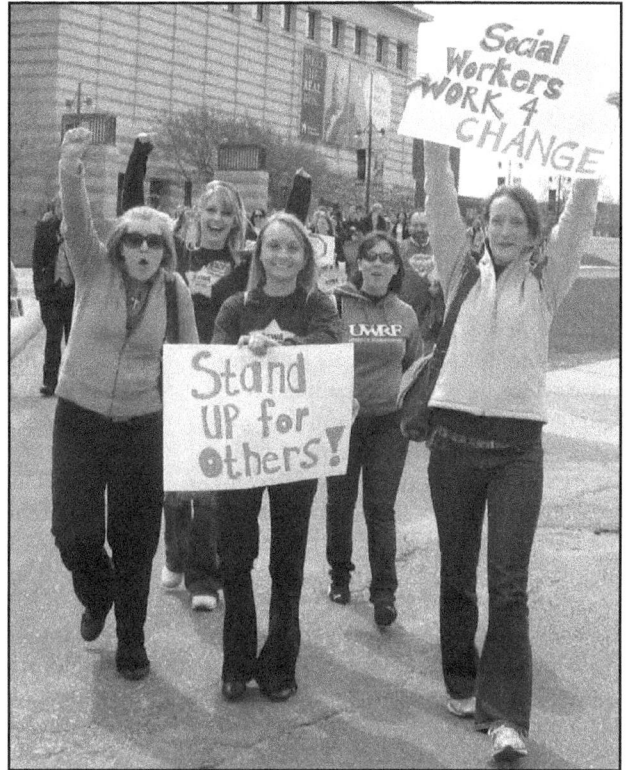

Elizabethtown College BSW students at lobby day at the Pennsylvania State Capitol.

University of Wisconsin River Falls social work students at Lobby Day at the Capitol.

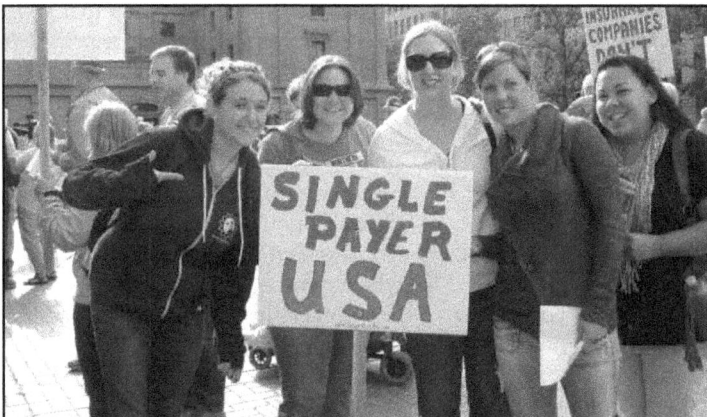

Social work students and Professor Jessica Ritter from Pacific University Oregon at a single-payer rally organized by the Mad as Hell doctors.

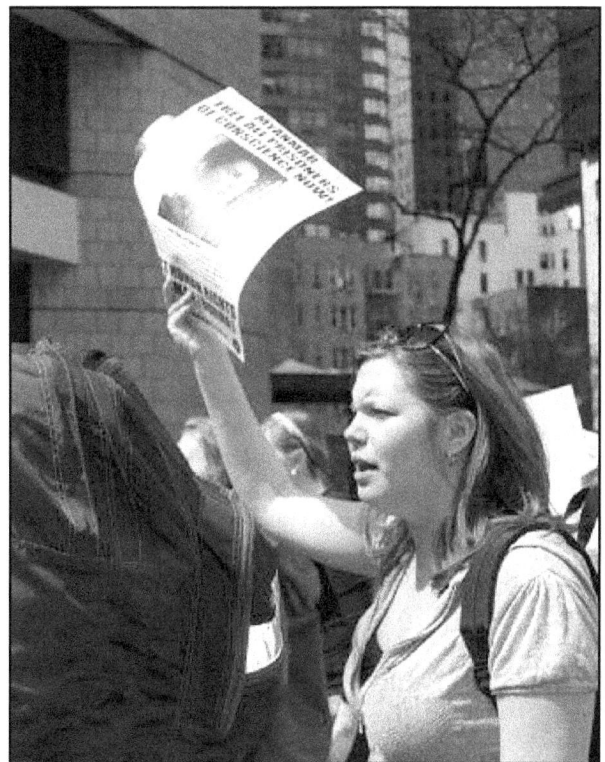

West Chester University MSW student at a human rights rally.

# ABCD in Practice: A Practical Lesson
# From the Field Placement
*by Mukerem Mifta Shafi, MSW*

Asset Based Community Development (ABCD), has most recently been well cherished by academia and practitioners alike. As most of its proponents argue, it is a radical shift from the needs/deficit based community development, to an asset based community development (Kretzmann & McKnight, 1993; Phillips & Pittman, 2009).

Even though we took almost half a dozen courses for the MSW first-year first semester, it was in the Integrated Social Work Methods I course that we dealt extensively with ABCD as an alternative model of community development. At the end of this semester, as part of the MSW first-year field placement, I was assigned to do my first social work field education at an agency. The field placement agency was called BLEA (Beza Lehiwot Ethiopia Association). It is an NGO—a charity organization that works with orphans and vulnerable children (OVC), persons living with HIV/AIDS (PLWHA), and the needy in the center of Addis Ababa, the capital city of Ethiopia. It was in this particular field placement agency that I had the opportunity to see how the ABCD model of community development actually worked in practice.

In this field placement, which lasted for a month, we were expected to go through the first two major goals of social work field education, according to the school of social work at Addis Ababa University. These are direct field visits/observations and carrying out assessments in the field placement agency. For this purpose, I had to undertake direct field visits, observations, and assessments. I took notes on the overall service provision patterns of the agency, challenges and opportunities associated with agency beneficiaries, local arrangements with which the agency works to address problems and challenges of the community where the agency operates, and the like.

It was in the middle of an interview, a kind of unstructured key informant interview with a local Idir (an indigenous self help arrangement/institution)

representative that I came to realize that the agency was actually, in fact, subconsciously working under the mainstream ABCD framework of community development. As I moved on interviewing additional representatives, it became clear that not only did the agency use local resources and means to reach out to those in need, but I was also able to unveil the structure under which the agency organized itself along the community. Although the program manager of the agency never heard of the presence of ABCD as an alternative model of community development, local resources, assets, human power, and local social institutions were mobilized and used as a springboard to bring about changes in the beneficiaries and client system. That would make the organization a community based organization, or CBO.

When we look at the overall structure of the agency—that is, the means it uses to reach out to its potential beneficiaries and address their causes of concern—the following arrangement emerges. First, the agency organized a community dialogue or conversation as to how the agency works with the local community. Following this dialogue, a decision has been made on how beneficiaries are selected; by whom they would be selected; who would be willing to give psychosocial support; how the indigenous social institutions (such as the Idir) work with the agency, how volunteers work with the beneficiaries, the Idir and the agency; and so forth.

Second, with the help of the agency, the local self help arrangement called Idir selected volunteers from the community neighborhood who would be willing to provide care and support for OVC and PLWHA. Third, the agency provided these recommended volunteers from the community a comprehensive psychosocial care and support training that would enable them become "para-social workers."

When it comes to the actual selection of potential beneficiaries, the Idir, as a union of local community members,

knows all the members of the community. This enables it to effectively identify major serious causes of concern in the community, including OVC cases, PLWHA, and the needy. Then, the Idir recommends "para-social workers" for these identified potential beneficiaries, and they undertake a comprehensive needs assessment and report to the agency. This way, the agency extends certain material help and support to these beneficiaries.

In spite of this minimal support, the actual care and support is provided by local residents of the community, the "para-social workers." As most of them are adult women, they know the needs and challenges of the OVCs and treat them as their children. In fact, as I have seen the practice directly through the field visit, they visit daily to check on the progress of the overall conditions of these children, especially their health condition and education.

The most astonishing part of this psychosocial care and support is that these children, the OVC, are known to have been born and grown up alongside with their own children, the "para-social workers'" children, in one village, playing and learning at the same school. The presence of this emotional proximity between the "para-social workers" and the beneficiaries enabled the agency to effectively carry out its principal goal of providing comprehensive psychosocial care and support to OVC and PLWHA in the community. I think this idea of trained "para-social workers" was, by far, successful, given that the training of social workers in Ethiopia is a very recent phenomenon.

The first direct social work field education was quite an eye opening experience. In fact, not only did it assure the efficient integration of theory and practice, but it also made it possible for students like me to capture the actual lived experiences of local communities to respond to local challenges and problems drawing on local community assets. Theory and practice integration is, I think, the ultimate goal of any social work field education, and of course, the essence of almost all professions and sciences alike.

## References

Kretzman, J. P., & McKnight, J. L. (1993). *Building communities from the inside out: A path toward finding and mobilizing a community's assets.* Chicago: ACTA Publications.

Phillips, R., & Pittman, H. R. (eds.). (2009). *An introduction to community development.* New York: Routledge.

*Mukerem Mifta Shafi, MSW, was born in Addis Ababa, Ethiopia. He studied sociology and social anthropology in the undergraduate program of Addis Ababa University, Ethiopia. Immediately after completing his BA degree with a distinction point in July 2009, he was assigned by the Ministry of Education, Ethiopia, to teach at Jigjiga University, Ethiopia. In this university, he served as an instructor and taught many courses in the department of sociology from 2009 to 2010. Following this, he had the opportunity to pursue his master's degree at Addis Ababa University. Given his prior interest in social welfare and social policy, he decided to study social work with a specialization in family, youth, and children at Addis Ababa University, where he received his MSW in 2012. He has written articles for a local English magazine called* Addis Standard *and also serves as a co-chair for a local book review club organized by Islamic Research and Cultural Center (IRCC) in Addis Ababa. He and ten close friends founded an NGO, Muslim Graduates Initiative for Education and Training (MGIET), in Addis Ababa.*

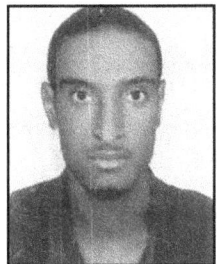

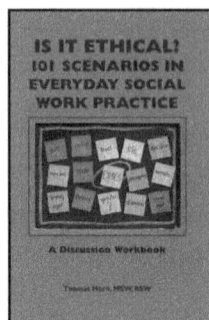

# Your Community Needs You

## Make a Difference at Home

Earn a Master of Social Work
Online from the Top-Ranked
USC School of Social Work

http://msw.usc.edu/NewSocialWorkerMag

**USC**School
of Social Work

# Reviews

*The Defining Decade: Why Your Twenties Matter—And How To Make the Most of Them Now,* by Meg Jay, Ph.D., Twelve: New York, 2012, $22.99 hardcover.

While society often touts slogans like, "thirty is the new twenty" and "you only live once," at the same time that the job market has become a more treacherous place than ever, it has become very easy for twenty-somethings to feel that this is the time to live it up and that the time to work is later. In this book, Dr. Jay, a clinical psychologist specializing in adult development in twenty-somethings, attempts to dissect the span of time that often seems vast and uncertain to those ranging from ages 20-29. Divided into three sections, this book covers the general areas of work, love, and the brain and the body.

In the "Work" section, Dr. Jay uses client interactions and parts of her clients' sessions to illustrate the frequency with which younger people find themselves unable to navigate the waters between finishing their education and settling into their careers. For some, this occurs because the person feels overwhelmed by the number of options that exist. For others, it seems that there will never be another opportunity to enjoy life and to be young and free, and the idea of focusing on work pales in importance. Regardless of the reasoning, Dr. Jay's work with her clients helps to show the reader ways in which to combat the uncertainty and to begin to make a plan to reach the professional place they wish to find themselves later in life, rather than to miss opportunities that, although they seem endless, might only be options for a short while.

In the "Love" section, clients' discussions and struggles with current relationships helps the reader to understand fears of not finding the right life partner, whether they are due to being in inappropriate relationships or being uncomfortable with the idea of seeking a relationship at all. Dr. Jay helps clients to clarify their own priorities, to figure out whether a current partner is the right long-term fit, or when to focus elsewhere rather than to put all of one's effort into finding a mate.

In "The Brain and the Body," Dr. Jay cites medical cases and personal client interactions in which there are discussions about the ability for the brain to create

new ideas and to take new risks, as well as pointing out that there are necessary considerations to be made physically, even when a person is at an age at which such has never had to be considered before.

Overall, this book may be used in three ways: for a clinician or parent looking to better understand the current life struggles of those in their 20s, for a twenty-something to read simply to enjoy the clients' stories, or for a twenty-something to read and use as a guidebook. Although the first two are very valid reasons to enjoy this book, its true impact is most evident when a reader chooses the third option. Although not every section may feel completely personal (if, for example, you've already married, the middle section might not be as poignant for you as the others, or if you do not want to have children, there are areas of the final section that won't apply), having a professional help the reader to begin to consider his/her life choices and how decisions made now will impact future life options is something that many find a gentle but effective wake-up call.

*Reviewed by Kristen Marie (Kryss) Shane, MSW, LSW, LMSW.*

---

*Bullying in Different Contexts,* edited by Claire P. Monks and Iain Coyne, Cambridge University Press, Cambridge, UK, 2011, 276 pages, $41.99 paperback.

Domestic violence, elder abuse, and workplace harassment: these may not be words that are generally grouped under different types of bullying, but that is exactly what the editors attempt to do in *Bullying in Different Contexts.* The definition of bullying is largely debated by the contributors; in the end, the editors contend that there are several definitions of bullying. This gives the reader an in-depth background on what bullying means in different areas. However, it makes the reader question how useful and prevalent the text is in an educational and/or social environment.

Monks and Coyne begin the book by giving a summary of the book's contents. The following nine chapters discuss bullying in various arenas. Chapters two and three introduce readers to bullying that happens at preschool to school age levels. Although it many times does not take place between school walls, cyberbullying is something that children and adolescents have to face as well (covered in Chapter

10). Other forms of bullying among youth are dating violence and bullying in residential facilities (Chapters 4 and 6).

Domestic violence and bullying issues that happen in a family context, not commonly categorized as bullying, are discussed in Chapter 5. Elder abuse is another type of bullying that can happen within families and many times goes unreported, because individuals are unaware of its existence (Chapter 9).

Chapters seven and eight stress the fact that bullying does not occur in a bubble in the prison and workplace areas.

The editors do an excellent job of categorizing bullying and suggesting areas of future research in the final chapter. However, the information about the Internet's virtual worlds and bullying may need to have more descriptive information. Professionals working in any of the areas described in the book would find this book beneficial, so as to broaden their understanding of bullying. By reaching out to others, more research will hopefully be conducted in the areas suggested, to help reduce bullying in several different areas.

*Reviewed by Michelle Sawyer, MSW, graduate of the University of South Dakota.*

---

*Republic, Lost: How Money Corrupts Congress—and a Plan to Stop It,* by Lawrence Lessing, Twelve, Hachette Book Group, New York, 2011, 381 pages, $26.99 hardcover.

In a poll commissioned for *Republic, Lost,* 75 percent of Americans stated that they believed "campaign contributions buy results in Congress." These results set the stage for *Republic, Lost.* Lawrence Lessig is a professor of law at Harvard Law School. Undoubtedly a man of brilliance, Lessig compels readers to take a look at how history has led us to the point of corruption in Congress today.

He offers insights not only about how America got into the mess of campaign corruption, but also offers four intriguing solutions to fix it.

Lessig makes a solid argument that money is not the corruption, but money in the wrong places causes corruption. He gives one specific example: "From 1998 to 2008, the financial sector spent $1.7 billion on campaign contributions and $3.4 billion on lobbying expenses. That's a faster growth in spending than with any other industry." The popular perception of Congressmen sitting in long meetings and shaking hands with constituents is far from reality. The more modern view of Congress is a "fund-raising Congress." Lessig compares current Congressmen to "junkies" addicted to raising funds for their next campaign.

His arguments are enough to turn the stomachs of unassuming Americans across our great nation. After he has finished turning stomachs, he then induces the desire for change.

There are several Thoreau references throughout the book, motivating the reader to strike at the root of evil, which he views as campaign corruption. *Republic, Lost* is an insightful book for the average American hungry for change. Lessig aims to inspire the reader to be "rootstrikers" and take down this current corruption in Congress.

*Reviewed by Alissa A. Lennon, MSW, graduate of the University of South Dakota.*

---

*Social Work With HIV & AIDS: A Case-Based Guide, by Diana Rowan and contributors, Lyceum Books, Chicago, IL, 2013, 576 pages, $59.95 paperback.*

Rowan has drawn together contributors from academia, agency administration, and front-line case management to create this guide. She describes it as suitable for classes on medical social work and social work with populations-at-risk, as well as a reference for service providers. I agree with her assessment of the book's utility in all respects.

The book's 17 chapters are divided into four topical sections. The first section (Chapters 1 through 3) addresses the current state of practice (Chapter 1) and the history of social work with HIV and AIDS as a stage to explore setting the next agenda for practice (Chapter 3). The second chapter reports an extensive conversation between Rowan and Alan Rice, a social worker with 28 years of experience working with HIV and AIDS. The chapter is conversational in tone and provides a comprehensive glimpse into one social worker's experience on the front lines of AIDS social work across most of the history of the crisis.

The second section comprises six chapters, each addressing a specific population group. Chapters 4 through 8, respectively, address HIV and AIDS among African Americans, Latinos, men who have sex with men (MSM), adolescents and young adults, and persons over

age 50. Chapter 9 explores the "ripple effect" of HIV and AIDS spreading concentrically outward from the person infected with HIV to families, friends, and communities. Rather than let this devolve into platitudes about "connectedness," the authors focus primarily on interventions across practice levels.

The third section (Chapters 10 through 15) is oriented around practice responses. Chapters in this section address case management (Chapter 10), medical care for HIV and AIDS (Chapter 11), and medication adherence issues (Chapter 13). Other chapters deal with some of the more emotionally-charged topics: sex and drugs (Chapter 12), spirituality and religion (Chapter 14), and work with the "Black Faith Community" (Chapter 15). These chapters have achieved an appropriate balance between sensitivity and frankness, though they may still present a challenge for those students accustomed to more concrete thought.

The last section (Chapters 16 and 17) addresses policy responses. Chapter 16 examines housing policy for people living with HIV and AIDS, and Chapter 17 looks at both the history and the current changes taking place in U.S. AIDS policy, e.g., the Ryan White CARE Act and the AIDS Drug Assistance Program. Readers will find the portion of the chapter devoted to the Patient Protection and Affordable Care Act (PPACA–the 2010 healthcare reform act) to be a good introduction to how the PPACA will affect treatment and coverage for persons living with HIV and AIDS. The chapter raises important questions about care going forward.

With the exception of the first three chapters, each chapter contains at least one case example, and several include multiple case studies. The case examples are well-developed and provide appropriate material for stimulating discussion or for classroom assignments. Reflection questions and discussion prompts add to the classroom utility of the text. Rowan and her contributors have produced a credible and useful resource for both students and practitioners.

*Reviewed by David H. Johnson, Ph.D., MSW, LSW, assistant professor at Millersville University of Pennsylvania.*

---

*Pinched: How the Great Recession Has Narrowed Our Futures and What We Can Do About It, by Don Peck, New York: Crown*

*Publishing Group, 2011, 223 Pages. $10.99 paperback.*

Don Peck discusses the current implications of the Great Recession in his 2011 book, *Pinched.* Peck's discussion of past economic downturns in our nation's history provides insight into our current situation. Examining the effects of the Gilded Age and Depression of 1893, the Great Depression of the 1930s, the stagnation of the economy from 1972 through the early 1980s, in comparison to the effects that we continue to feel from the stock market crash of 2008, Peck is convincing that we are a nation that will overcome.

Peck opens the first of nine chapters stating that our current recession began in 2008 and ended in 2009, but states that the cultural impacts are longer lasting. He discusses the changing marriages, relationships, and the widening division of the social classes.

In his next chapters, Peck notes gender differences in unemployment, historical depressions, and recessions, He discusses the American dream of home ownership, the 2008 housing crash, and its effects on our nation's communities. Peck discusses how previous effects of unemployment and economic downturns have had an impact on presidential elections. The author shares that if we remain stuck in an economic climate in which stagnation and disappointment are the norms for large numbers of Americans, the result will be low levels of public trust and political options that are stunted by a poisonous atmosphere and heavy discontent.

In his final chapter, Peck shares his remedies for our ailing economic structure. He presents a change to entitlement programs, including Medicare and unemployment benefits, which may cause alarm to those beneficiaries. His ideas for change may be unpopular but are worthy of review to bring change to national deficit spending.

Overall, Peck writes in an easy-to-read fashion, and not just for those highly interested in politics and economics. Although it doesn't sound appealing to read about the woes of our nation, this book manages to present our problems with a historical display of our ability to fix it, making it a worthy read during a presidential election year.

*Reviewed by Jennifer Hess, MSW, a July 2012 graduate of the University of South Dakota.*

# Tech Topics

## Red Cross Digital Disaster Volunteers (DDVs) Offer Support Through Social Media

### by John Weaver, LCSW, Valerie Cole, and Gloria Huang

In March 2012, partnering with Dell, the Red Cross launched its Digital Disaster Operations Center in Washington, DC. The digiDOC uses Radian6, a social media monitoring service, to gather large amounts of public social data (tweets, blogs, Facebook posts) via keyword searches. This data is filtered and sorted by event types (e.g., hurricane, earthquake, and wildfire), topic categories, and needs (e.g., emotional support, emergency assistance, shelter, safe and well). One of the goals in launching this digiDOC was to start using the information shared within these online communities to help the organization better assess and address immediate community needs during times of disaster.

**American Red Cross**

In August 2012, during Hurricane Isaac, the American Red Cross piloted the use of digital disaster volunteers (DDVs) to help the Red Cross Social Engagement team provide information and support to online communities. These virtual volunteers work from their homes to monitor and respond to social posts. Social media is perfect for engaging people in the Red Cross story and connecting with communities.

During a disaster, posts coming in from the Radian6 monitoring tool are reviewed by the DDVs, who are trained to respond and provide Red Cross mission-related services, such as virtual hugs, preparedness and safety information, tips for dealing with stress (positive coping messages), and–in some cases–referrals to other partners and resources. Red Cross Disaster Mental Health (DMH) is collaborating with the Social Engagement team to explore ways in which mental health professionals can be more involved in telling the Red Cross story and supporting the community.

The pilot period involved testing the software and the DDVs' abilities to sort through the high volume of data, triage the needs, and quickly respond to the individuals and organizations who posted. One of the major challenges was selecting the best key words and phrases to include in each search. To give you an idea of the kinds of messages used during the pilot, here are some sample messages and replies:

## Hugs

*I just want to cry...hurricane isaac ruining everything.*

> I am so sorry girl. Sending you a digital #RedCross ((HUG))

*The hurricane ain't no joke down here i'm scared as sh\*t.*

> Take a deep breath. Sending you some positive vibes and a #RedCross ((HUG))

*Lucy came to work with me today because she's afraid of #Isaac, but not when she's under my desk!*

> awww, so cute! I hope Lucy is doing okay! Here's a @RedCross ((hug)) for her!

## Preparedness and Safety

*Thankful to have weathered Hurricane Isaac. No electricity but family and friends are safe so feeling blessed. God is good! #Isaac*

> Glad you are safe! Make sure to download free [Hurricane App, First Aid App, Shelter Finder App] for your smart phone. Ready for next time! http://www.redcross.org/prepare/mobile-apps

*Kinda sorta really scared. Haha, moms in Sams while I'm sitting in the car and I can feel the car moving from the Hurricane wind.*

> Stay safe! I'm with @RedCross and I know it's scary. You can get safety info at http://www.redcross.org/prepare/disaster. ((hugs)) from us all.

*I'm terrified were going to drive through this hurricane weather.*

> Be careful driving and remember NOAA's message - "Turn Around Don't Drown" (more deaths occur due to flooding than any other weather hazard.)

## Stress Management

*I haven't eaten all day this hurricane was really stressing me.*

> I'm the opposite. Stress makes me eat. :( Try to grab something, even just a snack. Sending you a big ((HUG)) #RedCross

*STUPID WEATHER!!!! GOSH, THAT FREACKING HURRICANE HAS HAD ME SCARED!!!! :(*
*Were getting the hurricane Isaac winds here and I'm terrified. It's never been this windy before.*

> [Part 1 of 2 part reply] The storm stress sounds awful. Hang in there! (and don't be afraid to ask for help if you and your family need it)…
>
> [Part 2 of 2] If you need to talk, contact Disaster Distress Helpline 1-800-985-5990 or Text 'TalkWithUs' to 66746 http://disasterdistress.samhsa.gov

## Thanks for Supporting Red Cross

*Wow! Just learned Red Cross Va. Mountain Region has deployed 31 trained disaster responders to the Gulf to assist those affected by #Isaac.*

> Vicki from Red Cross. We're thankful for every one of them! {hugs}

*Honored to be able to support the @RedCross request for snacks for those impacted by #Isaac. @PepperidgeFarm @GoldfishSmiles on the way!*

> Thanks to Campbell for the tasty snacks! Those affected will appreciate it :) Thank you for being a #RedCross partner!

*To support the @RedCross' #Isaac Relief Efforts, you can donate $10 by texting REDCROSS to 90999 or visit redcross.org*

> Thanks so much for your support of @RedCross! There's a lot of work to be done and you've just helped us do it. :)

One challenge with offering service via social media is knowing the impact of the outgoing messages. Sometimes we get replies, often like these:

*Thanks for the encouragement! Done this before but it doesn't get any easier mentally. Thank you so much, I am just praying it's not a repeat of 7 yrs ago.*

Sometimes the information we provide gets retweeted. Many times we must simply hope for the best. We're hoping other friends/contacts of people we message will see our posts and offer additional peer support.

Social media will be an important tool in future responses to catastrophic events. It may even be the safest and preferred response option for something like a pandemic or any other event that involves sheltering in place. Red Cross anticipates greater use of DDVs, especially DDVs who also can serve as DMH responders, to help in these areas:

- providing mental health support for both disaster victims and responders;
- promoting community resilience; and
- educating all disaster relief workers about self care.

Red Cross is partnering with SAMHSA, APA, and the Disaster Distress Helpline for this initiative. The pilot utilized an initial group of about ten responders and Red Cross is seeking additional DDVs to expand the program.

## Become a DDV

Who is an ideal disaster digital volunteer? Someone who:

- is an experienced user of online social tools
- is an established member of online communities
- is trained on Red Cross social engagement and knowledgeable about Red Cross services
- has good judgment
- is extremely empathetic
- does not have a profane, political, or religious filled social presence
- is willing to use his/her personal social presence to act as an official rep of the American Red Cross
- is capable of handling many details at once.

Because of the time commitment and technical tools involved in this role, there are a few requirements that you must meet before you can get trained to be a DDV. If you match this profile and would like to become a Red Cross volunteer for the DDV team, see: *http://blog.redcross.org/disaster-digital-volunteer-training/*

And, in case you are wondering whether all of this will work in serving people without power, turns out it does.

Many messages that we responded to came from folks who managed to charge their smartphones and other tech equipment. So it turns out there is an APP (alternate power port) for that; people wisely use cars, transformers, 12-volt car battery jumpers with outlets, and even hand-crank flashlights that can charge phones *(http://www.redcrossstore.org/shopper/prodlist.aspx?LocationId=111)* to stay connected.

*John Weaver, LCSW, is a Disaster Mental Health and PA volunteer for the American Red Cross. John.Weaver@redcross.org.*

*Valerie Cole is a Senior Associate, Disaster Mental Health, American Red Cross. Valerie.Cole@redcross.org*

*Gloria Huang is Senior Social Engagement Specialist, American Red Cross. Gloria.Huang@redcross.org*

## Disaster Distress Helpline Available 24/7/365

The Disaster Distress Helpline (DDH) is the first national hotline dedicated to providing year-round disaster crisis counseling. This toll-free, multilingual, crisis support service is available 24/7 via telephone (1-800-985-5990) and SMS (text "TalkWithUs" to 66746).

The DDH began October 1, 2011. After a five-month transition of services from the former Oil Spill Distress Helpline, the service began taking calls and texts with its current network of crisis call centers on February 28, 2012.

### Disaster Distress Helpline
PHONE: 1-800-985-5990  TEXT: "TalkWithUs" to 66746

Christian Burgess, LMSW, is director of the Disaster Distress Helpline and oversees all DDH operations under Link2Health Solutions/MHA-NYC. *The New Social Worker* asked him to tell us a little about the helpline.

*Who does DDH serve and what needs does it address?* The Disaster Distress Helpline serves any individual or family experiencing emotional distress before, during, or after any natural or human-caused disaster in the U.S./territories. Symptoms of disaster distress may include temporary reactions to the disaster (such as fear, confusion, mild anxiety) or may be an indication of larger mental health concerns (persistent anxiety, substance use, patterns of unhealthy coping, depression, suicidal ideation/attempt).

*Who provides the services?* As a sub-network of the National Suicide Prevention Lifeline (1-800-273-TALK [8255]), all Disaster Distress Helpline counselors are trained in crisis assessment, intervention, and referral. Additional training is provided in psychological first aid and disaster crisis counseling for phone/texting. The majority of counselors staffing Lifeline/Disaster Distress Helpline are paid professional staff (including many with licensure). However, to staff our lines 24/7/365, many call centers also rely on paid staff from a variety of educational backgrounds, volunteers, and interns. Anyone who answers a call or text for the DDH has received up to 100+ hours of training. The Lifeline and the DDH are administered by Link2Health Solutions, Inc., a subsidiary of the Mental Health Association of New York City.

*Who has been helped, and how?* Through September 2012, the Disaster Distress Helpline has received more than 1,200 calls and has received more than 1,300 texts—these numbers do not represent individual callers/texters. While caller demographics and other trends of our service are still being established as this is our pilot year, preliminary data suggest that a majority of callers/texters are females ages 40-49, many with a caregiving role—however, again, it should be emphasized that the DDH serves any/all in the U.S./territories experiencing disaster distress, regardless of sex, age, and other identifying characteristics, including immigration status. Preliminary data also indicate that the following are reasons given for calling/texting:
- Overwhelming feelings of anxiety, confusion in face of severe weather forecast
- Anxiety regarding evacuation (including wildfires), especially if caregiver
- Current disasters triggering painful memories of past experience with disasters
- Feelings of despair, hopelessness regarding economic loss due to disaster and uncertainty over the future, especially if not eligible or denied claims

*What do you think is the biggest success of the helpline so far?* This is our first year of operations and the first national service of its kind, so its creation can be considered a success by the many partners who helped bring this service to the public. I consider it a great success that we have already been able to help so many individuals experiencing disaster-related distress.

*What else would you like social workers to know about the helpline?* Social workers can help by educating their clients about the benefits of calling or texting the Disaster Distress Helpline. It's accessible (available 24/7/365), confidential, and anonymous (unless imminent threat to self or others is indicated). Simply by reaching out to a trained counselor when in distress after a disaster and "talking with us," this connection can go a long way in easing symptoms of distress.

### For more information:
**Disaster Distress Hotline Web Site:** *http://www.disasterdistress.samhsa.gov*
**Facebook:** *facebook.com/distresshelpline*  **Twitter:** *twitter.com/distressline*

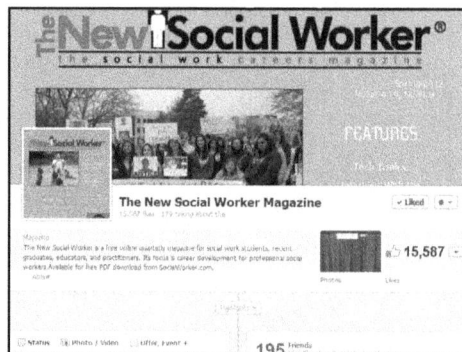

# DAYS IN THE LIVES OF GERONTOLOGICAL SOCIAL WORKERS

*44 Professionals Tell Stories From "Real-Life" Social Work Practice With Older Adults*

Edited by Linda May Grobman, ACSW, LSW, and Dara Bergel Bourassa, Ph.D., LSW

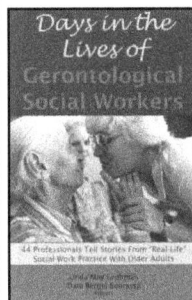

Highlights experiences of social workers in direct and indirect practice with and on behalf of older adults. Read about social workers in communities; hospitals, hospice, and home health; nursing homes; addictions, mental health, homelessness; international settings; research; policy and macro practice; and others. Photos by social worker/photographer Marianne Gontarz York are featured.

*ISBN: 978-1-929109-21-0, 2007, $19.95 plus shipping, 313 pages*

# DAYS IN THE LIVES OF SOCIAL WORKERS

*58 Professionals Tell "Real-Life" Stories from Social Work Practice*

Edited by Linda May Grobman, ACSW, LSW

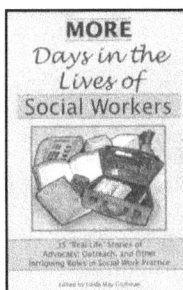

**"Thank you for ... the collection of 'typical days' from social workers! The students loved it." Naurine Lennox, Associate Professor and Chair, St. Olaf College Dept. of SW**

Fourth edition of our "best-seller." 58 social workers tell about their "typical" days in first-person accounts that cover a wide spectrum of practice settings and issues.

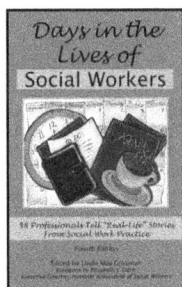

Settings covered in categories of health care, school social work, children and families, disabilities, mental health, substance abuse, private practice, criminal justice, older adults, management, higher education, and communities. Many rich case examples. Lists social work organizations and recommended readings.

*ISBN: 978-1-929109-30-2, 2012, $21.95 plus shipping, 433 pages*

## Macro roles and more

# MORE DAYS IN THE LIVES OF SOCIAL WORKERS

*35 "Real-Life" Stories of Advocacy, Outreach, and Other Intriguing Roles in Social Work Practice*

Edited by Linda May Grobman, ACSW, LSW

Now read about more social work roles and settings in this volume that builds on the narrative format introduced in *DAYS IN THE LIVES OF SOCIAL WORKERS*. Roles include: working on a national level, program development and management, advocacy and organizing, policy from the inside, training and consultation, research and funding, higher education, roles in the court system, faith and spirituality, domestic violence, therapeutic roles, and employment and hunger.

*ISBN: 978-1-929109-16-6, 2005, $16.95 plus shipping, 252 pages*

# THE FIELD PLACEMENT SURVIVAL GUIDE

*What You Need to Know to Get the Most From Your Social Work Practicum 2nd Edition*

Edited by Linda May Grobman, ACSW, LSW

Field placement is one of the most exciting and exhilarating parts of a formal social work education. It is also one of the most challenging. This collection addresses the multitude of issues that social work students in field placement encounter, including choosing a placement, getting prepared, using supervision effectively, working with clients, coping with challenges, and moving on to a successful social work career. This book brings together in one volume the best field placement articles from THE NEW SOCIAL WORKER. Packed with practical, essential information for every student in field placement!

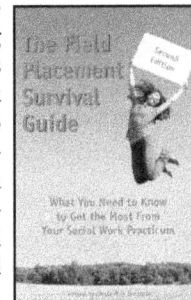

*ISBN: 978-1-929109-26-5, 2011, $22.95 plus shipping, 284 pages*

---

## ORDER FORM

Please send me the following publications: _____

_____

*Shipping to U.S.: $8 first book/$1.50 per add'l book. Canada: $14 first book/$4 per add'l book. Other countries: contact us for rates.*

*PA residents: add 6% sales tax to total cost of book(s) plus shipping.*

❑ Enclosed is a check for $_____ made payable to "White Hat Communications."
I want to pay with my: ❑ Mastercard ❑ Visa ❑ American Express ❑ Discover Card

Card # _____

Expiration Date_____

VISA/MC/Discover: 3-digit # on back of card_____ AMEX: 4-digit # on front of card____

Name as it appears on card _____

Signature _____

SHIP TO: NAME _____

ADDRESS _____

ADDRESS _____

CITY/STATE/ZIP _____

TELEPHONE NUMBER _____

Billing address for card (if different from above) _____

NSW1012

# Riding the Mutual Aid Bus and Other Adventures in Group Work
## A "Days in the Lives of Social Workers" Collection
Linda May Grobman, MSW, ACSW, LSW, and Jennifer Clements, Ph.D., LCSW, Co-Editors
### Foreword by Steven Kraft, Past President of IASWG (formerly AASWG)

Groups come in all kinds. Therapy groups. Support groups. Task groups. Psychoeducational groups. Online groups. Play groups. Experiential groups. Art groups. Drumming groups. Co-facilitated groups. Child groups. Adult groups. Family groups. The list goes on. Regardless of what setting you are in, if you are a social worker, you will work with groups at some time in your career.

You may have a picture in your mind of what a social work group looks like. It probably has people sitting in a circle, talking about their feelings. There certainly are groups described in this book that fit that image of a traditional group. However, the editors also introduce you to groups that take place on a bus or a train, in a public restroom, in cyberspace, or on a zipline 40 feet in the air! Each story takes the reader into the life of a particular social worker and shares practice wisdom about a time when that social worker worked with a group.

By reading each one, you will have a greater perspective on social work with groups. The diversity of the chapters, fields of practice, types of group, and populations will give you a greater idea of the power of group work. It can be quite an adventure!

Developed in collaboration with the International Association for Social Work With Groups (IASWG), this book includes the full text of the Standards for Social Work Practice With Groups.

"These captivating stories will inspire and inform social workers about the endless possibilities and power of practice with groups. Social workers will find strong connections with stories that are set across a wide range of organizational contexts with highly diverse populations, group models, and strategies. The accessible and poignant chapters will resonate with practitioners and students as the authors share their challenges in working with groups—as well as their successes. Ultimately, the stories provide examples of skillful practice and accompanying struggles that promote progress and change through group membership."

*Carol S. Cohen, DSW, Associate Professor*
*Adelphi University School of Social Work,*
*Garden City, New York*
*Co-Chair, Commission on Group Work in Social*
*Work Education, International Association*
*for Social Work with Groups*

## Table of Contents

See http://www.daysinthelivesofsocialworkers.com for more information.

## ABOUT THE EDITORS

TLinda May Grobman, MSW, ACSW, LSW, is the publisher/editor of The New Social Worker magazine. She edited the books Days in the Lives of Social Workers and More Days in the Lives of Social Workers, and co-edited Days in the Lives of Gerontological Social Workers. Linda received her MSW from the University of Georgia and has practiced in mental health and medical settings. She is a former chapter staff member of the National Association of Social Workers.

Jennifer Clements, PhD, LCSW, is currently an Associate Professor of Social Work at Shippensburg University of Pennsylvania. She is Vice President of the International Association for Social Work with Groups and a passionate group worker. She has worked in child welfare practice for 15 years, leading numerous groups with children and adolescents.

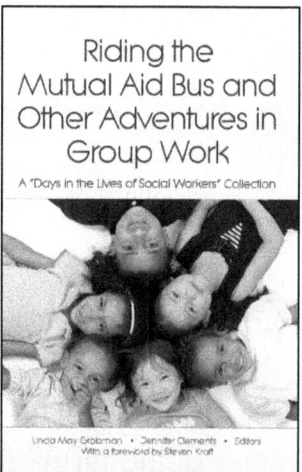

### Riding the Mutual Aid Bus and Other Adventures in Group Work
A "Days in the Lives of Social Workers" Collection

Linda May Grobman • Jennifer Clements • Editors
With a foreword by Steven Kraft

"This book presents a lovely compilation of group work vignettes—slices of practice life—that reflect a range of populations, issues, and settings in which group work takes place. The exercises at the end of each vignette offer many types of opportunities to help students work through some major practice issues, either as individual assignments or in small classroom groups. The informal approach to presentation makes the case examples very user-friendly and, accompanied by theoretical material, offers a creative way of bringing theory to life."

*Dominique Moyse Steinberg, DSW, Adjunct Faculty*
*Smith College SSW, CEO, CustomElderCare®*

"From children in residential treatment and adolescents in an outdoor adventure program to men charged with domestic violence and individuals living with AIDS, this book is chock full of examples of how groups benefit their members. A variety of practitioners from a range of practice settings write about their group work experiences in an approachable, appealing style. The core principles and benefits of group work practice are clearly illustrated in the multitude of case examples. This book will serve as an excellent accompaniment to a standard text on group work. Students will no doubt find the case material interesting and relatable. The editors' and authors' enthusiasm for the modality is infectious and should serve to motivate readers to make group work an integral part of their practice."

*Dr. Carolyn Knight, Professor, School of Social Work,*
*University of Maryland Baltimore County*
*Past Vice-President, International Association for*
*Social Work with Groups*

ISBN: 978-1-929109-33-3 • 2013 • 5.5 x 8.5 • $22.95 plus shipping   Order from White Hat Communications, PO Box 5390, Harrisburg, PA 17110-0390
http://shop.whitehatcommunications.com   717-238-3787 (phone)   717-238-2090 (fax)